MASTERS AND STATESMEN

NEW STUDIES IN AMERICAN INTELLECTUAL AND CULTURAL HISTORY

Thomas Bender, Consulting Editor

KENNETH S. GREENBERG

MASTERS AND STATESMEN

The Political Culture of American Slavery

THE JOHNS HOPKINS UNIVERSITY PRESS
Baltimore and London

FOR JUDI

This book has been brought to publication with the generous assistance of the Andrew W. Mellon Foundation.

Printed in the United States of America

Originally published, 1985
Johns Hopkins Paperbacks edition, 1988

The Johns Hopkins University Press
701 West 40th Street
Baltimore, Maryland 21211
The Johns Hopkins Press Ltd., London

Library of Congress Cataloging in Publication Data

Greenberg, Kenneth S.

Masters and statesmen.

(New studies in American intellectual and cultural history)
Bibliography: p.
Includes index.
1. Slavery—Southern States. 2. Southern States—Politics and government—1775–1865. I. Title. II. Series.
E441.G8 1985 305.8′00975 85-9786
ISBN 0-8018-2762-0 (alk. paper)
ISBN 0-8018-3744-8 (pbk.)

Contents

Preface and Acknowledgments

THE CENTRAL CONTENTION of this work is that slavery in the antebellum South was intimately connected to a distinct set of political values and practices. Ultimately, these values and practices—this political culture of slavery—helped shape the form and content of conflict with the North. The argument is rooted in the belief that the way a society produces goods is closely connected to such cultural features as its religion, law, literature, science, morality, and politics. I do not mean to suggest, in any simple sense, that slavery as a social and economic system caused the development of culture, but rather that socioeconomic and cultural elements came together to form a mutually reinforcing whole. Masters on plantations and statesmen in their seats of government supported, sustained, and reflected each other at countless points of intersection.

The assumption that social relations, economics, and culture are interdependent has significantly influenced the method of analysis used here. In large part, the book offers a description of that interdependence; it shows how the various pieces of the political culture of slavery related to one another and to other features of slave society. Hence, for example, I was not so much interested in simply describing the Southern vision of the ideal statesman (the man who "legitimately" exercised power over free people) as I was in showing how this ideal paralleled and complemented the vision of the ideal master (the man who "legitimately" exercised power over slaves). Moreover, I tried to show how ideas about these matters closely resembled ideas about political parties, representation, and secession. This approach led me to a rather startling realization: for each area of thought that I considered I uncovered the same fundamental themes and structures. For example, many Southerners believed that the ideal statesman should never seek political power and office. Yet, in a completely contradictory way, in order to be honored in his society, a political leader also had to assert his superiority and power. In parallel fashion, the ideal master had to indicate that he was not possessed by a lust for power motivated by greed. On the other hand, in order to be respected as a master he also had to prove his power and superiority. My discovery of the endless repetition of the contradictory admonition to remain powerless and at the same time to be powerful led me to conclude that this was not simply an abstract intellectual phenomenon. This admonition, I decided, represented the embodiment in thought of a tension inherent in the master-slave relationship.

As Hegel recognized, masters define themselves in terms of their relations with slaves. In a great battle for power and recognition, masters need slaves to acknowledge them as the victors. But a paradox is at the heart of this battle. The more the master seeks his own independence and power by transforming the slave into an extension of his will, the less the slave can confirm that independence and power. In fact, at the very moment when the slave is at his most slavish, at the very moment when the victory of the master seems most complete, at the very moment when the slave disappears as an independent entity, the being who confirms the freedom of the master also disappears. It is then that the master becomes fully aware of just how dependent he has become on his slave. And ironically, it is also then that the slave realizes how independent he has become of his master.

Of course, the existential impasse of masters imagined by Hegel could never occur in the real world. The complete slave, the human who is nothing more than an extension of his master's will, never existed. Nonetheless, Hegel's abstract discussion of the master-slave relationship does offer insight into the tensions and contradictions found in real communities of masters and slaves. Masters are always in search of power and independence and yet create conditions that constantly make them aware of their dependence. The structure of political thought, I concluded, paralleled the structure of this real social relationship. In countless ways, masters and statesmen simultaneously asserted their power and powerlessness; they simultaneously asserted their independence and dependence.

Another feature of slave society also receives repeated reflection and confirmation in its politics. Masters simultaneously live in two communities: in the community of masters and in the community of slaves. Both communities, of course, need to be governed, but each requires a different type of government. Masters want to participate as equals in the government of masters in order to avoid becoming slaves. On the other hand, masters want to participate as superiors in the government of slaves. If masters had really been able to keep the government of their statehouses totally separate from the government of their plantations, they could have developed two distinct forms of authority that could have coexisted in their separate spheres without tension or contradiction. But my analysis of the political culture of slavery indicates that they had trouble keeping the two areas apart. They seemed incapable of assuming one pose on the plantation and a different one in the statehouse. Much of what I have described here shows how thought in these two arenas of political activity came to resemble each other.

My search for the connections between the political culture of slavery and other features of slave society also included a behavioral component. For example, I discovered that many (although by no means all) Southern political leaders actually tried to act like ideal statesmen and masters. Their behavior often embodied the contradictions contained in those ideals. I even concluded that Southern duels offered strong evidence of the same pattern. The duel practiced by political leaders was a ritual that restated and reaffirmed the central values of slave society. Each of the parties in a duel tried to avoid becoming a dependent or an inferior, yet each depended on community opinion to confirm his status. Similar patterns reappeared in the behavior of Southerners in political parties and during the secession crisis. The structure of the master-slave relationship seemed to echo endlessly through all areas of Southern thought and behavior.

My central concerns, then, were to show how the elements of the political culture of slave society fit together and paralleled one another and ultimately to show how this political culture channeled and shaped conflict with the North. But I am also well aware that the political culture of slavery did not dominate all parts of the South. My judgment is that it achieved its most complete form of development in South Carolina. This distinction helps explain why the state was so alienated from the North at such an early date. But I believe one can also detect the political culture of slavery wherever the planter gentry congregated in large numbers—especially in the deep South. Still, it would be incorrect to suggest that the concept of the political culture of slavery could encompass all Southern political thought and behavior. Many areas of the South had few masters and few people who accepted the ideology of masters. Even in areas dominated by masters, influences other than slavery helped shape political life. Masters shared a common national heritage and a common set of political institutions with nonslaveholders; they traded with a free world from which they could never be isolated. The political culture of slavery did develop wherever slavery developed, but it was surrounded by and mixed together with competing political visions and practices. Although much of Southern politics, including secession and the Confederacy, cannot be understood without reference to the political culture of slavery, it should not be the only reference of consequence. I have tried to describe a core set of Southern beliefs and practices, not the only set.

It has not been my intention to suggest that the elements of the political culture of American slavery were unique to the antebellum South. In fact, just the opposite is true. At least two major traditions blended together in the political culture of slave society: republicanism and honor. Consider republicanism first. Historians have traced the long history of republican ideas from Aristotle through Machiavelli to James Harrington and Thomas Jefferson.[1] It was a complicated body of ideas and did not remain static over time. But whatever form it took, always at its heart was a fear of power, especially the power of government. Governments, according to this republican ideology, were established in order to protect the liberty of the people. But governments were also a major threat to that liberty because people in power tended to want to accumulate more power. One protection against this abuse was to create governmental structures that prevented power from spreading beyond narrowly defined limits. In order to do so, it was important to have the government divided into parts that were independent of one another. Moreover, each political leader was expected to be a statesman, independent of all influences other than a reasoned devotion to the good of the whole. But the ultimate protection for republican government lay in the virtue and independence of the people. Only the people—free of the corrupting influences of luxury and dependence, frugal, industrious, temperate, devoted to simple pleasures, ever watchful of the abuse of power—only the people could protect fragile republican government.

It should come as little surprise that this republican ideology flourished in the antebellum South. What group of Americans had more to fear from government than slave masters frightened by the possibility of abolition? Who else but slave masters should be so obsessively concerned with their independence? After all, they had before them black slaves, perfect examples in their thought of the degrading effects of dependence. Who else but masters—lords on their plantations yet insignificant cogs in a vast international commercial machine—should be so aware of the threats to their independent lives?

A very different tradition, "honor," was also a major component in the political values and practices of slave society.[2] The concept of honor is complex, but at its core it involves reputation. More broadly, in the words of anthropologist Julian Pitt-Rivers, honor is "a sentiment, a manifestation of this sentiment in conduct, and the evaluation of this conduct by others, that is to say, reputation. It is both internal to the individual and external to him—a matter of his feelings, his behavior, and the respect he receives." Orlando Patterson, in his monumental comparative study *Slavery and Social Death*, has elaborated on this idea by giving emphasis to the intimate relationship between power and honor. Patterson notes the importance of Thomas Hobbes's insight that "to obey, is to Honour; because no man obeys them, whom they think have no power to help, or hurt them. And consequently to disobey, is to Dishonour."[3] In other words, those who seek honor must also seek power over others but must simultaneously be ever watchful that others do not attain power over them. To the extent that a search for honor involves a concern for personal autonomy and a distrust of power, it is compatible with the republican tradition. But since the search for honor equally involves the assertion of power over others, it is also in tension with republicanism. The political culture of American slavery reflects both that compatibility and tension.

The point of my analysis, then, is not to sketch a portrait of a unique South, but rather to show how and why certain earlier traditions, such as republicanism and honor, fit with one another and with other aspects of slave society. I have put together a puzzle whose pieces are cut from earlier traditions as well as the social, economic, and cultural elements of slave society.

The book is organized into three parts. Part one explores republicanism and honor in Southern politics by focusing on the concept of statesmanship and the practice of the duel among Southern political leaders. Part two carries these themes forward through a discussion of Southern ideas and practices related to political parties and representation. The focus then shifts to the proslavery argument in order to demonstrate further the convergence between thought about governing slaves and thought about governing free people. Part three is devoted to a consideration of the origins of Confederate nationality and secession. It begins with a discussion of Anglophobia and its gradual transformation into "New Anglophobia." Here, it lays out the basis of Southern fears of enslavement by New England and the North. The final chapter tries to place the form and content of the secession movement into the context of the political culture of slavery.

A FULL DESCRIPTION of how my friends, family, and colleagues have helped me to write this book might be longer than the work itself. Some people gave generously of their time, some were friends who encouraged me just when I needed encouragement, some inspired me, some supplied comments and criticisms that have greatly strengthened the book, some loved me, and one did all of these. I wish to thank Judi Greenberg, Irving H. Bartlett, Anne Boylan, Steven Carlin, John Cavanagh, Paula Chisolm, Paul Conkin, David Donald, Stanley Engerman, Rudelle Fenty, Ronald Formisano, Amy Greenberg, Howard Greenberg, Laura Greenberg, Allan Guttman, Jean Guttman, Robert Hannigan, Edward G. Hartmann, Paul Havey, Peter Kolchin, Stanley Kutler, Joan Lewinson, Roslyn Marino, Randy

McGowen, Fran Olsen, Joanne Norman, Thomas V. Peterson, David Robbins, Daniel Rodgers, Michele Roos, Lynn Rousseau, Robin Turnbaugh, and Bertram Wyatt-Brown.

T. H. Breen and the members of his 1980 National Endowment for the Humanities Summer Seminar helped me develop my ideas on the culture of Southern dueling. My thought about dueling also benefited from Drew Faust and Michael Johnson, who commented on my paper at the American Historical Association. The Conference on Critical Legal Studies provided numerous opportunites for me to struggle with friends over difficult intellectual issues. William Cooper and John McCardell provided useful comments on my ideas about statesmanship at the Southern Historical Association meeting.

I owe special thanks to Suffolk University for reducing my teaching load at a critical stage in the writing of this book. Suffolk provided not only the time for me to complete this project but also the kind of humane environment that makes scholarly work a pleasure. My colleagues, students, and Dean Michael Ronayne contributed to these pages in ways that might surprise all of them.

An earlier version of chapter 5 appeared as "Revolutionary Ideology and the Proslavery Argument: The Abolition of Slavery in Antebellum South Carolina," in the *Journal of Southern History* 42 (August 1976), 365–84. A version of chapter 4 originally appeared as "Representation and the Isolation of South Carolina, 1776–1860," in the *Journal of American History* 64 (December 1977), 723–43. I would like to thank the editors of these journals for permission to use these materials here.

PART I

REPUBLICANISM AND HONOR

CHAPTER 1

The Rhythm of Southern Statesmanship

IMAGINE A WORLD of masters and of slaves. Masters compelled their slaves to work on plantations and sought to profit from their labor. In governing this work force, masters were sometimes harsh, but they were also often kind and affectionate. In a sense, these masters led a strange double life. Although they sought power and a position of honor, which was both cause and consequence of power, they justified their right to govern their slaves by denying their power and their greed and by emphasizing the paternal bonds that united them to their slaves. They sometimes even thought of themselves as the fathers of their slave children.[1]

Many masters sought to exercise authority over free people in a way analogous to the way they ruled their slaves. Their life as masters on the plantation was repeated as statesmen in the statehouse. As part of their search for honor, they hungered for the political positions that would symbolize the respect they had won from constituents. Yet, drawing on the republican heritage of their fathers, they justified their right to hold office by denying their power and their greed. They tried to act as if they were the fathers of their constituent children.[2] Both statesmen and masters justified their right to govern in similar ways, and both tried to exercise their power in a similar style. In such a world, authority in the statehouse and authority on the plantation reflected and reinforced each other.

This world of masters and slaves never existed, and such a simple description could never reveal a society. Certainly, as we will see in later chapters, the antebellum South could not be so simply described. But this abstract world does help us understand certain central elements of Southern political life. A world that never existed can help us understand a world that did exist.

4

REPUBLICANISM AND HONOR

I

SOUTHERN POLITICAL LEADERS, like masters on plantations, both loved and hated power. They sought power because it was the way to be honored by their communities. But they also feared that others might assume power over them or that the power they exercised over others might, in fact, corrupt them. This chapter is about the love and hatred of power among Southern politicians; it is about republicanism and honor and the way they strangely combined to produce a distinct rhythm of political behavior.

Let us begin with a consideration of the Southern hatred of power as it appears in their ideal of statesmanship. Most Southern political leaders throughout the eighteenth century and the antebellum period liked to think of themselves as statesmen. It was an ideal advocated most passionately by South Carolinians and Virginians, but it was widely accepted outside these states. This ideal of statesmanship was not uniquely Southern, nor was it the only vision of proper political behavior, nor was it ever fully implemented. Yet in most private and public statements statesmanship seems to have been a vitally important standard by which Southerners judged political behavior.

The Southern ideal of statesmanship, a vision of proper political behavior rooted in a deep distrust of power, was part of a body of ideas variously known during the course of its long history as the civic tradition; the commonwealthman, or opposition, tradition; country ideology; or, as I will refer to it here, republicanism. These ideas can be traced back at least to classical Greece, but they had most immediately reached America through the writings of a small group of eighteenth-century English opposition thinkers, gentlemen of the "country" anxious to oppose the encroachments of power from the "court" party. These writers, with their extreme fear of unchecked governmental power and a strong desire to maintain their independence, circulated ideas about the nature of republican government which proved persuasive to Americans as they came to justify their own revolution against an abusive English government. Although transmission of republican ideology to America underwent some modification (given the differences between English and American society and government), historians have noted that this body of ideas remained central to American political thought even into the Jeffersonian period. Many antebellum Southerners adhered to the tradition even longer. Slavery and republicanism proved compatible in many ways.

What, exactly, did Southerners mean by "statesmanship"? First, a statesman acted for the good of the whole community rather than for any single portion. Thus, representatives to the national legislature had to act for the "*whole nation at large*," explained South Carolina revolutionary leader Christopher Gadsden. John C. Calhoun echoed his words many years later when he repeatedly told the Congress that he contended for the "interest of the whole people of this community."[3]

Statesmanship also required exceptional wisdom and virtue. The interests of the whole society could only be determined by careful reasoning, and power entrusted to representatives must be free from abuse by the unscrupulous. "Honest, prudent, just, practicable, in short *wise*, these are the terms which should be used to characterize Statesmanship," reads an 1852 entry in James Henry Hammond's diary. "The mind of the statesman ought to be enlightened upon every subject," explained a *Southern Quarterly Review* article on the characteristics of the statesman, "however remotely connected with the policy of government. . . . The competency of the statesman," the article continues, "should be ample, to discover those living and eternal principles to which every system is to be adapted, to be ensured perpetuity." Yet none of the attributes necessary for statesmanship, according to this writer, were attainable without the "most precious ingredient—virtue."[4]

Moreover, because statesmanship essentially involved the exercise of disinterested reason in politics, independence from interested sources of power was one of the prime attributes necessary for political leadership. Political alliances based on expediency or friendship had to be avoided at all costs in order to keep the mind unfettered by nonrational influences. "Unbiased either by friend or foe," Christopher Gadsden wrote Thomas Bee in praise of his own political conduct in 1778, "intimidated by none: constantly attending to my duty while a member of the Assembly: making no promises but always keeping myself disengaged upon every question for any offices whatever wanted to any Department of the State, or concerning any other matter of moment till it came before the House and then voted according to *my own* best judgment for the good of the whole."[5]

Independence was a refrain Southerners endlessly repeated through the antebellum decades. "I would rather be an independent Senator," John C. Calhoun later explained in words that echoed Gadsden's, "governed by my own views, going for the good of the whole country, uncontrolled by any thing which mortal man can bring to bear upon me, than to be President of the United States."[6]

The worst enemy of the statesman, the enemy that might cloud the reason of any leader, was ambition. "An immolation of self, and an impersonality of country," as a *Southern Quarterly Review* writer phrased it, "is the statesman." It was in such a spirit of self-immolation that Francis Wilkinson Pickens, anxious to return home to South Carolina from his ambassadorial post in Russia, wrote to a friend in 1859 that he decided to remain because "I do not like to seem more devoted to my own inclination and private interests than to public concerns."[7]

The ideal of statesmanship required independence from popular influences as well as independence from personal ambition. "You may rely on it," Calhoun admonished the Congress in 1817. "The public wish and expect us to act on the convictions of our mind and will, and will not tolerate the idea, that either on this or any other important occasion you are acting a part, and that you studiously shape your conduct to catch the applause of the audience." Nearly forty years later Lawrence M. Keitt boasted in a similar vein to his fiancée: "I have never stopped to inquire, when a vital principle was at stake, whether the multitude would think as I did or not." James Henry Hammond detested a government in which power derived from popularity and in which, in order to be elected, it was necessary "to stoop, to cringe, to flatter the lowest people." Perhaps one *Southern Quarterly Review* writer summarized the position most succinctly: "You may always safely assume that he who lends himself to the corruption of the people;—who treats for votes, begs for votes, lies for votes, and buys votes, will himself, when occasion serves, and with sufficient temptation, be just as ready to sell his own."[8]

It was not that what the people wanted a statesman to do was always antithetical to what a statesman should do. It was simply irrelevant. The multitude did not have access to all the information available to the representative and did not collectively possess the wisdom and virtue of the man they had elected to office. Hence, the representative should not look for guidance from the people who elected him, but rather the reverse. The statesman was a kind of teacher, perhaps even a kind of father, whose function involved guiding the masses in the direction of their true interests, as opposed to their immediate, ephemeral, and often emotionally based temporary desires. "[T]he people expect that their leaders in whose . . . public spirit they have confidence will think for them," the nullification leader James Hamilton, Jr., wrote in 1830, "and that they will be prepared to *act* as their leaders *think*." Daniel Huger of South Carolina, when asked what his constituents thought of a proposed measure, exclaimed in amazement: "Think! They will think nothing about it—They expect me to think for them *here*." "When a new question arises," wrote another Carolinian in 1844, "the populace await anxiously for his [the statesman's] determination, and having ample confidence in his integrity and ability, he alone is called upon to solve the doubts and unravel the mysteries which are above the common apprehension."[9]

Of course, Southern definitions of statesmanship did not all converge on a single emphasis. But they tended toward a central core. Government, according to this vision, should be a matter of right and reason rather than of force and numbers. Ideally, a statesman, a man of virtue and good character, should have no body—only a rational mind emotionally devoted to the service of others. Needless to say, no human could ever live up to such a standard. But many tried.

Many Southern political leaders attempted to maintain a distinct style of political behavior. Statesmen, for example, were never supposed to seek office, for to search for power was to evidence selfish ambition. Moreover, even in office, one had to demonstrate independent behavior, for to be a member of an organization or group (with the exception of family membership) or to become a victim of routine was to cast suspicion on one's devotion to the common good and to imply devotion to oneself or to friends or to power. Hence, throughout the eighteenth century and into the Civil War era, many Southern political leaders sought to maintain a rhythm of political work involving passivity toward the exercise of power as well as independence from attachment to self-interested groups. Passivity and independence were the proper poses of the statesman. At the same time the tradition of Southern honor demanded that men aggressively assert themselves in order to express their superiority, and consequently almost no one could fully maintain the passive pose. But many diligently worked at it.

Consider, for example, the way many Southerners took great pains to deny that they were interested in government office. Never again have so many struggled so hard to remain so passive. South Carolina offers numerous examples throughout the eighteenth and nineteenth centuries, but other Southerners also struggled for the appearance of passivity. Typical of this phenomenon in South Carolina during the revolutionary period was the case of Rawlins Lowndes, elected governor of the state in 1778. "Mr. Lowndes, intreated not to chuse him," wrote an observer of the legislature's efforts to fill the high office, "but requested that those who had honored him with their votes could transfer their favours to his friend who was more Capable of the Office than he was." The legislature responded to this plea in predictable Carolina fashion: "We had another Ballot & Mr. Lowndes had a Majority of Votes." Lowndes, in turn, responded equally predictably: "He accepted considering the situation the State was in."[10]

Even more passive than Lowndes, John Parker, Jr., won election to the Jacksonborough legislature in 1784 although he was still in England and would remain there for another year. Similarly, when Christopher Gadsden explained to a public audience in 1784 that "the worthy man offices seeks; the designing man cabals for them," he voiced an ideal he believed had shaped his own behavior. "I have had," he boasted in a 1778 private letter to Thomas Bee, "without asking or soliciting any man's vote directly or indirectly the Honour to serve my country for many years in various stations always totally devoted to that particular post occasionally allotted to me." William Loughton Smith shared Gadsden's attitude. In 1792 he informed Edward Rutledge that he would remain a representative to Congress if elected, but the office "is not sought by me." The strategy of passive office seeking repeatedly succeeded for Smith. In 1794 he refused to return to the state to campaign for his congressional seat and yet he won the election despite the opposition of the powerful Pinckney and Rutledge families.[11]

Political leaders of nineteenth-century South Carolina couched their behavior in similar phrases. Frederick A. Porcher, for example, described his 1832 election to the House of Representatives in the following terms: "The October elections came on whilst I was in the upper country [away from his district] and I was re-elected." He later recalled that in 1836 "notwithstanding my long absence I found that my friends had done me the kindness to return me again to the Legislature." When the state legislature elected James Louis Petigru solicitor of Beaufort District, Petigru feared that others might believe he sought office. "I have been elected in Columbia," he hastily wrote a friend, "while sitting down innocent of solicitation in Coosawatchie." When Petigru later became a state senator, he believed it was the result of effort no more positive than he had used to become a solicitor. "I am in for it, according to my usual luck," he wrote. "They have impressed me for a senator—nothing less than impressment. I resisted stoutly, and howled lustily for help, but none would help me, so nothing was to be done but to take my place in the team."[12] When Francis W. Pickens resigned his ambassadorial post to Russia in order to return to South Carolina during the final secession crisis, he obviously desired to serve his state in some elected office, but felt constrained to write Milledge Luke Bonham: "I shall never intrude myself for any public position whatsoever, but shall never shrink from placing all that I have at stake for duty, honor, and right." Carolinians rewarded such admirable passivity and elected Pickens governor. David F. Jamison wrote a friend in 1860 that his election to the Democratic convention "took me completely by surprise." Isaac W. Hayne, who ran for a position at the same convention, was not told he was a candidate "until two minutes or less before it was announced."[13]

The South Carolina writer William Gilmore Simms complained privately to his friend James Lawson in 1846: "I am put in nomination as Lieut[enant] Gov[ernor] of the State. This has been done without my privity. . . . I heard of it by the merest accident a few days ago & have not been at all consulted in the business." Simms showed equal passivity in 1860 when he wrote William Porcher Miles: "It is just possible that I may be a member of the [secession] Convention. I am put in nomination in Barnwell. But I am no candidate, and dread the loss of time & money, & peace of mind & comfort to which it will subject me. It will be a serious loss, & I can hardly afford to be a patriot. But, I will not shrink, and neither ask nor decline." Simms did not achieve election in 1860, but William Porcher Miles did. With reference to his own political behavior Miles simply echoed Simms's words in a letter to Robert N. Gourdin: "I did not seek the position of a candidate."[14]

The letters of antebellum Carolinians abound with evidence of the desire to be viewed as passive toward political office. Francis W. Pickens boasted to John C. Calhoun in 1846 in words reminiscent of Christopher Gadsden's: "I have served a portion of the people of Carolina in some capacity or other for the last fifteen years, and I have never yet approached any man or set of men to seek favour or office." "I have a mortal aversion to asking for an office," James Henry Hammond wrote in 1860. Only in the peculiar context of South Carolina's devotion to passivity in politics is it possible for a modern reader to make any sense of the paradoxical, confidential confession of one statesman: "I very much fear, I shall again be a candidate before the people of this district. I have not desired this position and have so expressed myself to many gentlemen. But, the partiality of some friends has caused them (against my wishes) to use my name in connection with the *Senatorial Election*, so freely and repeatedly, that I feel like, an option was scarcely left me."[15]

Even the statements of the man historians regard as the chief political manipulator of antebellum South Carolina—John C. Calhoun—give evidence of the strength of the ideal of passive office seeking. It would, of course, be misleading to suggest that Calhoun never wanted political office and never sought to manipulate the machinery of politics. But his statements to that effect—both public and private over a long period of time in many different contexts—attest to his sincere conscious belief in the passive ideal. For example, during his 1824 race for the presidency Calhoun condemned what he believed was William H. Crawford's attempts "to attain favor, not by placing himself on principles and policy . . . but by political dexterity and management." Later Calhoun would spend a good portion of his public life condemning the abuse of government power and patronage by men such as Andrew Jackson and Martin Van Buren—men who seemed to seek office actively.[16]

Even in private, Calhoun struggled to maintain the pose of passivity. In 1837 Calhoun's close friend and political adviser Duff Green offered some detailed suggestions on how he should act if he wished to become president. Calhoun wrote back that such calculation "deeply mortified [his] feelings. No one knows better than yourself," he castigated Green, "that in the heat of youthful years, I never sought, or desired the Presidency, but through a faithful discharge of my duty, and as an instrument of high usefulness and distinguished service; and that when the alternative was presented between truth and duty on one side, and personal aggrandizement on the other, I never hesitated for a moment. You also well know, I never held out office or emoluments to those who followed me; nor have ever asked or sought the support of any." Duff Green might have been astounded by the rebuff, but it was just the kind of statement Southerners expected from their political leaders. In 1839 Calhoun informed Green that he was finished with the turmoil of politics. "I look on political power," Calhoun wrote, "as a sacred trust, full of responsibility and burthensome in its discharge, and rather to be shunned, than sought at my time of life." In 1842, in precisely the same tone, Calhoun wrote privately to Andrew Pickens Calhoun about his presidential prospects: "My friends are sanguine and by no means idle. They take a far deeper interest in my election than what I do." Perhaps Calhoun most directly expressed his attitude toward active campaigning in an 1843 letter to the Virginian Robert M. T. Hunter: "If I thought I could gain by it [active electioneering], and even secure the election, I could hardly bring myself to adopt it. . . . I am adverse to being made a spectacle, or considered an electioneerer, or to take a step, that would, in the public estimation, indicate a personal solicitude about the office which I do not feel."[17]

The same aversion to office seeking was repeatedly expressed throughout the South during the antebellum period. Some groups, such as Southern Whigs, tended to voice the ideal more frequently, but almost no one explicitly condemned it.[18] Several examples will illustrate the point. James C. Dobbin, a North Carolinian who had served in the Congress, wrote the Georgian Howell Cobb in 1848: "They have rather forced me to consent to become a candidate for our Legislature." Cobb himself wrote his wife in 1849 trying to explain his election as Speaker of the House of Representatives: "I have done nothing to procure my election. Indeed all my personal efforts have been directed to my defeat for the last two weeks." Cobb expressed similar feelings to his wife when he wrote her many years later about his attitude toward seeking the presidency of the Confederacy. It is an office, he wrote, "I cannot seek and shall feel no disappointment in not getting."[19]

Cobb's colleague from Georgia, Robert Toombs, expressed the ideal of passivity to his friend J. J. Crittendon in 1849. He asked Crittendon not to push for his appointment to the president's cabinet: "I have an unaffected repugnance to official station," he wrote, "and my interests harmonize with my inclinations in this respect." The third leg of the powerful Georgia political triumvirate, Alexander Stephens, also tried to strike a pose similar to those of Toombs and Cobb. In an 1857 circular to his constituents, seemingly framed for the purpose of gaining votes for his impending congressional race, he still felt constrained to note: "So far as I am personally concerned, I can say with truth, I would not give a day of rest at my cherished home for a whole life spent in Washington." Similarly, in 1860, Stephens wrote privately to a friend about his "forced" reentry into political life. "It was very much against my will. . . . This is a great embarrassment to me. I was almost offended at those who put it [his name] forward. I had expressly forbidden it. They ought not to have done it."[20]

Antebellum Virginians also repeatedly expressed the passive ideal. John Randolph spent a good portion of his public life denying that he wanted political office. Edmund Ruffin, the state's agricultural reformer and militant secessionist, repeatedly gave vent to his hatred of ambitious office seekers in his diary. Even in struggles for office full of accusations of corrupt bargains, political leaders felt constrained publicly and privately to maintain that they played no role in the process. The Virginian John Tyler, for example, maintained that no matter what others had done to arrange his 1840 nomination for vice-president, he used "neither intrigue nor solicitation." Appropriately, Tyler was ultimately nominated with the support of all convention members except his fellow Virginians who publicly affirmed their own passivity by abstaining from voting for their favorite.[21]

Hence, it was in a grand old tradition that the Mississippian Jefferson Davis decribed in his autobiography the "process" that resulted in his election to the presidency of the Confederacy. He had just been appointed commander in chief of the Mississippi army by the state secession convention. "I went to my home," he later recalled, "in Warren County in order to prepare for what I believed was to be a long and severe struggle. Soon a messenger came from the Provisional Confederate Congress at Montgomery, bringing the unwelcome notice that I had been elected Provisional President of the Confederate States. But, reluctant as I was to accept the honor, and carefully as I had tried to prevent the possibility of it, in the circumstances of the country I could not refuse it."[22] Political office, if we are to take Davis and the other Southern statesmen at their word, just seemed to appear uncalled and unwanted. But unselfish devotion to the community always compelled service after the position had mysteriously been offered.

II

OF COURSE WE CANNOT TAKE Jefferson Davis and the other Southern statesmen entirely at their word. Certainly, every student of antebellum Southern politics knows that many politicians, despite their sincere public and private poses of passivity, actually felt pushed by a strong desire to be elected to public office. Some seem to have used, even if only half-consciously, the passive pose as a way to win election to office. No one could ever suggest that such men as John C. Calhoun or William Gilmore Simms actually felt no urge for office. In fact, it is quite clear that, even as they repeatedly voiced the passive ideal, they passionately hungered for prominent political positions. This ambition should come as no surprise. In a rural, slaveholding society steeped in the old traditions of "honor," election to political office was one of the major ways in which a man's status and reputation could be publicly confirmed for all to see. Southern political leaders were not simply elected in order to govern. Election brought honor and the power that was both cause and consequence of honor. As much as Southern political leaders loved to assert their passivity they loved to assert their power as well.

Consider the Southern fondness for orations. Although the true statesman was supposed to maintain a passive attitude toward power, a certain amount of activity was expected both before and after elections. Statesmen were supposed to deliver orations—not public speeches but orations. Here, in the oration, we can detect the drive for honor—a drive that made many Southern politicians greedy for office even as they denied their greed.

The words "public speech" and "oration" are often used interchangeably but for this analysis a distinction is crucial. Speeches can have many different forms and purposes. They can be used to inform an audience or to arouse it to action. They can be used subtly to persuade or viciously to malign. Orations, in terms of their content, can also be used for these purposes, often making them hard to distinguish from speeches. What was different about an oration was that one of its primary functions was to inspire respect, even awe for the speaker in the minds of the listeners. An oration, in contrast to a speech, was the public display of a superior personality. Orations allowed statesmen to display their independence, as well as their superior intelligence and virtue. The subject matter was sometimes even secondary to this display. A good orator, in other words, may or may not have informed his audience about a subject matter other than himself.

It should come as no surprise, then, that the oration remained a central component of Southern political life long after it had begun to atrophy elsewhere during the nineteenth century. The public display of wisdom and virtue—the public display of character—was at the core of the politics of honor.[23] One student of oratory, for example, notes that throughout the process of education antebellum South Carolinians made no real distinction between learning (moral and practical) and speech. The spoken word embodied all aspects of a man's wisdom and character. Young children read aloud to parents in formal settings in the home—and they received careful criticism from their fathers. Recitation continued in school and college, ultimately reaching its highest levels in the public delivery of grand orations committed to memory. A good orator could speak about any subject because each oration placed on view "the whole man" for all to see. Hence, the best orator was likely to be the best statesman.[24]

Many Southern political leaders marked their entry into public life with a grand discourse. The young John Randolph, for example, began his career in Virginia politics in such a way. In an election-day gathering he spoke just after the aged and venerable Patrick Henry, orator of an earlier era. One listener reacted to Randolph's words in a way that would have warmed the heart of any statesman. Comparing him to Patrick Henry, the man exclaimed: "I tell you what, the young man is no bug eater neither."[25] Such a listener probably could not recall for long the content of Randolph's speech. But he would probably never forget that Randolph was "no bug eater," that he was a man of superior ability. In a man's maiden speech he strutted his character for the first time before the public.[26]

There were, of course, many different ways of strutting one's character before the public. The oration could assume diverse forms. Many Southerners were fond of a haughty style of discourse involving Latin and Greek quotations—a technique whose primary purpose could not possibly be to explain ideas to an audience. It was obviously intended to parade one's learned background. But another form of the oration was to use the crude humor of the stump orator. Much of that humor was intended to belittle political opponents and thereby raise the status of the speaker. One can also detect the style of the oration in the blusterings of the Southern Whig "statesman" who announced to the world, "I'm . . . David Crockett, fresh from the backwoods, half-horse, half-alligator, a little touched with the snapping turtle; can wade the Mississippi, leap the Ohio, ride upon a streak of lightning, and slip without a scratch down a honey locust. I'll wear no man's collar."[27] The subject of such a statement was as much about one's character as were the discourses of those who quoted Latin and Greek. Both kinds of men announced through their orations the central features of their superior character. Both kinds of orations were expressions of ego. They were ways of asserting superiority and being honored.

Sometimes an oration might even appear under the guise of a plain expository speech, as was the case with the powerful and influential John C. Calhoun. Although he certainly had some desire to inform his audience about a specific subject matter, the style of his discourse indicated an equally strong desire to demonstrate his superiority. Calhoun, for example, clearly hoped to persuade others when he delivered his orations, yet he never could lower himself to ask people for their support. As one historian noted, a typical Calhoun speech began with such phrases as "I rise simply to state my reasons" or "I propose to make a few explanatory remarks." Just as he could not bring himself to electioneer he could not bring himself in his orations to make any request of others. He simply stated facts in his various addresses. Those facts were the "truth" (to which he adhered) and others had to obey once they knew the truth.[28] For Calhoun, the style of the expository speech placed him in the role of the honorable statesman—a man above politics, guiding his constituents in a fatherly way. Little wonder that even though he did not use extensive Greek and Latin quotes, even though he used remarkably plain and clear language, many listeners found Calhoun haughty and overbearing.

The difference between Southern and Northern devotion to oratory during the antebellum period was really one of degree. Certainly Northerners such as Daniel Webster or Charles Sumner delivered orations (and aspired to statesmanship).[29] Yet the basic thrust of politics in the North was moving away from the oration. Frederick Law Olmsted, observing the Congress in action during the 1850s, noted the distinction. "The South," he wrote, "sends more 'orators' to Washington than the North, and the nuisance of Washington is 'bunkum' oratory. The South speaks more Greek at Washington than the North." Obviously, Olmsted's own conception of political activity had already moved away from "bunkum" oratory. "The valuable men at Washington," he believed, "are not speakers of Greek or aught else, but the diggers and builders of the committees, and the clerks of the departments, and the best of these are men trained in habits of business by the necessities of what is called private business, and who have been drawn directly from private business."[30] Businessmen, Olmsted believed, made better organizers than orators, and organization was at the heart of the emerging new political order in the North.

Another observer of antebellum political life, Carl Schurz, also described the decline of oratory in the North before the Civil War. Perhaps the best example of the newer style of politics can be found in Schurz's description of Thurlow Weed, a masterful organizer, and a founder of the Republican party. Schurz watched him at the 1860 Republican nominating convention as he moved among his followers "with ceaseless activity and noiseless step, receiving their reports and giving new instructions in his peculiar whisper, now and then taking one into a corner of the room for secret talk, or disappearing with another through a side door for transactions still more secret."[31] The characteristic voice of the new politics, it seems, was the whisper and not the oration; its characteristic style was the secret transaction and not the public display. The new politics certainly involved the exercise of power, but since it occurred in secret it had little to do with honor.

Orations had not suddenly ceased to exist in the antebellum North, but organization became increasingly important to political success. Even the nature and function of the remaining public speaking had begun to undergo a subtle change. Again, Carl Schurz nicely illustrates the point. Schurz was clearly a Northern political leader who condemned the "secret whispers" of Thurlow Weed. But he was no orator. He relied on speeches. Schurz described his style as he moved among German-American communities in the Midwest and Middle States. He met them "face to face, without the noise and formality of a large assemblage," and he talked to them "in a conversational way, without any attempt at oratorical flourish, about the pending questions to be decided. . . . There they sat," Schurz noted with pleasure, "for an hour or two, hard-working farmers, and small tradesmen, and laborers, with earnest and thoughtful faces, some of quick perception and others of more slowly working minds, listening with strained attention, sometimes with a puzzled expression, which made me go over the same ground again and again, in clearer language and with different illustrations."[32] Schurz, in other words, sought to inform his audience about something other than his own superior character. He even answered their questions. He had no need of Greek, or even of Davy Crockett's backwoods bluster. Schurz did not use Weed's whisper nor did he use oratory. He used the style of the conversation—a kind of exchange between equals—and that too had become common in the antebellum North.[33]

Schurz hinted at these same differences between North and South in his discussion of speakers in the United States Senate. He described the Northerner Stephen Douglas as a "parliamentary pugilist." "There was nothing ornate, nothing imaginative in his language, no attempt at 'beautiful speaking.' " The Republican William H. Seward had "elocution . . . of dull sound, scarcely distinct," and Salmon P. Chase's speech "did not borrow any charm from rhetorical decoration." On the other hand, Senator Butler of South Carolina was "fond of quoting Horace," and when slavery was attacked he assumed "the haughty air of the representative of a higher class," using "fluent and high-sounding phrase to make the Northern man feel the superiority of the Cavalier over the Roundhead." Although Schurz did not view the speech of the Georgian Robert Toombs as aristocratic in tone, he described his language as "boisterous, always fluent, and resonant with vigorous utterances." Mason of Virginia, although "stupid," gave speeches that presented himself as "better than other people," leaving them with the insistence "that they must bow to his assumed aristocracy and all its claims." Mason spoke with "pompous utterances" and an "overbearing tone."[34]

III

HERE, THEN, IN THE STRANGE mixture of the passive ideal of statesmanship along with the assertive ideal of the oration, we have before us the essential double nature of Southern political life. How is this to be explained? Why did men who were apparently hungry for power and place feel so compelled to deny their hunger? One possible explanation is to suggest that one part of the doubleness was "real" and the other part was rhetorical. In other words, one could make the argument that Southerners really were pushed by their greed for office and honor but they found it "useful" to act as if they had no desire for power. It was useful for a variety of reasons. A society in which many people sought the few political offices that could bring honor could have generated extraordinary passion and violence. The rhetoric of passivity provided peace and stability. Moreover, free people who were worried about their own autonomy would refuse to elect and honor men who threatened their independence and equality. The only way to win election was to act as if one did not want to win election. In this sense the pose of passivity served the interests of aggression.

But this kind of explanation too readily dismisses passivity as merely rhetorical. It downplays the premise that in a society that values honor the way one "poses" is the way one is; it tends to ignore the apparently sincere private statements of passivity; and it does not adequately acknowledge the passive actions that often supported the passive statements. A far more satisfactory explanation must involve a recognition of the "reality" of both passivity and aggression. They existed equally and together in the Southern political world. As we will see, they were aspects of a world of masters and slaves that endlessly repeated themselves in all areas of Southern life.

In fact, many of the rhythms of Southern political life reflect this double quality in a way that makes it impossible to separate the doubleness and rank the rhetorical and "real" components. Republicanism and honor seem to have existed side by side in many patterns of Southern political belief and behavior. In fact, one can even detect the doubleness within the ideal of statesmanship and the practice of the oration themselves. As we have just suggested, passive statesmen often won power. Moreover, orators fit into the republican tradition because even as they expressed their superiority and power, they simultaneously expressed their wisdom and virtue—traits necessary for all political leaders who needed to defend the people against abusive power.

One can also detect the doubleness in another common rhythm of Southern political life: the tendency of Southern political leaders to retire or resign from office or to make a sudden switch. These techniques simultaneously indicated personal independence, won the kind of popular esteem flattering to a man in search of honor, and also expressed the passive attitude toward power demanded by the republican tradition. Rather than carefully to organize for an ultimate triumph or quietly to weather the storm of opposition, Southerners seemed to prefer the dramatic gesture of withdrawal or reversal. Such a gesture asserted superiority and passivity at the same time.

The tendency of Southern political leaders to retire, resign, or reverse themselves is easy to miss if we study each such action in isolation. The specific issues involved in an assertion of independence may cloud our ability to detect the larger pattern. And, most definitely, there was a larger pattern. It is almost impossible to find a Southern political leader who did not either resign, retire, or dramatically and publicly break an alliance at some time during his career. Some did it many times during the antebellum period. For example, of the sixty-nine Southern Democrats elected to Congress in 1831, twenty-five later joined the Whig party. During the same period, when John C. Calhoun came into open conflict with Andrew Jackson, he became the only vice-president in the nineteenth century to resign that office. In 1837, Calhoun pushed himself into an uneasy truce with Martin Van Buren. Several prominent Southern congressmen joined him in the switch, including Dixon H. Lewis of Alabama; Edward J. Black, Walter T. Colquitt, and Mark A. Cooper of Georgia; Samuel T. Sawyer and Charles Shepard of North Carolina; and Robert M. T. Hunter of Virginia.[35]

John Tyler was elected as a Whig in 1840, but he quickly broke with that party and vetoed its economic program in 1841. He was publicly joined by, among others, the Virginia Whig Henry A. Wise, along with several prominent Southern Democrats including William C. Rives and James Garland of Virginia, as well as Hugh Swington Legaré of South Carolina.[36] Legaré's reaction to his break with the Democratic party and defeat at the polls indicates the way assertions of independence seem to have affected many Southerners. "I feel like an eagle turned out of a cage," he wrote his mother.[37]

The career of the Georgian Alexander Stephens is illustrative of the kind of switching and retiring common during the life of a Southern politician. He was a Whig who joined with the Democrats on the Texas annexation issue. In 1850 he worked with the Democrat Howell Cobb in support of the Compromise of 1850. He rejected Winfield Scott, the Whig nominee for president in 1852, because Scott did not explicitly endorse the Compromise of 1850. Stephens then voted for the Whig Daniel Webster, even though Webster had just died. (Webster after death was clearly the most independent statesman available.) He even supported Democrat Stephen Douglas's Kansas-Nebraska bill in 1854 but ran for Congress as an independent in 1855. Then he became a Democrat, but ultimately resigned from Congress in 1859 when he could not get Kansas into the Union under the Lecompton constitution. Finally, he did what every real statesman always secretly desired: he delivered a "farewell address," explaining his position to the people after he had stepped down from office. In retirement, he could be almost as independent and passive as the dead Daniel Webster. Such behavior was well rewarded. Stephens became vice-president of the Confederacy.[38]

Perhaps the most notorious example of independent behavior came from the Mississippian Henry S. Foote, dubbed "General Weathercock" by contemporaries. Foote was a Democrat in 1834, a Whig in 1835, a Democrat in 1836, a Whig in 1837, and a Democrat again in 1840. That he was not unique in his state is evidenced by the switch of allegiance of four Mississippi senators who were elected as Democrats and became Whigs during their terms.[39]

Southern devotion to retirement, resignation, and the dramatic switch of alliance may also help explain the remarkable turnover rate among state officeholders. For example, the vast majority of Southern legislators in the lower South served only briefly. During the 1850s in Mississippi over 60 percent of the state legislators served a single term and in Florida 80 percent served only one term. These are remarkable figures for years when state legislative office still carried a great deal of prestige. No single factor can explain this turnover. In part the explanation is the economic inconvenience of officeholding. In part it is the formidable competition for some position. But some portion of it, perhaps a good bit of it, is the desire to retire and resign. This behavior allowed Southern political leaders to achieve public recognition of their honored position in the society, assert their independence, indicate their passive attitude toward the exercise of power, and make room for others who wished to do exactly the same thing. This was certainly the case in Florida where many legislators resigned before their terms were even complete.[40] Think of the wondrous opportunities for farewell addresses.

Of course, some of the most skillful retirees, resigners, and quitters were the Southern fire-eaters—those political leaders most anxious for secession. Their behavior is often studied in isolation, but it acquires a deeper meaning in the larger context of the rhythms of Southern statesmanship. When John A. Quitman resigned as governor of Mississippi in 1851 and refused to run for reelection; when Robert Barnwell Rhett settled into "profound political retirement" between 1852 and 1859; when William Lowndes Yancey resigned from the Congress in 1846; when Preston Brooks resigned after being condemned by Congress for his brutal caning of Massachusetts Senator Charles Sumner; when Southerners walked out of the Charleston Democratic presidential convention of 1860; when individual Southern statesmen resigned from the government and stormed out of the nation's capital during the dark days after Abraham Lincoln's election—they were all acting the way statesmen in the South were expected to act. Each resignation or retirement had its own unique motives and circumstances yet it conformed to a general pattern. Other responses were possible at each crisis point. Turning away from conflict was never the only option, and yet it was used with remarkable frequency.

The sudden reversal, retirement, or resignation was an accepted part of Southern political life. Statesmen did it often, and, as Alexander Stephens's experience indicates, frequently they gained in popularity for having done so. Independent behavior was expected and often admired. Even independence of a concern for public opinion sometimes seemed to win admiration. Unpopularity, in other words, was popular—or so at least many Southern statesmen liked to think. Passivity was, in fact, a route to power. The South Carolinian Lawrence M. Keitt, for example, reminisced about his entry into politics: "I was first elected seven years ago, a mere boy, against the opinion of nine-tenths of my constituency, and upon an issue which excited so much animosity that not one in the parish except myself avowed his opinion against the mass; audacity drew the people to me and gave me a hold upon them greater than any one ever had there. This experience has taught me no reason why I should stoop to namby-pamby dalliance, a blue blazing, melodramatic flirtation with public opinion before I made up my mind."[41]

John C. Calhoun had an experience similar to Keitt's during the 1830s when he voted against the attempt to recharter the national bank. He had been warned that such a position would be unpopular in the state, but unpopularity in South Carolina was a kind of political virtue. Calhoun sensed that, paradoxically, the very unpopularity of his vote showed the people he was qualified to be their representative statesman, that he was qualified to be honored. "[I]n being prepared to sacrifice her confidence [his popularity in the state], as dear to me as light and life, rather than disobey, on this great question, the dictates of my judgement and conscience, I proved myself not unworthy of being her representative."[42] In other words, to do the unpopular but principled act (short of challenging such a basic assumption as the virtue of slavery) produced popularity.

IV

THE IDEALS AND RHYTHMS of statesmanship or honor were not uniquely Southern or uniquely related to slavery. Just as the public and private statements of Southerners exhibit instances of passivity toward office, so do those of Northerners. Not only did such men as Daniel Webster and Charles Sumner seek the posture of the passive statesman, but so did Abraham Lincoln in 1848 when he wrote William H. Herndon about running for Congress: "To enter myself as a competitor of others, or to authorize any one so to enter me, is what my word and honor forbid." The language and pose of honorable passivity seem to have been part of the political culture of antebellum America rather than of the political culture of slavery.[43] Similarly, given the rise and fall of new parties during the 1830–60 period, many Northerners also engaged in the practice of suddenly switching allegiance and asserting their independence.[44]

Despite the overlap between the political ideals and rhythms of Northerners and Southerners, they showed important differences of degree and differences of tendency—the kinds of differences evident to Frederick Law Olmsted as he discussed Southern oratory. Similarity is to be expected in the political ideals and practices of regions sharing a common history and common institutions, and consequently the differences become more important. The point is simple: although the rhythms of statesmanship can be seen all over the nation during the eighteenth century, they fit more easily into the social and intellectual texture of nineteenth-century Southern life than they could ever fit into the nineteenth-century North. These political practices did not go unchallenged in the South, but rather they were more firmly rooted. And slavery provided the soil. Republicanism and honor were part of a larger system of relations in slave society. They reappeared on the plantation as well as in the statehouse. Plantations did not cause ideals and behavior in statehouses, but ideals and behavior in both places were part of the same mutually reinforcing system.

The connection between the rhythms of statesmen and masters is complex. The best way to begin to see the relationship is to note the way masters increasingly tended to dominate the political leadership of the antebellum South. The domination increased dramatically as the Civil War neared. Not every political leader was a great planter owning large numbers of slaves, but most owned slaves. Slaveholders, for example, overwhelmingly dominated the state legislatures of all the lower Southern states by the eve of the Civil War. Although masters seem to have been most significant in South Carolina, where over 80 percent of the legislators owned slaves by 1860, over 70 percent owned slaves in the Georgia, Alabama, and Mississippi legislatures. Louisiana and Texas were not far behind. All of these legislatures experienced increases of slaveholders between 1850 and 1860—increases that advanced at a far greater rate than the general increase of slave ownership in the population.[45]

The connection between political leadership and slaveholding in the antebellum South is actually of little significance in itself. A society can be ruled in the interests of a class without the personal involvement of any members of that class. That so many slaveholders participated in government is suggestive of domination by masters, but it does not establish domination. More suggestive, however, is the way in which this slave-owning leadership seems to have won popular support by exercising a rhythm of political work similar to the rhythm of its work as slave masters. The statesman in the legislative hall and the master on the plantation exercised the same style of government. It was a style widely admired by other Southerners—even by many who were not actually masters themselves.

That the statesman and the master actually exercised the same style of authority may seem absurd at first glance. The differences in their positions seem obvious. Citizens of a state are not the personal property of public officials in the way that slaves are owned by masters. Masters exercise personal power directly over individual slaves, whereas statesmen dispense public authority. The power of legislators is restricted by the formal restraints of a constitution, whereas the master is not so formally restricted. Moreover, the purposes of governments and plantations are quite different. While plantations are the setting for the government of people they are also the setting for the accumulation of profit. This is not the case with legislatures. Furthermore, masters exercised authority over people of a different race. How could the ideal master really be the ideal statesman?

Given these seemingly obvious differences between the position of masters and that of statesmen, the fundamental similarity of style is striking. Consider first the republican ideas that often appeared in masters' discussions of their plantations. The ideal statesman of the republican tradition—the independent man of intelligence and virtue, utterly devoid of personal ambition, and anxious to act for the good of the entire community—was also the ideal master. Consider, for example, the way slave owners constantly emphasized the burden of their position and repeatedly told of their reluctance to undertake the task. Eugene Genovese, in his complex and masterful study of slavery, notes the recurrence of the words "duty" and "burden" when masters described their relation to slaves.[46] Masters, like statesmen, were supposed to assume the burden of their office without greed. At the center of their thought was the solemn obligation to care for their "people." "To clothe the naked, feed the hungry, and soothe the sick should be our ceaseless duty toward the slave," wrote one planter. "Our slaves are our solemn trust," explained a South Carolina professor of theology, in a phrase that summed up the thought of many. A Mississippi planter advised other masters: "We should love our slaves in order to make them love us. . . . Let us first be just and generous toward them and not be too covetous of riches—for the 'love of money is the root of all evil.' " Perhaps few masters ever stated the case so boldly as one who responded to a question about runaway slaves with the comment: "It's pretty hard work to keep me from running away from them!"[47] But it was a comment that revealed what every planter liked to think about his position as slaveholder—it was an office not sought by him.

But masters, like statesmen, also sought honor. They aimed to exercise authority through the public display of superior virtue and intelligence. They constantly wanted to win the respect and admiration of their "people"—a respect and admiration centered on their personal characteristics as virtuous masters.[48] One can see this wish in the way masters tried to deal with the issue of punishment. The use of the whip, it might at first seem, was an aspect of plantation life in which no master could possibly detect honor. Certainly, some masters did find themselves uncomfortable with the whip. Those who could afford it placed the burden of punishment on the shoulders of overseers—and then hated them for their brutality.[49] But often, when a master personally had to use the whip, he tried to turn it into an instrument that supported his position of honor.

Although I may carry the analogy between statesmen and masters a bit far, there is a fundamental similarity between the punishment of the slave and the delivery of the oration. In both cases, they thought that the superior virtue and intelligence—in short the character and honor of a man in authority—were on display. A master might whip a slave for many different reasons, but a slave was always informed about the character of the master by his style of delivery. "Never inflict punishment when in a passion, nor threaten it; but wait until perfectly cool and until it can be done rather with sorrow than in anger," explained a Louisiana planter. A South Carolinian advised that, when punishing, "all abusive language or violence of demeanor should be avoided, they reduce the man who uses them to a level with the negro, and are hardly ever forgotten by those to whom they are addressed." Perhaps a Virginia planter most clearly (but unwittingly) expressed the relationship between oratory and the correction of slaves. "Anger begets anger," he wrote. "A low tone of voice is recommended in speaking to negroes. This is a wise suggestion, as it must necessarily be attended by a low tone of temper. All conversation with a negro is forbidden, except about his work. This is important; he should be kept as far from his master as possible, but with no accompanying harshness; he ought to be made to feel that you are his superior, but that you respect his feelings and wants."[50] Just as the oration, regardless of its subject, established the superiority of the orator, so the words of admonition to a slave established the superiority of the master. And, of course, both the orator and the master rejected conversation as a way of establishing authority. Conversation was the style of discourse to be used only between social equals. It was not the way to achieve a position of honor.

To understand the basic similarity between the style of the statesman and the style of the master is to begin to understand the political culture of slavery. In the statehouse and on the plantation statesmen and masters sought power and simultaneously denied they sought power. They were both aggressive and passive. They were republicans and men of honor.

CHAPTER 2

The Duel as Social Drama

VIRTUALLY ALL ANTEBELLUM Southern political leaders participated in duels during some portion of their careers. Even if public figures could avoid an actual exchange of shots, they found it almost impossible to escape the verbal interactions and formal notes characteristic of the culture of dueling and the gentlemen's code of honor. The central contention of this chapter is that the duel was a theatrical display that attempted to resolve conflict and reaffirm the political values of the dominant group in the society.[1] All societies use social dramas as an essential component to resolve disputes. In contemporary America, for example, the courtroom and the legislative chamber sometimes provide the settings for such displays. These are the theaters in which antagonists publicly meet and antagonisms are resolved or contained within a structured, formal context. Social dramas are important techniques for handling conflicts that seriously threaten a society. The participants in a social drama recognize that there has been a significant breach in their relations, but their participation in the performance allows them publicly to reaffirm their unity by engaging in ritual forms of behavior that embody common ideals. Hence, just as both plaintiff and defendant accept the procedures of the courtroom and the values embodied in those procedures, both participants in a duel abide by the code of honor and the values embodied in that code. In other words, if we can understand the duel as a social drama, we can both see the kinds of disputes that threatened to disrupt Southern political life and come to a deeper understanding of the central values that united that life. The duel seen in this way embodies in ritual form key elements of the political culture of slavery. Passivity and power, republicanism and honor are all displayed in the duel.

I

DUELING WAS A VITALLY important institution in the antebellum South. The practice first appeared in common use in America among revolutionary war officers during the 1770s and quickly spread to the rest of the nation, but it retreated into the South by the early nineteenth century. It flourished in the slave states even though it was both against the law and widely condemned in public. Even in states without antidueling statutes common law prosecution was possible. But Southern prosecutors, unlike their Northern counterparts, rarely enforced laws against dueling. When a possibility of enforcement existed, duelists crossed borders or even dueled on borders in order to create just enough ambiguity in legal jurisdiction to discourage indictment. Even when duelists did come to trial, Southern juries almost never found them guilty. If dueling laws provided that public officers swear they had never fought duels, Southern legislatures routinely passed special exception laws.[2]

To understand the importance of duels in Southern political life we must recognize that they were a public activity that involved large numbers of people. Perhaps only a few thousand Southerners ever exchanged shots on dueling grounds, but it is misleading to judge the importance of duels simply by the number of bullets fired. Duels directly and indirectly involved many more people. Even if one defines a dueling encounter narrowly—as the first exchange of formal notes—it is clear that the number of encounters far exceeded the number of shots. Such notorious duelists as Andrew Jackson and John Randolph engaged in dozens of dueling encounters that they peacefully resolved for each one that ended with a bullet.

Many factors could help forestall hostilities. Since most duels began with a formal letter from the offended person requesting confirmation, clarification, or explanation for words spoken, a gentleman could avoid shooting if he apologized or satisfactorily explained the insult. Seconds generally assumed the responsibility for negotiating agreements and they often suceeded. John Lyde Wilson, governor of South Carolina and author of a widely circulated code of proper dueling practices, assumed that seconds could almost always prevent an exchange of shots. This role was their prime purpose. "Use every effort to soothe and tranquilize your principal," Wilson suggested. "Endeavor to persuade him that there must have been some misunderstanding in the matter." Seconds followed this advice. Rear Admiral Daniel Ammen, for example, recalled that, during his antebellum naval career, "in the twenty-one years I have passed on board of vessels, although challenges have frequently occurred, no duel has resulted, from a reasonable consideration of the difficulty by the seconds."[3] Sometimes gentlemen could avoid an exchange of shots even without an apology or explanation. Sheriffs might temporarily arrest them or a judge might require them to post bond not to duel. Moreover, parties had to agree on the mechanics of the confrontation, and trouble often developed on this issue. In 1856, for example, Preston Brooks of South Carolina, after his vicious caning of Massachusetts Senator Charles Sumner, never fought because his opponent wanted the duel held in Canada. Brooks feared traveling through the North. On another occasion, Congressman George McDuffie of Georgia refused to duel with Congressman Thomas Metcalfe of Kentucky because Metcalfe chose rifles rather than the more conventional pistols.[4] An 1855 duel between B. Gratz Brown and Thomas C. Reynolds was avoided (although they later did duel) because Brown chose rifles and Reynolds rejected them since he was "so near-sighted that he could not, even with his glasses, in ordinary weather recognize any person at a greater distance than 30 paces."[5]

Even an understanding of the duel as involving more than just an exchange of bullets does not allow us fully to appreciate the large number of people involved in Southern dueling activity. Each encounter directly involved more than the two principals and their seconds. Friends gave advice or lent weapons; physicians came to the dueling grounds; public officials sometimes tried to stop the duel; worried or angry family and kin sought to interfere in various ways. For example, even if we exclude family and later investigators, thirty-four people directly participated in the Jonathan Cilley–William J. Graves duel of 1838.

The extent of public involvement in duels went well beyond the direct participants. Those who dueled often represented groups.[6] The Haley-Delancey duel in 1771 in Charleston, for example, symbolized group conflict. Delancey represented the Royalists and, when he died after the duel, "the Whigs . . . defended Dr. Haley, and concealed him until his trial came on." In the same spirit, soldiers frequently fought for the "honor of the regiment." When Preston Brooks caned Charles Sumner in 1856, he wrote to his brother, "I have lost my individuality in my representative capacity. I am regarded to a great extent as the exponent of the South against which Black Republicanism is waring [*sic*] in my person." William L. Yancey, describing his position in the 1845 duel with Clingman, noted: "I was a Southern representative who in defending Southern rights and the honor of the whole Southern delegation was called to account."[7]

S. S. Prentiss, recent Northern immigrant to Mississippi, fought a duel with General Henry S. Foote because "he had persuaded himself too, that not only his own reputation but that of New England was at stake; he fancied he was challenged because he was 'a Yankee, and would not fight.' "[8] Duels by legislators often originated in heated debates between parties or factions. In 1840, for example, Whig leader Henry Clay led a bitter battle to fire the Democratic printers of Senate documents. Democratic Senator King replied in harsh words, Clay responded with harsher words, and for a time a duel seemed unavoidable. The Thomas L. Clingman–William L. Yancey duel of 1845 developed because of words spoken in debate over the annexation of Texas.[9] In 1831, Democratic congressional candidate Spencer Pettis so brutally attacked the Bank of the United States that he received a challenge from Thomas Biddle, brother of bank president Nicholas Biddle.[10]

Sometimes elections themselves generated duels—duels in which the participants symbolically fought for their supporters as well as for themselves. Harsh words spoken during campaigns often provoked a challenge. In Mississippi during the 1811 congressional election, the most enthusiastic Federalist campaigner, Abijah Hunt, challenged the victorious Democratic-Republican George Poindexter after Poindexter's election victory. In 1819 General Armistead Thomson Mason and his brother-in-law, John Mason McCarty, stood at ten paces and fired muskets at each other after a bitter Virginia congressional campaign.[11]

Young duelists sometimes fought for the honor of older leaders. During the revolutionary war, John Laurens could not bear to have George Washington maligned by General Lee, so he challenged Lee to a duel. When, in 1856, Preston Brooks of South Carolina caned the startled senator from Massachusetts, he explained, as he raised his hand to strike the first blow, that he was vindicating the honor of his cousin, Senator Andrew Pickens Butler, as well as his state. As late as 1880, Tom Smith, son of the governor of Virginia, fought against a man who had maligned both his father and Confederate President Jefferson Davis. "Just before the order was given to fire," explained a contemporary in a letter to Davis, "Col. Smith took his cane, which you [Davis] had given him . . . and suspended it to an overhanging limb. . . . When his adversary fell, he took down the cane, upon which your name was engraved, and putting it to his lips bowed to his adversary—The scene to those who understood it was very touching."[12] Clearly, Tom Smith's duel was more than his own private battle.

Newspaper editors, who were also public figures, often resorted to the duel in the antebellum South. Since newspapers were nearly always affiliated with a political party and since the duelists were almost never from the same party, editor's duels were also sometimes party battles. In 1843, for example, a Democratic candidate for Congress challenged the editor of a New Orleans Whig newspaper for articles written against his election and uncomplimentary to his character. In 1846 John Hampden Pleasants, editor of the Richmond *Whig*, fought with Thomas Ritchie, Jr., son of the editor of the Democratic *Richmond Enquirer*, because of an

Enquirer article accusing Pleasants of abolitionist leanings. Here was another Democratic-Whig battle fought with bullets rather than at the polls.[13]

As some of these examples indicate, sometimes duelists represented their families. Thomas Biddle fought for his brother, Nicholas Biddle; Preston Brooks fought for his cousin, Andrew Pickens Butler. There are many other examples. When Judge A. G. Magrath ran for Congress from Charleston, the editor William R. Taber insulted him. In his absence, Magrath's brother, Edward Magrath, challenged and killed Taber for the insult. In 1823 an article in the *Missouri Republican* accused the surveyor general, William Rector, of corruption. Rector was away in Washington; his brother assumed the quarrel and shot and killed the author of the article.[14]

Several other features of the duel indicate that it was less a private contest between two individuals than a clash that intimately involved large publics. Knowledge that the duel would ultimately undergo careful public scrutiny shaped the behavior of all participants. For example, throughout the period of preliminary negotiations each party maintained the threat of publicly "posting" his opponent as a coward. In posting, one could print a notice in a newspaper, as did a Missouri duelist who, assuming a large audience, addressed himself "TO THE WORLD!" about J. Quinn Thornton: "Having resorted to low, cowardly and dishonorable means, for the purpose of injuring my character and standing, and having refused honorable satisfaction, which I have demanded; I avail myself of this opportunity of publishing him to the world as a reclaimless liar, an infamous scoundrel, a black hearted villain, an arrant coward, a worthless vagabond and an imported miscreant, a disgrace to the profession and a dishonor to his country." James Wilkinson used a slightly different technique, printing handbills and posting them all over the District of Columbia. "Hector unmasked," he announced. "In justice to my character, I denounce John Randolph, M.C., to the world as a prevaricating, base, calumniating scoundrel, poltroon and coward." Sometimes all one had to do to post a "scoundrel" was to tack the sign up in a public place and stand under it with a gun for a few hours.[15]

Another indication that participants regarded their duels as subject to public scrutiny is that duelists generally kept copies of notes leading to the duel. These letters were extremely important because after the duel it was not unusual for each side to publish the entire correspondence or full accounts of the episode. In 1806, for example, Thomas Swann published his account of his conflict with Andrew Jackson, submitting it "to a candid and impartial public" to judge. Jackson published his own account as well. Sometimes duelists or their seconds published joint accounts, as did the seconds after the Cilley-Graves duel of 1838. Henry Wise of Virginia called on Cilley's second, George Wallace Jones of Wisconsin, to suggest the possibility of a joint statement. Jones consulted Thomas Hart Benton who advised: "That's just right, General, for when I had my duel with Lucas, Judge Lawless, my second, . . . and Mr. Lucas' second, Barton, made a joint statement to the public at St. Louis, as to all the facts and circumstances attending that duel." Sometimes duelists publicly acknowledged agreements reached before the exchange of shots, as was the case with Henry Clay's apology to Senator William R. King or with the settlement between John Rodgers of the navy and Captain James Barron who printed circulars of the adjustment which they sent to friends.[16] Since most duels involved injuries to reputation, duelists needed to make their audience—either their friends or the general public—aware of their honorable behavior in the encounter. Duels, in other words, could never really be private battles; they had to be public.

II

WHAT SOCIAL FUNCTIONS did the duel perform in the antebellum South? The best way to begin a consideration of this issue is with a careful look at one encounter—the Jonathan Cilley–William J. Graves duel of 1838. This duel, in some ways, was rather unusual. It was the only American duel that led to the death of a sitting congressman; it involved Northerners as well as Southerners; and it broke several of the conventions of proper dueling behavior. But it is a good duel to examine in detail, in part because we have so much information about it. All the major participants (short of Cilley, who died) wrote accounts of the affair, and the death of a congressman led to a full-scale investigation and report. No other nineteenth-century duel, with the exception, perhaps, of the Alexander Hamilton–Aaron Burr encounter, generated quite so much documentary material. Moreover, despite the unusual elements of the Cilley-Graves affair, the confrontation did embody the central features common to most antebellum Southern duels.

The story of the Cilley-Graves duel begins neither with Cilley nor with Graves, but with Virginia Whig Congressman Henry A. Wise.[17] On February 12, 1838, Wise spoke to the House of Representatives in favor of a resolution to establish a new committee to investigate charges of corruption in Congress. As evidence to support these charges, he referred to an anonymous article written in the Whig newspaper the *New York Courier and Enquirer*. In passing, Wise noted that the editor of the newspaper, James Watson Webb, vouched for the reliability of the accusations. Jonathan Cilley, Democratic congressman from Maine, spoke against the resolution to establish an investigating committee, referring specifically to the untrustworthiness of any report derived from the editor of the *Courier and Enquirer.* Offhandedly, he accused Webb of corruption—of being opposed to the continuation of the Bank of the United States until it loaned him $52,000.

Nine days later the irate and insulted James Watson Webb arrived in Washington. But, despite his anger, he did not immediately confront his adversary. He asked his friend, Congressman William J. Graves of Kentucky, to carry a note to Cilley requesting him to "explain" his remarks. This note was the first formal communication required by the code of honor preparatory to a challenge. When confronted by Graves in the House of Representatives, Cilley declined to receive the note. It was this action and the accompanying explanation that shifted the immediate issue of the confrontation away from a Cilley-Webb dispute toward a Cilley-Graves dispute. There are two versions of what happened at this point. The official congressional investigation concluded that Cilley did not want to be held "personally" accountable for what he said on the floor of Congress and that he "chose to be drawn into no controversy" with Webb. Moreover, since the refusal to receive a note might be an indication that the challenged party denied that the challenger was a gentleman worthy of recognition in an affair of honor, Cilley declared that he "neither affirmed nor denied any thing in regard to his [Webb's] character." This wording, of course, left open the possibility that Cilley did not regard Webb as a gentleman. It was this message that offended Graves. Since Graves had agreed to carry Webb's note, according to the code of dueling he had acknowleged that Webb was a gentleman. Cilley's refusal to do the same might be understood as an indirect insult to Graves. That Cilley wrote Graves he intended "no disrespect to you" did not soothe the furious Graves. Graves himself, a year after the duel, gave a slightly different version of this incident in a speech to his constituents. Graves maintained that Cilley had verbally assured him that he did not object to Webb as a gentleman. But Cilley later refused to commit this acknowledgment to writing. This refusal implicitly denied Graves's version of Cilley's verbal remarks and implied that Graves had lied.

At any rate, Graves then called upon Congressman Richard H. Menafee of Kentucky to deliver a note to Cilley which directly asked him to "disclaim any exception to him [Webb] personally as a gentleman." Cilley, still not wanting to be drawn into a personal dispute over his public remarks, answered by refusing to "admit the right on your part to propound the question to which you ask a categorical answer." Graves then issued a challenge.

Cilley, through his second, Congressman George Wallace Jones of

Wisconsin, accepted the challenge and submitted a copy of suggestions for the conduct of the duel to Graves's second, Henry A. Wise (the man whose original remarks began the dispute). The proposal was highly unusual—rifles at eighty yards. The note specified such details as how the rifles should be held before firing, how the word to fire should be given, that the dress should be "ordinary winter clothing," that each should have on the grounds a second, a surgeon, and two other friends. The seconds could have pistols, for if a principal fired out of turn, it was the obligation of the opposing second to shoot him down. Wise, after consulting with Graves and noting that it was unusual to use rifles in a duel, accepted the terms. Graves, as a matter of fact, had some trouble finding a rifle. At one point, Cilley's second actually brought him one, but finally he found his own.

On the dueling grounds in Maryland, selection by lot gave Wise (Graves's second) the choice of position. Jones (Cilley's second) would give the word to fire. The two seconds measured the distance together but, probably in their eagerness to avoid a death, they measured ninety-two yards rather than the agreed-upon eighty. Congressmen John Calhoon and Richard Hawes of Kentucky stood at a distance; the audience included two others (unidentified and uninvited) along with the hack drivers. Cilley came with Jones, his second, Congressman Jesse Bynum of North Carolina and Colonel James W. Schaumberg as his friends, and a Dr. Duncan as his surgeon. Graves came with Wise as his second, Senator John J. Crittendon and Congressman Menafee, both of Kentucky, as his friends, and a Dr. Foltz of Washington as his surgeon.

Shortly after 3 P.M. Cilley and Graves fired at each other and missed. The seconds and friends began to negotiate a resolution while they occasionally consulted the principals who stood their ground. Throughout the negotiations everyone conceded that the matter could be resolved if Cilley would remove any doubt that he did not recognize Webb as a gentleman. They all agreed that this duel involved only "a mere point of honor," that no animosity existed between the duelists, and that there was no need to continue fighting until someone had been shot. But Cilley would not change his position and Graves would not change his, so they fired again and missed. Once again, the seconds and friends conducted frantic negotiations and once again they failed. On the third exchange of shots a bullet hit Cilley, who died within three minutes.

Perhaps the most interesting part of this duel concerns what happened away from the dueling grounds while Cilley and Graves exchanged shots. James Watson Webb, the man who had received Cilley's original insult, leaped around in frenzy. Earlier, he had tried to prevent the duel because he did not want Graves to fight his battle for him. The day of the duel Webb joined with two friends and planned to confront Cilley at his boardinghouse, force him to fight with pistols on the spot or agree to fight a formal duel before he met Graves. If Cilley refused to do either Webb planned to break his right arm in order to prevent the duel with Graves. But Webb and his friends discovered that Cilley already had left his room, so they raced to the Maryland dueling ground. They agreed that if they came upon the duel in progress Webb would ask Cilley to fight. If Cilley refused and raised his rifle at Graves, Webb would shoot him. Webb and his friends considered the possibility that someone might first try to kill Webb—perhaps even his good friend Graves! Webb agreed that under these circumstances he would first shoot Cilley and then they would all defend themselves as well as possible. None of this, of course, actually happened because Webb missed the duel entirely.

What motivated the men involved in the Cilley-Graves duel? At its core the struggle involved injuries to reputation. It began with Cilley's public statement that Webb's word could not be trusted because he had accepted a bribe. It continued because Cilley refused to recognize Webb's status as a gentleman. It did not, it should carefully be noted, originate in a desire to kill a hated enemy. It is easy to misunderstand the duel as a substitute for murder. The men who fired at each other had no special desire to cause injury or death. Cilley had said he intended "no disrespect to Graves." During the negotiations after the first exchange of shots Wise had told Jones that "these gentlemen have come here without animosity towards each other." Jones answered that Cilley "meant no disrespect to Mr. Graves, because he entertained for him then, as he now does, the highest respect and the most kind feelings." When the eighty-yard distance originally had been proposed, Wise smilingly told Jones: "The distance is so great that they will not be apt to hit each other." Still, when they measured the distance they made it even longer. Notice that Graves, the "killer" in the duel, did not even own a rifle.

The Cilley-Graves duel, as a matter of fact, was unusual in that it involved a death at all. Most duels, like the ritualized combat of medieval warfare, operated as substitutes for deadly encounters. Just as Cilley and Graves did not come to the dueling ground with a strong desire to kill each other, few duelists were motivated by a lust for blood. There were, of course, exceptions. Given its nature, the duel could be easily perverted into a legitimation of murder.[18]

But most dueling encounters never involved the exchange of shots and most "participants" were not principals. Even those who exchanged shots did not view death as a primary goal. Many of the most famous duelists so clearly understood this attitude that they often intentionally fired their pistols ineffectually into the air. Christopher Gadsden did so in a 1778 duel with William Henry Drayton. In Andrew Jackson's 1788 duel with Colonel Waightsill Avery, both parties fired into the air and shook hands. When John Randolph and Henry Clay fought a duel in 1824 Randolph aimed at Clay's knees on the first shot and fired into the air on the second. He later told Thomas Hart Benton: "I would not have seen him fall mortally, or even doubtfully, wounded for all the land that is watered by the King of Floods and all his tributary streams." In an 1833 duel between S. S. Prentiss and Governor Henry S. Foote of Mississippi, Prentiss later wrote: "I threw up my pistol as I fired, not intending to hit him at all, but so near had I been to killing him that my ball, even as I threw up my pistol, hit him on the shoulder, slightly wounding him in the flesh." In 1846 John Hampden Pleasants "went upon the field with no desire to take his adversary's life; that in his last moments, he declared that previously to the combat he had extracted the ball from his pistol to lesson the chances of a fatal result."[19]

Of course, some of these magnanimous duelists ended up being killed by their less magnanimous adversaries. But death in a duel was not so common as one might suspect, given that the encounter involved two men shooting at each other. One historian of dueling in the old navy discovered a 22 percent mortality for those who exchanged shots. But naval duels, fought by military men anxious to prove their manhood, were probably more murderous than civilian duels. A June 12, 1800, newspaper article noted that in twenty-one duels in recent weeks only six people had died. This is a 14 percent death rate. Even this figure may exaggerate the casualties because duels involving deaths had a greater chance of being reported in the newspaper. These figures demonstrate that, while death was a distinct possibility, it was not the usual experience of duelists—even duelists who aimed at each other. The duel certainly involved the risk of death, but not usually death itself.[20]

That death was not the usual intention even of those who killed someone in a duel is evidenced in the behavior of the "successful" duelist. "Gentlemen," explained one 1830 duelist, "I assure you that I had no enmity against that man." In an 1835 encounter, the duelist fell down by the side of his fallen opponent and "implored his forgiveness." "My despair," he later wrote, "at his fate knew no bounds."[21] Such feelings as these gave rise to the common stories of the duelist who went insane with remorse or whose career was destroyed because he had killed a man in a duel. Andrew Jackson may be the exception here, but even he had to explain away his killing of a man in a duel. Aaron Burr is probably the most famous example of the failed duelist—the duelist who destroyed his own career by killing his opponent.

Unbearable remorse rather than career advancement seems to have been the fate of most duelists who killed. William Henry Harrison wrote after the Cilley-Graves duel that "in the grave of the fallen duellist was frequently buried the peace and happiness of the survivor." One Virginian reported a Washington duel in which the man who fired the fatal shot "became a fugitive, his life and happiness ruined." In the Trotter-Wickliffe duel in 1829 in Kentucky, the killer was reported to have "become insane and died in the lunatic asylum." Even if we assume that these tales of insanity resulting from duels were much exaggerated, they tell us a great deal about the attitudes of people in the society. The duelist who killed was not regarded as the victor.[22] Graves became quite aware of this fact as a storm of public criticism—criticism from both North and South—descended on him during the months after his duel.

But if duelists fought more to preserve their reputation than to kill an enemy, exactly how did a duel perform that function? Why should an exchange of shots wash away an insult? What could an insulted man hope to gain by risking his own life in a dueling encounter? James Watson Webb clearly understood the answer to these questions. Duelists were in a common club—a club of self-professed gentlemen. To duel was to join the club, publicly to affirm that one had the qualifications for membership, to restore a tainted reputation. To be excluded from a duel by a recognized member of the club was to be denied status as a gentleman. Webb, having acknowledged Jonathan Cilley's status as a gentleman by sending him a note of inquiry about an insult, refused to allow himself to be excluded by Cilley's refusal to receive the note. William J. Graves, having recognized both Cilley's and Webb's membership by agreeing to carry a note between them, had to get Cilley to recognize Webb as a gentleman or it would cast suspicion on his own status. A duel, in other words, whatever else it may have involved, publicly and dramatically defined the members of a gentlemen's club, bound them together, and distinguished them from others in the society.

It is easy to see how duels bound together principals and their own seconds. These major participants publicly reaffirmed close personal connections through their common involvement in the encounter. In the duel itself the principal and second became almost interchangeable. When Cilley and Graves stood on the dueling ground their seconds stood by ready to assume their places should it become necessary. In fact, this shift is precisely what happened when Graves moved from his position as Webb's second to his position as Cilley's primary antagonist. Graves had bound himself to Webb by agreeing to carry his note, and an insult to Webb had become an insult to Graves. Not surprisingly, duelists almost always referred to seconds as "friends." Andrew Jackson in 1798 actually used brother Masons as his seconds and kept referring to them as brothers. Seconds recognized the binding role of their position. Nathaniel Pendleton, for example, explained in a letter that, when Alexander Hamilton asked him to become his second in the fatal duel with Burr, he felt he could not hesitate a moment before accepting. "You know," he wrote, "that besides the love, the admiration and respect I always had for the amiable qualities, the Sublime talents the generous spirit of that man [Hamilton], I was under particular obligations to him for particular acts of kindness, and of late much more in the habits of confidence with him than any other man in New York."[23]

Principals likewise recognized the special bond. Andrew Jackson, after an 1804 duel in Knoxville, wrote his second John Coffee a note of thanks. "I have treasured the act in my bosom," he explained, "that neither length of time nor change of circumstances can eradicate or eface, and as long as my bosom beats with life, it will beat high with gratitude on viewing the event." After his duel with Henry Clay in 1824, John Randolph gathered with his friends and produced an envelope—an envelope he had earlier left with instructions to be opened in the event of his death. It contained a note that directed that the gold coins Randolph carried in his pocket be made into seals and given to the seconds. "But Clay's bad shooting shan't rob you of your seals," Randolph announced, "I am going to London and have them made for you."[24]

That the duel reaffirmed the bond between principals and seconds should come as no surprise, but that it also bound opponents seems less obvious. When tensions grew to a point that implied fundamental, irreconcilable conflict—conflict that was highly disruptive to society—the duel served to end the conflict and reestablish harmony. Consider the form of the dueling encounter. As in the Cilley-Graves duel, the notes were always couched in terms of polite requests. Even the euphemisms implied the purpose of the duel. The encounter was a "meeting" or "interview"; the challenge an "invitation." Once the parties planned to meet they had to plot together in secret in order to avoid intrusion from authorities. Duelists shared the secret of their encounter with each other even while they kept the information from their wives. Hamilton's wife, even as Hamilton lay wounded in bed, remained ignorant that he acquired his bullet wound in a duel. On the dueling grounds each faced the other, hemmed in by the same set of formal rules. Each, often not wishing to kill, watched to guess the intentions of his opponent and adjusted his behavior accordingly. Each faced an identical danger.

The proper duel involved the extension of a host of courtesies. John Lyde Wilson's code of dueling advised that, once on the dueling ground, "each second informs the other when he is about to load, and invites his presence, but the seconds rarely attend on such invitation, as gentlemen may be safely trusted in the matter." If one party is hit, Wilson advised the second of the other party to "forthwith tender any assistance he can command to the disabled principal."[25] It was in this same spirit of extending courtesies that B. Gratz Brown in an 1856 Missouri encounter spent the night before the duel as a guest at the house of his adversary's second. In an 1817 duel one duelist fired before the other could pull the trigger. The one who shot demanded that he be shot at in turn, but the other refused. Finally he discharged his pistol into the air and they were reconciled.[26]

The very act of sending a note to someone, even in confrontation, meant that you regarded your opponent as a social equal. Cilley's rejection was the cause of James Watson Webb's fury. He had acknowledged Cilley as a social equal by sending him a note, but Cilley had refused to reciprocate. Wilson's code of dueling clearly stated that dueling encounters could occur only between social equals. It was in this spirit that S. S. Prentiss of Mississippi refused to duel with the editor of the Vicksburg *Sentinel* when he received a challenge. The editor was not his social equal. But Governor Tilghman Tucker's attendance at a dinner to honor the editor indicated an alliance to Prentiss, so he challenged the governor—his social equal. Similarly, Benjamin F. Perry, a frequently insulted South Carolina Unionist, decided not to challenge men who were beneath him in status. He wrote in his 1832 *Journal*: "I am not going to challenge any blackguard of an editor. The next man I fight or challenge shall be a man of distinction."[27] This assumption of equality between opposing duelists extended to the form of the duel. Both parties on the field, according to Wilson's code, were "entitled to a perfect equality." Consequently it was dangerous to fight a duel with a poor shot. In order to eliminate the difference in shooting ability, the distance had to be decreased and therefore the likelihood of death became quite great.[28]

This view of the relationship between duelists made "strangers" a special problem in the culture of dueling. Strangers were people with an undetermined position in the social structure. Wilson's dueling code offered special instructions for dueling confrontations with strangers. First of all, he warned seconds: "If a stranger wish you to bear a note for him, be well satisfied before you do so, that he is on an equality with you; and in presenting the note, state to the party the relationship you stand towards him, and what you know and believe about him." As for the person challenged by a stranger, Wilson advised, "you have a right to a reasonable time to ascertain his standing in society, unless he be fully vouched for, by his friend." In 1806, when Andrew Jackson decided to refuse a challenge to a duel, he explained, "I will not degrade myself by the acceptance of a challenge from a stranger whose acts and conduct had been inconsistent with that of a gentleman."[29]

The understanding of the duel as a ritual of admission to a gentleman's club may have caused some Southerners to see the duel as a vehicle of social mobility. To be shot at by a man was to assume his social status. It was probably no coincidence that shortly after revolutionary general Robert Howe wrote Henry Laurens, "I have been long upon the Brigadier's list and pant to get higher," he was involved in a duel with Christopher Gadsden. One enterprising British soldier even faked a duel in order to gain acceptance among American revolutionary officers. In 1778 John Laurens wrote about a British soldier, Cope, who came to the American side seeking protection because he had just killed a man in a duel and feared the consequences. He was treated with "generosity" by the Americans until they discovered he was an "imposter." "A duel has lately been fought," wrote Laurens, "in which an officer was killed, but Cope was not concerned in it." Laurens warned others of the lie. In 1829 Edward Bates, member of Congress from Missouri, challenged George McDuffie of South Carolina. According to one historian of the encounter, "He afterwards gave as his reason for the challenge that, being a representative from a frontier state, McDuffie seemed to consider him inferior to the representatives of the older commonwealths."[30]

To be excluded from a duel was a terrible insult, for it denied one's membership in the group of "gentlemen." Those excluded struggled mightily to gain admission. James Jackson, for example, refused a challenge from Jacob Waldburger in 1798 because Waldburger had once been whipped by a gentleman. Waldburger tried to explain the whipping in the newspaper, noting that it happened "when I was really but a boy." James Wilkinson, disgraced by involvement in Aaron Burr's schemes to detach the Western states, practically begged John Randolph for a duel in 1807. "I have no hesitation," he wrote, "to appeal to your justice, your magnanimity and your gallantry, to prescribe the manner of redress." Randolph denied his request. "I cannot descend to your level," he wrote.[31]

Perhaps the most dramatic example of a man begging for a duel occurred in an Andrew Jackson encounter in 1806. Jackson decided that Thomas Swann was not a gentleman, so he caned him. Swann was distraught, as he later confessed in a newspaper article. Jackson, he said, "was told I had letters of introduction, and could procure certain certificates to prove I was entitled to that character." Swann even subsequently published his letters of reference to clear his tarnished name.[32]

The same intense social pressures operated on the other side of the dueling encounter. To refuse a duel once offered by a recognized gentleman, or to refuse to challenge once insulted by a gentleman, was to resign your membership in the club. James Thatcher, surgeon in the revolutionary army, described an officer who was forced to duel because "his brother officers treated him with contempt, and threatened to hoot him out of camp." When, in 1804, the volatile John Randolph splashed wine and broke a glass in the face of a young congressman, and then threw a bottle of wine at him, a contemporary observer reported that "the men of the Pistol say that so gross and deliberate an abuse cannot be pocketed or compromised—that A. [Congressman Alston] must fight—or leave the place in disgrace."[33] Similarly, S. S. Prentiss explained in a letter to his brother after his first duel that if he did not fight "life will be rendered valueless to him, both in his own eyes and those of the community." Willie Mangum, commenting on the Clingman-Yancey duel of 1845, noted that Clingman had to fight: "It was unavoidable, & to have declined would have disgraced him here & destroyed his just Weight & influence." Mississippian Henry S. Foote noted that short of being closely associated with a religious group no one could turn down a challenge "without being consigned to permanent discredit and coldly shut out from all intercourse with gentlemen."[34]

Since the duel always occurred between social equals it should come as no surprise that duelists frequently admired their opponents. The greater the status of your foe, the higher your own status. When Thomas Tudor Tucker was shot by Ralph Izard in revolutionary South Carolina he expressed his respect for a man who "did not scruple to acknowledge what he had said, to insist on the right of saying it, and to wish every man in the parish had been present to hear it." In a 1783 duel, after the first exchange of shots, James Jackson shouted across to the man aiming at him: "Damn it, Gibbons, you're a brave man and a good marksman, for I believe your ball hit my pistol." Gibbons replied: "You are a brave man, General Jackson." In the John Laurens–Charles Lee duel, when Laurens was late for the dueling ground, Lee's second remarked that he might not come at all. Lee was quick to answer that that was impossible for Laurens was a man of "unquestionable bravery." Even after Lee was shot and lay on the ground bleeding he remarked: "How handsomely the young fellow behaved. I could have hugged him!"[35]

As one would expect from an institution that upheld and reinforced the equality of participants, reconciliation rather than death was more often the result of duels. The number of duels that produced good friendships or, at least cordial relations, was extraordinary. John Lyde Wilson's code mandated that, when both parties in a duel were satisfied after an uneventful exchange of shots, the second of the challenger should announce: "We have agreed that the present duel shall cease, the honor of each of you is preserved, and you will meet on middle ground, shake hands and be reconciled."[36] The formal language of Wilson's code captured the spirit of the real experience of many duelists. Several years after the Laurens-Grimke duel in revolutionary South Carolina, Laurens casually referred to Grimke in a letter as "my good friend John Paul Grimke." After the Clay-Randolph duel of 1824 the two men shook hands. Clay had put a bullet through Randolph's coat. Randolph noted: "You owe me a coat, Mr. Clay." Clay answered: "I am glad the debt is no greater." According to Randolph's biographer, a few days after the duel "the parties exchanged cards, and social relations were formally and courteously restored." After Henry S. Foote shot at S. S. Prentiss in two Mississippi duels he noted: "We were good friends, and lived in the greatest amity and harmony up to the period of his death." One Louisiana duel, rather than ending in a death, ended in a jolly breakfast for all at a nearby restaurant.[37]

Even when a duel ended in blood, the wounded duelist more often spoke words of love than of hate. As James Barron and Stephen Decatur lay on the ground both thinking themselves mortally wounded, "Barron proposed that they should make friends before they met in Heaven. . . . Decatur said he had never been his enemy, that he freely forgave him his death." As two duelists lay dying together on the ground in New Orleans, the last to die noted of his old "schoolmate" who lay dead beside him that "they had been on terms of great intimacy and friendship for fifteen years; and he bore honorable testimony to his character as a man of science and a gentleman." It was clearly another good reference letter to take to heaven.[38]

The duel not only permitted men to display their membership in the dominant social group in the society, it also allowed them to define publicly the proper behavior of the members of that group. After all, an "insult" involved words spoken or written that damaged a reputation. These words indicated improper behavior and by negative implication suggested proper comportment.

What words so damaged the reputation of a Southern political leader as to make him want to risk his life in order to erase their effect? Only a very few kinds of insults generated duels in the South. Although many duels had their ultimate origins in longstanding rivalries and political disagreements, the movement from a dispute to a duel could only be accomplished by a handful of magical words. James Watson Webb, for example, although he disliked Cilley's political position, did not initiate a dueling encounter until Cilley had accused him of corruption—of having accepted a bribe. A slightly different insult generated the Clingman-Yancey duel. Clingman opposed the annexation of Texas, and Yancey charged him with being a traitor to the South, of betraying both his principles and his friends, of becoming mired in "the dark purlieus of party." "Ambition" was the insult tossed at A. G. Magrath by the editor of the *Charleston Mercury.* Other insulting words included calling a young man a "puppy" or calling any man a scoundrel, a villain, a coward, a dastard, a poltroon, or an abolitionist. But perhaps the most common precipitant of Southern duels involved the charge of lying. This charge, in part, was what bothered William J. Graves according to his account of his duel with Jonathan Cilley. Graves claimed he had a verbal acknowledgment of Webb's status as a gentleman, but Cilley refused to confirm it in writing, thereby casting doubt on Graves's word. The 1771 Charleston duel between Haley and Delancey began because Delancey "gave him the lie." In 1809 Henry Clay challenged Humphrey Marshall because Marshall called him a liar. The Thomas Hart Benton–Charles H. Lucas duel began after they met as opposing lawyers in a trial and accused each other of lying.[39]

Although there are numerous exceptions, most insults—especially insults involving unprincipled political alliances, corruption, ambition, or lying—struck at the very heart of a man's status as a statesman, and not coincidentally at his status as a master as well. Southerners believed that a statesman and a master could be trusted with power in part because they shared the interests of their community, but the ideal leader also had to be a man of good character. An ambitious man, an unprincipled man, a man who deceived could not be trusted with power—power that could so easily be abused. An insult, in short, struck at the core of a man's claim to exercise authority in the South. It struck at the very thing that, in a gentleman's own eyes, made him a man.

Why did the duel seem the appropriate remedy for the kinds of insults that challenged a man's right to exercise power? Why, for example, did not James Watson Webb respond to the bribery charge by amassing proof of his innocence and printing it in his newspaper? Although Cilley, because he spoke his insulting words in Congress, may have been immune from a legal suit, why did not people like Benton and Lucas sue for slander when they accused each other of lying? The problem was that neither the publication of evidence of good character nor a suit for slander was the right theatrical display to erase the implications of an insult. To amass evidence in one's own behalf implied a kind of self-interest and self-absorption that did not conform to the disinterested pose of the gentleman and the statesman. If a man really had no ambition why should he go to such trouble to prove his innocence? If a man's word could be believed why should he need to amass additional proof? Similarly the suit for slander or libel carried the wrong message. To sue in court for one's reputation did not simply involve a great deal of time, expense, and keeping the issue in public view. The legal suit also carried the improper implication that reputation and character once injured could be repaired by the payment of money damages. A man who would take money in exchange for an insult was just the kind of man who might take money in exchange for his vote.

The duel, on the other hand, allowed a gentleman to display the proper qualities of character necessary for him to be trusted with power.

The duel, in fact, duplicated the rhythms of the statesman. Just as statesmen periodically asserted their individual independence by resignations, reversals, and the breakage of political alliances, the insulted gentleman asserted his independence by issuing a challenge, stopping his normal worldly activities and connections, writing out his will, and facing his opponent alone in a moment that threatened death. Moreover, duels proceeded in a form that paralleled the ideal statesman's election: "friends" carried out most of the activity while principals remained passive. John Lyde Wilson's code of dueling offered advice to an insulted gentleman that John C. Calhoun might have given to a statesman: "When you believe yourself aggrieved, be silent on the subject, speak to no one about the matter, and see your friend who is to act for you as soon as possible." Once a gentleman acquired a second, Wilson suggested that he "leave the whole matter to his [the second's] judgement and avoid any consultation with him unless he seeks it. He has the custody of your honor, and by obeying him you cannot be compromitted." Wilson advised that, once on the dueling ground, duelists, like candidates for office, "are to be wholly passive, being entirely under the guidance of their seconds."[40] Furthermore, the duel, like the oration of the statesman, inspired a kind of awe among people. Like the orator, the duelist never asked people to respect him, he simply displayed himself in a way that commanded admiration, even awe. Like the orator he did not directly converse with people by defending his character in the newspapers; he placed himself on a stage for all to see and admire. The form and style of his behavior carried the substance of his message. The duel embodied both the passivity demanded by republicanism and the assertion of power demanded by honor.

Orlando Patterson's comparative study of slavery and social death offers further insight into the reasons why masters saw the duel as a ritual that justified their right to govern. Masters in virtually all slave societies think of slaves as having chosen a subservient life—a life without honor, a social death—in order to avoid real death. It is the slave's fear of actual death that (according to the mythology of masters) makes him a slave. Masters on the other hand do not have this fear.[41] And, of course, the duel perfectly demonstrates this. After facing death, the duelist is reborn into the world ready to assume his position as a master. This behavior, of course, reduplicates the actions of the statesman who resigns from office only to reemerge with an enhanced reputation and greater power. Both the statesman and the master must face death in order to be reborn into a position of honor and power.

Overall, then, the duel seen as a social drama offers a reflection of some of the central elements of the political culture of slavery. It displayed the ideals and rhythms of statesmen and masters. It demonstrated that strange mixture of passivity and aggression that appeared in the statehouse and on the plantation. Moreover, it publicly expressed the unity of the gentlemen who exercised authority—that they all belonged to the same club. Even though these men might sometimes engage in bitter conflict—might belong to different parties or different families—the message of the duel was that they all were united. In short, the duel reaffirmed the hegemony of the ruling group in the South, displaying their values and their solidarity for all to see.

PART II

THE GOVERNMENT OF MASTERS AND THE GOVERNMENT OF SLAVES

CHAPTER 3

Party and Antiparty

BETWEEN 1789 AND 1840 the United States underwent a transition from factional to party politics. Since party and faction are terms that defy precise definition, and since the transformation did not progress at the same rate all over the country, historians disagree over exactly when this change occurred. Some perceive the emergence of American political parties in the years before the Constitutional Convention, whereas others do not recognize true political parties until the 1830s. Perhaps Ronald P. Formisano is correct in noting that no single date separates faction from party politics in America, but that the change spans fifty years. Old political habits did not die suddenly or easily.[1] Nonetheless, there is general agreement that the political practices of the nation underwent a significant transformation between 1789 and 1840. One way to characterize this change is as a switch from faction to party.

Party and faction are difficult to distinguish precisely because they are demarcated by differences of degree. Among other things, the relations between leaders and followers are more stable in parties than in factions; parties involve more people, both among the leadership and the electorate, who are more formally linked; and parties have more formal, stable structures for handling such political functions as nominating candidates, electioneering for office, compromising and mediating between groups, and providing connections among the various levels and branches of the government.[2] In short, parties are characterized by formal organizational structures, stability over time, and mass participation, whereas factions are informal, unstable, and elite oriented.

The central argument of this chapter is that political parties never developed so fully, nor were they so firmly rooted, in the antebellum South—especially the deep South—as in the rest of the nation. Parties, of course, were important in many Southern states, but elements of instability often underlay their development. Slavery, as we will see, provided poor soil for party growth. Political parties did not flourish in the world of republicanism and honor.

I

TO ASSERT THAT ANTEBELLUM Southern political parties differed from those in other parts of the country is not to ignore the vast body of evidence suggesting the contrary. William J. Cooper, Jr., in his sweeping study of Southern politics, argued that most antebellum Southerners fully embraced the new mass party tactics and organizations. Conceding that a few Southerners, "patricians and radicals," adhered to the older ideals of statesmanship and lamented the decline of morality they saw in the new political order, Cooper believed that such skeptics (with the exception of John C. Calhoun) remained on the periphery of Southern politics. Despite the repeated cries of many Southerners that they were poor organizers, Cooper argued: "The reality of conventions, clubs, executive committees, correspondence committees, circulars, addresses, rallies, and, most important, victories belie such lamentations."[3]

Cooper's judgment is supported by a host of other studies. Several historians have noted the remarkable loyalty of the mass of the Southern population to the new antebellum political parties—a loyalty no different from that evident in other parts of the country. Thomas B. Alexander discovered a great deal of continuity in Democratic party loyalty between 1844 and 1856, reaching similar conclusions for both Northern and Southern counties.[4] Richard P. McCormick's analysis of party formation in the Jacksonian era described the rise during the 1830s of a tense rivalry between two evenly matched parties all over the nation. Numerous state studies have noted the elaborate party organization and rivalry that were common everywhere in the South during the 1830s and 1840s.[5]

That political parties in each state assumed a roughly similar form should come as no surprise to any student of nineteenth-century America. State party structures and practices, after all, did not develop in isolation from one another. For one thing, the political institutions that provided the setting for party development resembled each other all over the country. State governmental structures, despite local variations, assumed a similar form because popular political values largely overlapped, and the writers of state constitutions copied one another. Moreover, common participation in national elections and national political institutions linked the various state political parties. The presidential election—the election that vitalized party activity everywhere (except in South Carolina)—demanded some kind of national coordination and cooperation, even if only once in four years. Furthermore, the Congress and other federal institutions required political leaders from all parts of the country to work together continuously. Given these circumstances, it is not at all remarkable that state political parties should resemble each other. What is noteworthy is that they should differ at all in any systematic way. The differences are not extreme, but they are significant.

One difference between Northern and Southern political parties is suggested by an analysis of electoral competition during the antebellum years. Organizational development and stability, as well as mass loyalty, could not long survive in America unless parties seriously competed with each other. Political competition was both cause and consequence of party organization.[6] Although the patterns of political competition in the states of the upper South do not easily lend themselves to simple generalization, it seems quite clear that within the deep South (including states with the greatest concentration of slaves) competition was never quite so intense over so long a period as it was in non-Southern states during the antebellum period. Even though some deep Southern states had a great deal of competition, especially during certain periods, overall they had less electoral competition than was common in most Northern states.

One good way to compare degrees of electoral competition is to examine elections to the House of Representatives. Congressional electoral districts uniformly divide the nation into units of roughly comparable size (with the exception of the 3/5 clause in the South), and congressional elections regularly recur every two years. If electoral competition were essentially the same all over the nation then we would expect to find little variation in the competitiveness of House elections between regions. But that is not the case.

If we define a noncompetitive election as one in which the winner attained more than a 20 percent margin of victory over the second-place candidate, then the deep South had fewer competitive elections than the rest of the nation. During the period 1824–60, of the 347 congressional elections for which returns are available in the deep South, 170, or nearly half, were not competitive. In the rest of the nation, outside the South, only about one-quarter of the elections involved margins of greater than 20 percent. Even if we divide the period into three parts, roughly corresponding with the rise and fall of the second party system and compare the deep South with non-Southern states, a similar pattern emerges for each period (see table 1).

Analysis of presidential election returns also illustrates the lower competition within deep Southern states. Approximately 42 percent of all popular presidential electoral contests in the deep South between 1824 and 1860 involved margins of victory greater than 20 percent. This result compares with a showing of only 25 percent of noncompetitive elections outside the South. Calculation of the average difference between the percentage of the popular vote for the winning and second-place candidates for each state during the period 1824–60, and the consequent regional average, echoes this pattern. The average difference for the deep South was almost 25 percent; it was approximately 16 percent for the rest of the nation.[7] What is even more striking about these figures is that the calculations do not include the least competitive deep South state. South Carolina had no popular presidential elections before the Civil War and it cannot be incorporated in the analysis.

Of course, averages of electoral data hide a great deal of variety. In particular, the regional categories and the long-term periodization used here do not reveal that many New England states were sometimes as uncompetitive as deep Southern states; they do not show that some of these Southern states during some periods were more competitive than any others in the nation; and they do not indicate electoral competition at the local or county level. All this is simply to point out that the data considered here are highly aggregated—lumping together in grand averages many years

TABLE 1
Noncompetiveness (Margin of Victory Greater than 20 Percent) in Congressional Elections

Region[a]	1824–34	1835–53	1854–60	1824–60
Deep South	65%[b]	41%	54%	49%
Non-South	35	19	32	25

Source: U.S. Congress, *Congressional Quarterly's Guide to U.S. Elections* (Washington, D.C., 1975).

Note: This table was constructed according to the following criteria: (1) The data only include elections that took place in districts. All at-large elections have been eliminated. This excludes a large number of elections during the period 1824–34. (2) All elections for which the *Congressional Quarterly's Guide* lists no vote returns have been excluded. (3) All multimember districts have not been included. (4) I have not included the upper South in this table. The pattern is more ambiguous, although overall approximately a third of all upper South congressional elections were not competitive between 1824 and 1860.

[a] The states within each region are as follows:
Deep South: Alabama, Florida, Georgia, Louisiana, Mississippi, South Carolina, Texas
Upper South: Arkansas, Delaware, Kentucky, Missouri, Maryland, North Carolina, Tennessee, Virginia
Non-South: Connecticut, Illinois, Indiana, Iowa, Maine, Massachusetts, Michigan, New Hampshire, New Jersey, New York, Ohio, Oregon, Pennsylvania, Rhode Island, Vermont, Wisconsin

[b] Rounded to nearest percent.

and many large political units. They have all the defects of aggregate data but also some of the virtues. Sometimes, to divide the world into little pieces for analysis can be misleading. Division makes it easy to overlook important, large patterns. The technique of aggregation, for example, was useful in our earlier discussion of the tendency of Southern leaders to resign from political office. Each resignation considered in isolation could always be explained by unique circumstances. But to detect the overall tendency to resign, to recognize the aggregate number of resignations, was to arrive at an explanation that transcended any individual or particular cause or motive. The aggregate data made us aware of the operation of a general political culture of slavery.

Similarly, the electoral data presented here in aggregate form could be divided into pieces for analysis. But such a procedure would remove the focus from the overall pattern. The aggregate data include in summary form many separate circumstances which could be considered in isolation but which should also be considered in relation to each other. For example, embedded in the data is the slow development of party and party competition in the South during the 1830s. Although most New England and Middle states had developed political parties by 1829 or 1830, most Southern states did not begin to process until 1834. Even then they seem to have progressed at a slower pace.[8]

The data also reflect the weakness of the Whig party in some Southern states. Even during the 1840s—during the period when it achieved its greatest strength—the Whig party was often a minority party. Whigs in Alabama, for example, never controlled the lower house of the state legislature and only captured the state senate twice. They never won a statewide office, and could never muster more than 40 to 45 percent of the vote.[9] Whigs never gained a significant following in South Carolina. Moreover, the Whig party totally collapsed very early in all the states of the deep South—as early as 1850—and interparty competition never reemerged throughout the decade of the 1850s. The 1852 Whig presidential vote plummeted 66 percent in Georgia, 50 percent in Alabama, and 30 percent in Mississippi. With this election, organized party combat virtually ended in the lower South and most future contests were between rival factions of a disorganized party system.[10]

Also embedded in the data—at least in the data on House elections—is the extreme case of South Carolina. Eighty percent of South Carolina's elections to the Congress were not competitive (elections with a margin of victory greater than 20 percent). The vast majority of these elections involved no opposing candidates at all. No other state approached this total.

Historians have isolated for analysis each of these developments—

the delayed growth of the second party system in the South, the weakness and early collapse of Southern Whiggery, the end of party combat in the deep South during the 1850s, and the peculiar political culture of South Carolina. For example, one historian attributed the slow growth of parties in the South to the position of Andrew Jackson as a regional favorite who stifled any potential Southern opponents. Another historian explained the end of interparty competition in the lower South during the 1850s by describing the elimination of traditional issues from state politics.[11] But individual explanations are not entirely adequate if we consider these separate developments as part of a general weakness of party activity and organization in the South. They identify only the precipitating causes that expose the general weakness.

Additional evidence of underdeveloped Southern parties (even outside the deep South) is scattered throughout the antebellum years. It cries out for an overall explanation. Even during the period before the 1830s, the old South (Virginia, North Carolina, Kentucky, Tennessee, and Georgia) never developed the elaborate party organization characteristic of some Northern states. In states where parties did develop to some extent—Virginia and North Carolina—they had disappeared by 1824.[12] Similar evidence of party weakness repeated itself at the end of the second party system during the 1850s. Not only did the states of the deep South (Alabama, Mississippi, Georgia, Florida, Louisiana, and Texas) fail to redevelop a system of interparty competition after the collapse of the Whig party in 1850, but the weakness of party organization and activity continued into the secession crisis and the Confederacy.

By the time of the 1860 secession conventions, political organization had become so fragmented in the deep South that it virtually ceased to exist. Nothing tells the story quite so eloquently as a list appended to the secession convention of Mississippi, which summarized the "party" labels used by delegates: Democrats, States Rights Democrats, Southern States Rights Democrats, Secession Democrats, Whigs, Old Line Whigs, Secession Old Line Whigs, Secession Whigs, Old Whig, Clay Whig, State Rights Whig, Southern, Southern Rights, Secessionist, A Mississippian, State Rights, Independent Southern, Disunionist Per Se, Inflexible States Rights, Independent, Extremely and Intensely Southern, No Preference, and Opposed to Universal Suffrage. Such a list demonstrates not the wide variety of Southern political organizations but the absence of any organization at all. These were, in large part, not the names of political parties but they were the creations of individual delegates. The collapse of party in Mississippi was repeated in many other Southern states.[13]

The Confederacy, unlike the Union during the Civil War, had no political parties. Seceded Southerners did not join together in political organizations, caucuses, or elaborate political committees. The memory of old party affiliations may have played some role in the politics of the Confederacy. There may even have been an "unconscious spirit" of party, but there was little overt attempt to formalize political relations into organizations.[14] The problem, of course, extended into the postwar years.

What made the South so different from the North? Why did political parties have such a difficult time establishing firm roots in the region? Why did parties appear so late and disappear so early?

II

SLAVE SOCIETY ITSELF helped sap the strength of political parties in the South. It did so in two main ways. The political culture of slavery helped sustain values about political behavior that were not and probably could never become entirely compatible with political parties. Slavery was also related to social conditions that inhibited party growth. Parties developed, of course, in spite of slavery, but never so fully as in nonslave states.

Let us first consider the problem of values. The political ideals described in our earlier discussions of statesmanship and honor were antithetical to political parties. For example, men who liked to think of themselves as statesmen—as independent men of reason who never sought office—could hardly feel comfortable in the new political organizations of the 1830s. These parties and many of their members actively and openly pursued power. Moreover, a good bit of the cement that held parties together was the promise of patronage to loyal followers—the promise of subordinate jobs in a bureaucratic organization. It was hardly the route to honor.[15] Many Southerners might convince themselves for a while that the ideals of statesmanship and honor were not inconsistent with party devotion, but most, even as they joined the new organizations, sensed a tension. Similarly, men who believed that the best protection against the abuse of power lay in establishing a community united by a single interest could never feel comfortable with the clash of interests permanently embedded in the new political order. The implications of these ideas for the development of party loyalty in the South are worth examining in some detail.

Many who accepted the values of masters found it difficult to become loyal members of formal organizations of any kind. Impermanent voluntary associations with limited goals and few demands might be tolerated, but the political party seemed much more threatening. To become a devoted member of a party was severely to reduce one's autonomy, to submit to an external authority, to be "at the will" of other people. This submission, of course, was exactly what masters dreaded when they spoke about their fear of enslavement. Not surprisingly, many Southerners who objected to political parties couched their arguments in the form of such a fear. Hugh Lawson White, Southern Whig presidential candidate, was typical of the kind of leader who joined a party and yet at the same time distanced himself from it. He saw devotion to party as a form of bondage. "I feel," he explained in an 1835 speech, "that I was not intended to be the *slave* of any man or set of men—that I have some mind, and that the author of my existence intended that I should exercise it—that I should form opinions as to *politics and religion*, and freely and fearlessly act upon them, without being intimidated by what either man or devils can do."[16]

A fear of parties as organizations that reduced individuals to slavery was, of course, much exaggerated. Still, this attitude had more than a hint of reality in it, that is, if we accept the broad Southern definition of slavery. For the purposes of elections, for example, an interrelated (even if loosely connected) series of committees and conventions, arranged in an elaborate hierarchy, provided the structure of state and national party unity. For the purposes of government, caucuses bound party members within legislative bodies. Whether in committees, conventions, or caususes, individual preferences had to be subordinated to the good of the organization. Ideally, although not always in practice, lower levels of the organization had to conform to upper levels in the hierarchy. The best situation for parties was the one described in an 1840 report of an Ohio Whig organizer: "Conventions named the men and all personal considerations are sunk in devotion to party."[17] Such a political system had little need for the statesman or voter of independent mind or the man in search of honor. Such a political system needed managers and the party soldiers they controlled.

But the concept of management in politics frightened many people in ninteenth-century America, especially Southern masters. Men who seemed openly to embrace the techniques of political managers—Thaddeus Stevens of Pennsylvania or Thurlow Weed of New York—represented a strange perversion of proper political values. Southerners repeatedly voiced their condemnation of management in a wide variety of contexts. It was on the lips of John C. Calhoun as he explained to Lewis Cass in 1823 that the nation was exposed not only to the danger of aristocracy, but also to the "speret [*sic*; of co]mbination and poli[tica]l management." An Alabama priest also had it in mind in 1857 when he wrote "that in the policy of parties there is over much trickery and management." It was in the thought of Howell Cobb in 1860 when he voiced his fear about being accused of "managing" the movement for his nomination for president in the Democratic convention.[18] What would such men have thought of Senator Richard Brodhead of Pennsylvania who, after avoiding a discussion of the great political issues of the 1850s, openly told Carl Schurz: "On the whole, I do not take as much interest in measures and policies as in the management of men."[19]

Southerners, of course, knew all about the "management of men." That was how some masters described the way they handled slaves. A Georgian, for example, noted in 1851: "No question of domestic economy . . . demands more the attention of the slaveholder and philanthropist than the treatment and management of slaves." An 1846 Alabama agricultural society committee explained to readers that "with prudent management prosperity on the part of the master and happiness on the part of the slave is the inevitable consequence." An 1852 Virginia planter called attention to the single most important issue involving the prosperity of masters: "the management of Negroes."[20] In other words, in the minds of many Southerners management was the activity that masters performed on slaves. It was intimately associated with treating the slave as an object to be used for purposes understood only by the master or manager.[21] Even if some masters softened the relationship by refusing to use the term "management" at all, even if some masters thought of their love for their slaves as a management tool, even if some masters convinced themselves that slave management could be in the interests of both master and slave—everyone knew that only inferior people could become the objects of management. Although such powerful associations might have been absent in the mind of a Pennsylvania senator who openly described himself as a political manager, masters could not help but make the connection. Little wonder that so many Southerners so often described their fear of party managers as enslavers. Little wonder that formal organizations and their managers frightened Southerners. It was this same fear which reduced the effectiveness of another formal organization—the Confederate army—during the Civil War. Just as many Southerners resisted the role of loyal party soldier in the antebellum period, they resisted the regimented life of the armed camp, refusing to follow unreasonable or even unpleasant orders, objecting to marching in tidy lines, and determining their own length of service.[22] They treated the army as they had treated the political party—joining the organization in one sense, but remaining at a distance in another; marching, perhaps, but not always in straight lines.

Many Southerners also firmly maintained that real statesmen could never become good party managers or loyal party workers. Party loyalists, they believed, sought power rather than principle. This belief is ironic, of course, because it was precisely power that Southern statesmen in search of honor really wanted. But they hoped to obtain power rooted in the pose of passivity rather than the active power of the party organizer. John C. Calhoun, for example, disliked the idea that a supporter of Andrew Jackson did not assume a political position based on a commitment to principle and reason, and could remain a Jackson man as long as "he shall submit to party discipline and sustain the party candidates for office." A writer in the *Southern Quarterly Review* objected to "the utter shamelessness with which they [political parties] grasp at power, in the teeth of principle." The editor of the South Carolina *Unionville Journal* echoed the familiar theme when he objected to the absence of a discussion of slavery in the 1856 Democratic platform. "This looks," he argued, "like putting party success forward as the first consideration, and leaving principles in the background." Another writer voiced a similar objection to the 1860 Democratic Convention and warned Southerners not "to cling with blinking eyes to party, and scramble with the shortsighted or corrupt in the low game of office seeking and party promotion."[23]

Many Southerners assumed that party loyalists inevitably became obsessed with a self-interested concern for personal power rather than with a disinterested devotion to the general good. Party membership inevitably perverted the stateman.[24] "Let the statesman regard alone the helm of state," a writer in the *Southern Quarterly Review* declared in 1844. "Let him divest himself of the degrading livery of party . . . let him characterize his action by devotion to truth and principle." In 1858 the South Carolina *Lexington Flag* praised a political leader who had remained free of any party connection: "He has preferred to take an independent position as was taken by all the pure and illustrious statesmen of our country!"[25]

John C. Calhoun applied these ideas in many different situations during the forty years of his public career. Calhoun warned in 1814 that "opposition, in free States, is strongly inclined to degenerate into a struggle for power and ascendency, in which attachment to party becomes stronger than attachment to country." Whenever charged with party loyalty during the rest of his career, he struggled to deny the imputation. "I appeal with confidence to my life," he told the 1836 House of Representatives, "to prove, that neither hostility nor attachment to any man or any party, can influence me in the discharge of my public duties." In 1840 he reaffirmed his independence of party in a letter to his daughter: "My political position remains of course just where it was; ready to sustain the administration, when right and oppose them when wrong, and on all occasions to express my opinions freely." When accused of party voting in the 1847 Senate, Calhoun fumed in reply to his attacker: "If he means to say that there is any organized opposition here,—as far as I am concerned, or my friends . . . never, never was a man more mistaken—never!"[26] Even if we believe that Calhoun really did seek power for himself, even if he did not always live up to the ideals embodied in his statements, we can still see their relationship to his behavior. He was never a conscious party manager or good party soldier.

The antiparty themes so often touched by Calhoun remained vital to many others in the antebellum South. One can see them in Hugh Lawson White's 1836 campaign for the presidency when he condemned the Jacksonians as "having no common bond of unity save that of a wish to place one of themselves in the highest office known to the Constitution, for the purpose of having all the honors, offices, and emoluments of the government distributed by him among his followers." Alexander Stephens of Georgia, like many other Southerners, supported Zachary Taylor's "no-party" campaign for the presidency. Taylor, Stephens wrote John J. Crittendon, was above political parties and had been elected "without the aid of schemers and intriguers and without any pledge save to serve the country faithfully." Stephens voiced the same ideals in 1860 when he broke free of political parties for the last time. "Parties may rise or fall," he wrote, "but principles with me are the pole star of my existence. What is the matter now with the country is that a class of men are in power who have no loyalty to principle, no attachment to truth for truth's sake. They are governed by a desire for office, for place and spoils, and change principles with any change of popular [breeze?] in their eagerness to get it." Southern fire-eaters, the men who pushed most strongly for secession, also repeatedly gave voice to the same fear of selfish party men. This, of course, was an old refrain in the chorus of republican thinkers. Over and over again they warned of the danger of party placemen and "political hucksters" and "tricksters." Even in the Confederacy, political opponents accused each other of acting in the spirit of party, of acting out of their concern for personal gain or the spoils of office. The charge was always hotly contested.[27] The numerous circumstances in which these ideas reappear attest to their powerful hold on the minds of many in the South.

Political parties also seemed to challenge the ideal of a society based on harmony—a society in which all groups shared a common interest. Unity was a favorite theme in South Carolina but it won increasing support elsewhere in the South, especially as the final secession crisis approached. Depending on their perception of the source of conflict, South Carolinians emphasized the need for unity in the state, the region, or the nation. They needed to eliminate conflict. And party always seemed associated with conflict. "We must not again mix up our [South Carolina's] complaints with mere party questions," Robert Hayne wrote James H. Hammond on the eve of South Carolina nullification. "We ought to keep aloof from everything calculated to divide our own citizens." After Calhoun began to see conflict within the state as nullification approached, he hoped that "our divisions sprang from accidental circumstances" and looked "forward with confidence to Union." In 1838 Calhoun feared to permit the people to elect the governor directly because "instead of producing unanimity at home, as is now the case, two violent parties would spring up, which would nearly equally divide the State." When the 1840 governor's election passed without serious party division, Calhoun rejoiced: "It is in the sperit [*sic*] of our noble little state."[28]

The secession crisis of 1850–52 also provided the occasion for the expression of faith in consensus in South Carolina. Francis W. Pickens pleaded with an audience at Edgefield "to produce union, concert of action, cordial and kind feelings at home, in every citizen of the state and between all classes and parties," William D. Porter asked Carolinians for "that union of feelings and sentiment, that concert of will and action . . . which are the chief sources of national strength." Another Carolinian looked back on the workings of the 1852 secession convention and rejoiced that it had obliterated division within the state. "The convention met last week," he wrote with approval, "and laid down a platform . . . which has reconciled parties and has made South Carolina once more a united people."[29] The unity evidenced in the 1860 secession decision greatly pleased Carolinians.

Carolinians shared the idea that the consensus generally prevailing in the state made South Carolina a particularly formidable defender of republican government. This belief was corollary to the idea that party drained the power of republics. Calhoun rejoiced that national parties never penetrated into the state: "it is because there is no powerful local party in the State, through which to act, and by which the State might be controlled, that we are enable[d] to interpose and nullify an unconstitutional act of Congress, which no other state can do, except on some local question." W. F. Colcock explained in 1851 to a Southern Rights Association meeting in Charleston why South Carolina was quicker to react against federal government aggression than other states: "But the chief cause for this state of forwardness on the part of South Carolina is the entire absence of party division within her borders. . . . In our sister states the people have been drawn away from the calm and unbiased consideration of great Federal questions, and have been engaged in eager strife for party ascendency. But with us there has always been a 'unity of sentiment' which has emphatically 'constituted us one people.' " J. C. Coit believed that "there is a more determined spirit of resistance in South Carolina" because her people "are free from the prejudices and bondage of national parties." Two years before the final secession crisis, James L. Petigru, after lamenting the rise of division within the state during the revolutionary war, proclaimed that nineteenth-century South Carolina had solved the problem of conflict: "The unanimity which for years has marked the republican counsels of the state deserves to be mentioned as the unexpected solution, a successful development of the long continued drama. From the most heterogeneous we have become the most united of all the political communities on this continent."[30]

Those Carolinians who sought protection from Northern aggression in a Southern Confederacy pleaded for the extension of South Carolina's unity to the whole South. They especially hoped to destroy the divisive influence of national political parties. In 1849 Iveson L. Brookes rejected any connection to national political parties and advised "that the Southern people at the present crisis should know but one party; the great mass of the South should as one man stand forth in defense of Southern rights." The Carolina novelist William Gilmore Simms objected to the way the Whig and Democratic parties "divided the people upon false issues" and, in another context, urged "the Union of all our [Southern] powers."[31]

In fact, much of Simms's literary career was devoted to cataloguing the horrors of factional squabbling during the revolutionary period in South Carolina. He referred to the revolution in the state as a civil war and condemned the bitter conflict that divided the young Republic. Simms was a romantic novelist, always more concerned with the "moral truths" than the "facts" of history, and the consensus ideal was one of the principal moral truths that informed his 1842 history of South Carolina: "Unanimity among our citizens will always give them unconquerable strength, and invasion will never again set hostile feet on the shores of our country."[32]

Perhaps one of the most peculiar features of antebellum Carolinians' continuing belief in the ideal of unanimity was their revival of the old notion that a republic could not long exist over a large expanse of territory. The argument flourished only briefly, achieving its clearest expression during the movement for single state secession in the early 1850s, but that it appeared at all is noteworthy. William D. Porter, for example, developed the idea when he demanded that South Carolina secede alone in 1851. While noting the strength of such small republics as Athens, Sparta, Rome, Venice, Genoa, and Florence, he concluded that among "the elements of strength in a state are compactness of territory, union of interest and feeling" and that "while small states have sometimes afforded substantial liberty, large ones have always been despotic."[33] Such ideas help explain tiny South Carolina's sense of invincibility as it repeatedly faced hostility from overwhelming forces.

It is quite appropriate that the most significant achievement of political thought in the antebellum South, John C. Calhoun's *Disquisition on Government,* should be so concerned with the problem of consensus. Although Calhoun disliked diverse interests in a community and feared that one group would always oppress another, he believed that diversity of interest was inevitable, even in the smallest state. Even if all people in a community had the same occupation, the action of the government that collects and disburses tax revenues would operate unequally on the citizens and thereby create conflicting interests. Parties, a collection of partial groups, would inevitably rise to fight for government offices in order to control the taxing and expenditure process.[34]

James Madison, like John C. Calhoun, had conceded the inevitability of faction, but Madison sought to nullify the effects of faction by extending the size of the Republic, thereby increasing the number of factions, relatively diminishing their individual strength, and decreasing the likelihood of control by a single interest or group of interests. But Calhoun's solution to the problem of diversity went beyond Madison's attempt simply to control the evil effects of faction. For while in one breath Calhoun conceded the inevitability of faction, in the next he devised an organism, as he called it, or constitution, that would not simply check the consequences of conflicting interests, but would, in effect, totally destroy faction. Calhoun's constitution was based on the notion of the concurrent majority and provided a veto to each faction as a protective device. "By giving to each interest, or portion, the power of self-protection," he explained, "all strife and struggle between them for ascendency, is prevented; and, thereby, not only every feeling calculated to weaken the attachment to the whole is suppressed, but the individual and the social feelings are made to unite in one common devotion to country. Each sees and feels that it can best promote its own prosperity by conciliating the goodwill, and promoting the prosperity of the others."[35] Calhoun assumed that reasonable men would avoid anarchy, which he considered the greatest political evil, and that under the concurrent majority, factions would realize that their selfish interest coincided with that of the general good. When the interest of the parts coincided with the interest of the whole, factions, in effect, would disappear. Men and groups, of course, would continue to act in their self-interest, but their self-interest would also be the general interest. Calhoun viewed with pleasure the happy prospect of a society based on consensus:

> *And hence, there will be diffused throughout the whole community kind feelings between its different portions; and, instead of antipathy, a rivalry amongst them to promote the interests of each other, as far as this can be done consistently with the interest of all. Under the combined influence of these causes, the interests of each would be merged in the common interests of the whole; and thus, the community would become a unit, by becoming the centre of attachment of all its parts. And hence, instead of faction, strife, and struggle for party ascendency, there would be patriotism, nationality, harmony, and a struggle for supremacy in promoting the common good of the whole.*

It is a tribute to the power of the consensus ideal that Calhoun, who believed that men would always act in their self-interest, should struggle so hard to develop an ideal community where for all practical purposes self-interest was eliminated from politics.[36]

South Carolinians were certainly the most devoted to the ideal of a polity based on consensus, but they were not alone. The appeal for unity and harmony, though never fully achieved, was an important theme elsewhere. For example, Georgians, on the eve of the Civil War, repeatedly gave voice to the vision of homogeneity. Sometimes they spoke as if the state already had achieved the ideal, as when Governor Joseph E. Brown told the state legislature in 1861 that "our whole social system is one of perfect homogeneity of interest, where every class of society is interested in sustaining the interest of every other class." Georgia had not achieved, nor would it ever really achieve such unity, but Brown's statement of the fact in this context is a reaffirmation of his devotion to the ideal. Even though political groups fought each other during the final secession crisis, even though cooperationists (those who wanted to act only in concert with other Southern states) fought against immediate secessionists, each side assumed that the ideal society was one united by harmony and consensus. Similar visions are evident all over the South. Many saw secession as finally ending political party activity, as finally destroying those divisive institutions organized for permanent combat. "We have now no political parties in the South," one Georgia newspaper gleefully observed in 1861. "We are united as a band of brothers . . . and a glorious career of unity, harmony, prosperity, and renown awaits us."[37] Just as many masters believed that the plantation prospered as a little community united by a common interest, so they believed that the elimination of political parties would bring prosperity to their state or section.

Given the popularity of antiparty ideas in the slave states, one wonders why political parties developed at all. Why did men who expressed a general distrust of parties frequently join them in practice? For, despite the great vigor of antiparty thought in the South, parties did emerge for some period nearly everywhere. Why did men who hated parties, men who hated political management and organization, who believed that parties could easily corrupt political leaders, and who maintained that the best society was united by consensus—why did these men still join party ranks?

One answer to this question—perhaps an answer that is a bit too simple—is that party organization worked. That is, when two candidates opposed each other the one who engaged in management, the one who could draw on organized support, won the election (especially if he could convince everyone that he did not engage in management). When men with spears face those with guns, the guns win in two ways: they kill more people, and they become objects of universal desire, even as they are hated. Moreover, political organization which had developed earliest and most fully in Northern states such as New York, Pennsylvania, and Ohio had a tendency to spread because its practitioners won elections. Bonds of union connected the South to these early party states. National political institutions helped spread the move toward organization in several ways. In the Congress, for example, it became difficult for representatives to have any impact at all unless they either joined outright the new parties or cooperated with them so closely that they, in effect, joined. As one representative stated the case: "A member of Congress has very little standing in that body who vacillates from one side of party politics to the other in excited party times." Another congressman wrote of the inevitable fate that awaited those who shunned parties: "God help the victim that dare express an opinion in opposition to the orthodoxy of party. Excommunication and proscription is his inevitable destiny." Many Southern congressmen had to use the new weapons even though they hated them, or they would be destroyed.[38]

But on the level of party formation among the masses of voters, the popular election of the president had a much greater impact on the slave states. As Richard P. McCormick has demonstrated, it was the popular presidential contest—a contest involving the mass of the voters—that spurred the establishment of a two-party system in the United States after 1830.[39] The quadrennial popular election for the presidency created the need for permanent party organizations on a national level, molded lasting loyalties between leaders and followers, and formalized and stabilized the fluid lines of politics in all the states of the Union—in all the states, that is, except South Carolina. South Carolina is really the exception that proves the rule, for only South Carolina remained aloof from the mass presidential contest between 1832 and 1860, and only South Carolina completely avoided the development of political parties. Only in South Carolina could the antiparty attitudes compatible with the larger world view of masters develop largely outside the context of nationalizing political institutions because South Carolina never made the fundamental institutional change essential for popular participation in the election for president. By 1828 all states of the Union except South Carolina and Delaware had removed the power of electing presidential electors from the legislature and placed it directly in the hands of the people. From 1832 to the Civil War, South Carolina stood alone.

The issue of direct election of presidential electors was debated in the state, but its advocates failed to muster the strength necessary to achieve victory.[40] Why this reform never succeeded in South Carolina is difficult to determine. It is not enough to suggest that the question was merely sectional—that the low country had a disproportionate representation in the legislature and sought to maintain control over the presidential election. Disproportionate representation certainly played some role but too many other states of the Union had malapportioned legislatures that did relinquish power over presidential electors. South Carolina's legislature clung tenaciously to its power over presidential electors because it clearly perceived direct election as the cause of party formation in other states, and it sought to prevent the rise of parties in the state. James Henry Hammond, for example, believed in 1846 that the citizens of South Carolina were the "finest mass that is or ever was united under any form of government—intelligent, high spirited and almost entirely free from party or factious political influences." But he feared they would be transformed by a popular presidential election. They would be corrupted by "the constant exercise of political power . . . the party lines, the miserable factions that must speedily arise." Lewis Malone Ayer, Jr., explained to a separate state secession meeting in 1851 that South Carolina was quicker than other Southern states to protest the aggressions of the federal government "because they [other states], by direct popular vote, elect all the high officers of the State and General Government. And these elections so often recurring, have maintained among them permanent party divisions producing more and more bitterness of feeling, and greater and greater diversity of views and interests year after year."[41]

It was with this explicit antiparty intention that Carolinians avoided all popular statewide elections for any office, including that of governor. It was the proud boast of Paul Johnston in 1856 that the absence of a general state election in South Carolina prevented the kind of expedient political compromises, intended solely to attain office, that were typical of the politics of other states. "[I]t may be said of all parties among us, that they have no means, by our mode of conducting elections, to attract strength outside of their own creed." "No people," Johnston explained, "are more dependent upon party leaders, than those among whom prevails the popular mode of conducting a canvass over so large a surface as the whole state." Such a general election would give rise to "that bane of public virtue—party organizations."[42] South Carolinians, in other words, understood very early that their political ideals—political ideals rooted in slavery—were fundamentally incompatible with the mass elections that swept through the rest of the nation. They avoided this institutional change and hence avoided mass political parties. Thus, the antiparty ideals of the political culture of slavery developed relatively undisturbed in South Carolina, but other Southern states—states where masters were weaker or where they did not so clearly understand the connection between the mass election and party organization—did not wall themselves off from the rest of the nation.

But even during periods when party organization flourished in the antebellum South, it seems as if antiparty attitudes both underlay their development and contributed to their instability. For example, much of the political organization in the South was undertaken for essentially anti-organizational reasons. Whether the enemy was the monster bank, the local aristocracy, the power-hungry Andrew Jackson and his spoilsmen, party conventions, nullifiers, antinullifiers, secessionists, or cooperationists—they seemed to be threatening at least in part because they were elaborately organized and managed. Parties formed to counter these threats invariably included anti-organizational and antiparty rhetoric in their appeal.[43] Parties that fed on such antiparty values could hardly be stable for very long. As we will see, they stimulated the very sentiments that would lead to their destruction.

III

SLAVERY ALSO PROVIDED social conditions that inhibited party development. First of all, certain aspects of slavery served to mute conflict in the South and thereby slowed the growth of political parties. The ways in which slave society deadened conflict are important for a full understanding of the political culture of slavery and the subject will be given close attention in chapter 4. For now, it is worth noting that in the South the relative absence of foreign immigrants and ethnocultural conflict, the small numbers of cities and a muted interurban rivalry, as well as the domination of the slaveholding interest—all tended to diminish the number of groups in conflict. Parties emerged first in America in areas of the country with highly developed and divided economic and social structures—in places like New York and Pennsylvania. In part, parties arose to bring into order, to make governable, a society fractured into tiny competing blocs.[44] To the extent that slavery helped sustain conditions of relative homogeneity, it eliminated an important stimulus to party development.

But slavery also operated in several other ways to weaken political parties. For one thing, even among Southerners who joined the new political organizations, slavery made it somewhat more difficult to use patronage as a unifying device. Consider, first, just how important patronage had become to the parties of antebellum America. Patronage was one of the major ways in which the loyalty of local political organizations became tied to national parties. Local parties hoped to reward the faithful after the election by arranging for their appointment to federal positions. Moreover, once appointed, once the party workers had become government employees, they could easily be mobilized for concerted action. They might be assessed for contributions to a campaign or they might be "encouraged" to poll watch, deliver speeches, or even to intimidate reluctant voters.[45]

Southerners who committed themselves to political parties used patronage as party cement as eagerly as the politicians of any section.[46] But the rural nature of the South reduced the total amount of patronage available. Fewer cities meant fewer government jobs; a sparse population meant fewer post offices—and this situation, of course, pleased a population fearful of government taxes and centralized power. Moreover, there was one important kind of patronage that Southerners could not use so frequently as party workers in the North: the customhouse. To the extent that slavery, and its intimate relation to cotton culture in the South, discouraged the growth of cities and of great port towns, it also diminished the influence of customhouse patronage as a mechanism of party solidarity. Aside from Baltimore and New Orleans (on the edges of Southern political life) and the port of Charleston, the South lacked major customs facilities. This lack was by no means a trivial loss for party formation. It was no coincidence that New York and Pennsylvania had the most highly developed political parties and that New York City and Philadelphia had large customhouses. As Cornelius P. Van Ness, collector of the port of New York, wrote Secretary of War William Marcy in 1845: "I am sure you perfectly understand the bearing which the management of the Custom House has had, for the last 10 or 15 years, upon our city elections; which is, that when well managed, we have gained, otherwise, lost."[47] The political parties in few Southern states could make use of such a powerful mechanism of control.

Southern parties also suffered from disproportionately high rates of illiteracy in the slave states. The 1850 census concluded that over 20 percent of the adult white population of the South could not read, compared with 3 percent in the Middle States and less than one-half of one percent in New England.[48] The precise reasons for this high rate of illiteracy are difficult to determine. It seems another form of the general phenomenon of stunted urbanization, scattered population, and an unwillingness to spend money on public services, all of which were in some way connected to the structure of social life in a slave society. All these features of slave society deadened movement toward public education and hence contributed to illiteracy. It was more difficult to establish schools in Southern rural areas because of the widely scattered nature of the population and the poor condition of roads. Moreover, since masters and those who aspired to be masters tended to distrust the external authority of the state, large numbers of Southerners seemed reluctant to support an adequate public education system.[49]

Illiteracy may have stunted party growth in a few ways. One kind of connection becomes obvious once we remind ourselves that parties are abstractions. They can become stable and win devotion over time only if they assume an existence beyond the particular personalities who are their leaders. But for an illiterate, scattered population, personal exposure to a candidate will be a major source of political knowledge; the party will be harder to conceive in abstract terms as an organization beyond the particular orator standing in front of the crowd. Literacy permits exposure to ideas divorced from particular personalities. Even an oration, when placed on the printed page, becomes, in a sense, free of the personality and social status of its creator. Illiteracy, then, may have deadened the movement toward abstraction so essential for the growth of stable party organizations.

Illiteracy, along with the rural nature of slave society, also diminished the number of newspapers available in the region. The total circulation of political newspapers to the white population was almost three times as great in New England and the Middle States as in the South. The disparity was even greater for literary publications. In terms of numbers of different publications of newspapers and periodicals, Alabama heads the list for the deep South with the total of 60. In comparison, Massachusetts had 209, Ohio 261, Pennsylvania 310, and New York had 428. Even Illinois and Indiana sustained over a hundred different publications.[50]

The smaller number of newspapers in the South may also have blunted party development. All over the nation, party organization grew along with the growth of newspapers.[51] Newspapers became associated with parties and funneled the party line to the masses; they published campaign material; they were rewarded with the public printing for their party loyalty; newspaper editors acted as lobbyists and as political organizers. Parties used newspapers for all these purposes in the South as well as in the North, but to the extent that the South had fewer newspapers—both in absolute and in per capita terms—overall, they had to have been a less important force.

The tendency for antiparty values to flourish in slave society, the deadening of internal conflict, the inability to use the customhouse patronage, illiteracy, and the smaller number of newspapers—though no one of these factors could explain the weakness of party in the South, together they can. Parties did develop in the South, party values and practices did appear, but the new organizations did not possess a solid foundation. They would crumble under stress.

CHAPTER 4

Representation

THE CENTRAL IDEA TO BE developed in this chapter and the next is that slaveowner thought about the political representation of free people paralleled the proslavery argument. Both tried to resolve the irresolvable contradictions of Southern social life—the simultaneous experience of independence and dependence, the simultaneous experience of power and powerlessness, the simultaneous need to live as ruler and ruled. In the end, both moved toward a resolution of the contradictions by asserting mutuality of interest to legitimize the relationship between the governors and the governed.

South Carolina, more than any other Southern state, came closest to handling the problem of representation in a way most consistent with the proslavery argument and the general logic of the political culture of slavery. South Carolina's experience is worth examining in detail for it allows us fully to appreciate the underlying connections between the ideas and institutions designed for slaves and those designed for free people. It allows us to see the remarkable connections between political thought in statehouses and on plantations.

I

HISTORIANS HAVE LONG recognized that the American Revolution significantly affected American thinking about representation. Perhaps more important, since the break with England necessitated the creation of new governments, these new thoughts helped mold new institutions. In South Carolina, however, the Revolution altered neither the assumptions nor the practices of representation.

During the years of crisis before 1776, South Carolinians, like other Americans, repeatedly argued that England could not tax them. It is "repugnant to the rights of the people," explained the revolutionary General

Committee of South Carolina, "that any taxes should be imposed on them, unless with their own consent given personally or by their representatives."[1] But from the time of the first opposition to the Stamp Act of 1765, Parliament and its supporters insisted on the right to legislate for the colonists in all cases, even in matters of taxation. Some English pamphleteers, such as Soame Jenyns of the Board of Trade, even went so far as to argue that the power to tax was not dependent on consent, but most writers simply contended that the colonists were in fact represented in Parliament and that they consented to all the taxes imposed.[2]

Although argument over whether or not Parliament represented the colonists proved relatively unimportant in the larger conflict with England, and although the dispute ended a few years after the Stamp Act crisis, historians see in this debate evidence of a much more basic disagreement between the colonies and England about the nature of representation itself. Americans during the colonial period, living in autonomous towns and counties, one historian has argued, were attracted to a medieval conception of the representative as an attorney or agent for the locality that elected him. In a world where real power lay in the hands of small, decentralized units, the particular group that elected a representative expected him to speak for its special interests. According to this view, the representative might even be bound by specific instructions from his local constituents. Massachusetts town meetings, for example, frequently instructed their delegates to the colonial assembly. Having such a conception of representation, Americans thought it absurd for anyone to argue that Parliament represented the colonists when Parliament contained no men actually elected by them. For "no member," explained the Georgia pastor John Joachim Zubly in a 1769 pamphlet published in Charleston, "can represent any but those by whom he hath been elected . . . representation arises entirely from the free election of the people."[3]

In contrast to the American emphasis on the explicit nature of consent through "actual" representation, the English during the late-eighteenth century adhered to the idea of "virtual" representation. As one London pamphleteer stated: "Every member of Parliament sits in the House not as representative of his own constituents but as one of that august assembly by which all the commons of *Great Britain* are represented. Their rights and their interests, however his own borough may be affected by general dispositions, ought to be the great objects of his attention and the only rules for his conduct, and to sacrifice these to partial advantage in favor of the place where he was chosen would be a departure from his duty."[4]

According to this reasoning, the local constituency that happened to elect a man to Parliament should have no special influence over his conduct in office. Each representative spoke for the whole nation and not a particular local district. Hence it did not seem at all ridiculous to suggest that "the colonists, like the 'nine tenths of the people of Britain' who do not choose representatives to Parliament, were in fact represented there."[5]

Recognition of the change in emphasis from virtual to actual representation in American political thought is of greater significance than may at first seem apparent. To defend actual representation is invariably to defend a rather distinctive system of related political ideals, institutions, and practices. The concept of representation is just one element of a larger political culture, and the change from virtual to actual representation is a reflection of a more general political transformation. In a way it is misleading to isolate for emphasis the idea of representation since the concept is embedded in a whole series of assumptions about politics and society, no one of which is a determinant of the others, no one of which can long exist without the others. For example, to emphasize the value of virtual representation is to defend deferential relations between represented and representative, to expect representatives to be the exceptionally wise and virtuous men of the society (statesmen), to require representatives to decide issues on the basis of reasoned judgment rather than out of concern for popularity, and to denigrate the importance of election as the mandate for representation. Similarly, to defend actual representation is to emphasize distrust in the attitude of constituent to representative, to require representatives to be the most "typical" men of the society, and to expect representatives to refer to popularity and the popular local election as the mandate for action. Thus, a change in the concept and practice of representation is of profound significance.

But the divergence between American and British beliefs about representation is not so sharp as this analysis may at first suggest. Most eighteenth-century Americans could never wholly repudiate the idea of virtual representation. It still made sense under circumstances where the interests of voters and nonvoters seemed truly identical. No revolutionary leader ever suggested that women or children needed actually to vote for legislators in order to be represented in government. Even in the dispute with Parliament, Americans generally did not deny the validity of virtual representation in all circumstances. It was more usual to argue that the absence of common interest between the colonies and England made any kind of representation seem unreasonable.[6] In just such a spirit South Carolina's General Assembly resolved in 1765: "That the people of this province are not and from their local circumstances cannot be represented in the House of Commons of Great Britain, and further that in the opinion of this House the several powers of legislation in America were constituted in some measure upon the apprehension of this impracticability."[7] With this type of argument Carolinians and other Americans could deny they consented to Parliament's taxes without repudiating the general principle of virtual representation.

Moreover, the American devotion to a particular notion of "republican" government during the revolutionary period may have made the idea of virtual representation seem plausible. The English conception of virtual representation could obviously only be meaningful under circumstances in which the interests of voters and nonvoters seemed to coincide. In the minds of the revolutionaries, republican government—literally meaning government in the public interest—posited a society in which all partial interests recognized their mutual dependence and worked together for a general interest; a society, in short, in which each legislator although elected by a local district virtually represented the interests of all.[8]

The equivocal attitudes toward representation generated by the revolutionary struggle were further confused by ambiguities inherent in the ideas themselves. Both virtual and actual representation become impractical when defended absolutely and unwaveringly. Virtual representation requires some degree of actual representation or else there would be little reason to have elections or to require citizenship of elected officials. No member of Parliament would ever claim he virtually represented the entire world nor would he ever permit a Frenchman to be elected to English office. Similarly, fully to implement actual representation and require elected officials literally to be the agents of particular electors would be to abolish totally the deliberative function of a representative assembly. To be sure, some Americans during the revolutionary period almost did follow the logic of actual representation to its ultimate conclusions. A few even suggested extreme actualization of representation by denying elected officials all discretionary powers and by binding them to a particular electorate. But the problematical nature of the concepts generated at least as much confusion and equivocation as conviction.[9]

If the defense of actual representation could rarely be carried to its logical extreme in revolutionary America, the structure of the new state governments clearly indicates the American desire at least to actualize representation to an extent hitherto unknown. In the years after 1776 the mechanisms of actual representation flourished: constituents bound representatives by instructions, election laws tied officials to local districts by residence and property qualifications for officeholding, the suffrage broadened, and legislatures reapportioned themselves to reflect more accurately the actual distribution of population. The revolutionary struggle generated a distrust for all forms of authority, and local districts, in numerous ways, tied the hands of their elected officials. Although the revolutionaries did not actualize representation to the degree acceptable to later generations, they at least headed in that direction.[10]

Yet, as is often the case before the Civil War, what was central to American politics in general was not necessarily central to the politics of South Carolina. Whereas other states may have gradually endorsed the premises and practices of actual representation, South Carolinians remained staunchly committed to virtual representation. The revolutionary struggle strained South Carolina's devotion to this old political ideal, yet during the antebellum decades it continued to flourish. The point is not that a clear line demarcated antebellum Carolinians from other Americans, especially Southerners, but only that in no other state did eighteenth-century English political ideas remain so powerful so long into the nineteenth century.

To be sure, the pressures generated by the American Revolution in favor of actual representation did not leave South Carolina entirely untouched. The need of the low country—the eastern, older, wealthier, and slave-owning section—to gain the support of the newly settled areas of the colony in the dispute with Great Britain encouraged the extension of representation to highly populated but relatively poor upcountry areas previously unrepresented in the House of Assembly. Once the upcountry gained a foothold in state politics, it continued to enlarge its influence. Even before the first shots of the war, the revolutionary General Committee in Charleston divided the western part of the state into electoral districts for elections to the provincial Congress.[11] From the time of this reapportionment until 1808 the upcountry, which continued to increase its proportion of the white population, kept expanding its share of the representation, although, on the basis of white population, it never achieved what it deserved.

South Carolina's Provincial Congress of 1776, claiming to be "a full and free representation of the people of this colony," adopted a constitution that gave added voting strength to the western sections of the state.[12] The constitution of 1778 required reapportionment in seven years and then again every fourteen years "in the most equal and just manner according to the particular and comparative strength and taxable property of the different parts of the [state], regard being always had to the number of white inhabitants and such taxable property."[13] Although the representation of taxable property is alien to the spirit of actual representation, the commitment to counting the number of white inhabitants and, for that matter, any commitment to a reapportionment that would invariably increase the representation of the rapidly growing upcountry, is in harmony with that spirit. A constitutional amendment of 1808 even further equalized according to population the representation of the various sections of the state. These developments, coupled with passage of a state constitutional amendment to end property qualifications for voting, moved South Carolina sharply toward actual representation.[14]

A movement for the instruction of representatives by constituents also flourished in South Carolina during the revolutionary period. Impelled by a distrust for all forms of authority as a result of their revolutionary experience, and especially fearful of the aristocratic, low-country, "nabob" members of the South Carolina legislature, popular leaders of the 1780s such as William Hornby, Alexander Gillon, and Thomas Tudor Tucker enthusiastically advocated instruction. Their ideas received wide circulation in Gillon's *The Circular Letter* and in Tucker's *Conciliatory Hints.* Advocating the explicit participation of the represented as the essential ingredient of any system of representation, Tucker even brought his views to national attention when, in Congress, he proposed to include the right of instruction of senators as one of the first amendments to the Constitution.[15]

Despite the revolutionary movement toward actual representation, South Carolina between 1776 and 1860 remained fundamentally attached to the ideals and institutions of virtual representation. On the question of instructions, for example, it was not Gillon or Tucker who spoke for the future of South Carolina politics, but rather the revolutionary leader Christopher Gadsden. Instructions, Gadsden argued in 1784, would "prove a dangerous *Jesuitical* imperium in imperio and serve to put the legislature into *leading strings*, and make them as a body contemptible." Instructions, Gadsden contended, need not be avoided under all circumstances. In matters of purely local interest instructions should be obeyed, but the representative was also "charged to attend to the *general combined* interest of *all* the state *put* together, as it were upon *an average*."[16] Obviously, Gadsden reasoned, the representative had to discover this general interest through deliberation and reasoned debate rather than through binding instructions from local constituents. Gadsden did not believe ultimate power should rest anywhere but in the hands of the people. Yet, during the usual operations of government, the people should exercise this ultimate power only on election day and should not interfere with their representatives once the election had ended, except under the most extraordinary circumstances. If "any representatives wantonly counteract the *plain* sense of their parish, choose them no more," he admonished, "which is much better *upon the whole* than sitting them with absolute instructions."[17]

The strength with which South Carolina political leaders continued to adhere to anti-instruction sentiments even during the strong pro-instruction movement of the revolutionary era is nowhere more evident than in the state's convention to ratify the federal Constitution in 1788. A ratifying convention is one of the least likely places to find anti-instruction ideas since, in American political thought, such a convention is supposed to be the direct voice of the people acting in their sovereign capacity as a constituent assembly. Yet even here, Alexander Tweed, representative of Prince Frederick Parish, in one of the few extant recorded speeches from that body, "spurned at the idea" that his district should attempt to direct his vote. "For my own part," he explained to the convention, "I came not here to echo the voice of my constituents."[18]

Even though many Carolinians in the nineteenth century disagreed with Tweed's anti-instruction sentiments for conventions, few denied the argument as it applied to the more usual governmental relations between constituent and representative. For example, J. C. Coit, speaking to the people of Chesterfield District on the eve of elections to the 1852 secession convention, explained that he regarded a delegate to such a body as an "agent or factor" of the people, "to express and execute their sovereign will and purpose." Yet he carefully distinguished this idea of a representative in a constituent assembly from that of the more usual representative in "*civil government*" who had to act "according to the convictions of his own judgment and conscience as to the public welfare." "My conception of a representative being this," he explained to the voters before him, "that the people choose men to *rule*, and do not themselves directly or indirectly, *govern* the subjects of civil law."[19]

These ideas were echoed by nineteenth-century South Carolina's most influential political leaders. Thomas Cooper, president of South Carolina College during the 1820s and 1830s, influential instructor of the state's most prominent citizens, and key figure in the nullification movement, shared the anti-instruction sentiments of his eighteenth-century forebears. Explicitly siding with Sir William Blackstone and Edmund Burke against Tucker of Virginia and Secretary of State Henry Clay, Cooper argued in 1826 not simply that state legislators should be virtual representatives but that "every man called to the national legislature, is a national and not a local representative. . . . You are sent to the national council," he admonished a hypothetical instructed representative, "to deliberate for the nation, and not for the petty district where you reside."[20]

John C. Calhoun, the man who dominated South Carolina politics for nearly a quarter century, fully agreed with Cooper on this point. Calhoun found particularly convincing the anti-instruction sentiments expressed in Burke's famous "Speech to the Electors of Bristol." "That mind must be greatly different from mine," Calhoun explained, "which can read that speech, and not embrace its doctrine." Burke's doctrines largely centered on the idea that since Parliament represented the interest of all, no representative should be bound by instructions from his local constituents. As Burke stated the case: "Parliament is not a *congress* of ambassadors from different and hostile interests, which interests each must maintain, as an agent and advocate, against other agents and advocates; but Parliament is a *deliberative* assembly of *one* nation, with *one* interest, that of the whole—where not local prejudices ought to guide, but the general good, resulting from the general reason of the whole. You choose a member, indeed; but when you have chosen him he is not a member of Bristol, but he is a member of *Parliament*." It was with such thoughts in mind that Calhoun admonished a Congress he believed to be instructed: "Instructions! Well, then, has it come to this? Have the people of this country snatched the power of deliberation from this body?" All who accept instruction "abandon the plain road of truth and reason."[21]

John Townsend, author of such pamphlets as *The South Alone Shall Govern the South* and *The Doom of Slavery in the Union, Its Safety Out of It*, referred with praise to both Burke's ideas and this Calhoun speech in an 1858 pamphlet directed to his constituents. "I regard the claim of *coercive* instruction," Townsend explained, "on the part of his constituents which the Representative is bound to obey, against his reason and conscience, as at war with the very spirit of our republican Representative institutions."[22]

Aside from the instruction issue, it should be recognized that much of what may appear to be a movement of the Carolina revolutionary generation toward actual representation was not really inconsistent with a fundamental adherence to virtual representation. Burke, one of the strongest advocates of virtual representation in eighteenth-century England, noted that "virtual representation cannot have a long or sure existence if it has not a substratum in the actual. The member must have some relation to the constituent." Such reasoning simply recognized the obvious absurdity of carrying virtual representation to its extreme. Hence, when the Carolina revolutionaries took care to send representatives from major interest groups to the Stamp Act Congress or when the western part of the state pushed for the more equitable apportionment of representation, they did not necessarily have to challenge the fundamental presupposition of virtual representation—that government was a matter of reason and deliberation in the interests of the whole. Despite challenges by some revolutionaries, this assumption remained dominant in South Carolina through the antebellum period.[23]

Certain persistent political practices in South Carolina between 1776 and 1860 served to block any lasting movement toward actual representation. South Carolinians during the revolutionary period did make some attempt to equalize representation according to population, but the reforms, still incomplete, came to a halt around the turn of the century. The constitution of 1778 had provided for periodic reapportionment, but the constitution of 1790 avoided the issue. After a great deal of agitation, the constitutional amendment of 1808 did provide for more equitable apportionment and for periodic reapportionment based on white population and taxes paid. But this new method of apportionment still left the relatively unpopulated low-country districts with excessive representation in the legislature. The problem was not resolved until after the Civil War.

More important, the state never developed the kinds of institutions that would have strongly linked voters and legislative representatives to specific electoral districts. During the revolutionary period other states of the Union required property and residency qualifications that clearly bound both elector and electorate to a single district. True, South Carolina's revolutionary constitutions did continue the colonial requirement of residence and property qualifications for voters and legislative representatives, and the constitution of 1790 even made these requirements more stringent, but nevertheless the state still maintained a strong commitment to plural district allegiances for propertied members of the body politic.[24] Colonial Carolina simply had required slightly higher property qualifications for nonresident political participants than for residents. A wealthy landowner, in other words, could both run for office and vote in as many districts as he held the requisite amount of property. Hence, the same man might try to be elected from different districts in the same election and often, in mimicry of the English rotten borough system, the same man could represent different parishes in different assemblies; furthermore, since elections were held over a period of two days, a man on a fast horse might vote in several parishes during a given election.[25]

None of South Carolina's revolutionary constitutions, not even the constitution of 1790, prohibited these practices; nor did the 1810 amendment, which abolished property qualifications for resident voters, deny the franchise to propertied nonresidents.[26] The less propertied upcountry districts, for obvious reasons, consistently opposed these practices, and in 1800 they did succeed in getting the legislature to adopt a resolution condemning voters who cast ballots in more than one district in a given election. But the majority vote was so marginal and sentiment so equivocal on this issue that the House almost immediately adopted another resolution reversing itself. The issue of plural district voting in a single election was never definitively resolved during the antebellum period. Although the practice gradually came to be confined by custom and administrative ruling to plural district voting for local offices only, it seems clear that the practice of voting in one district for one election and in another for a subsequent election still continued to be widespread. This certainly was a significant factor in closely contested elections such as the 1832 senatorial contest in Georgetown in which nonresidents participated heavily. Even as late as 1856, Josiah J. Evans, senator from South Carolina, felt compelled to defend the practice of nonresident voting when it was ridiculed as unrepublican by Senator Charles Sumner.[27]

The representatives themselves also took full advantage of the plural district participation permitted by the state's electoral laws. Perhaps the classic case is that of the politician and land speculator Robert Goodloe Harper. It is easy to see how laws for the political participation of nonresidents may have benefited low-country plantation owners who also held residence in Charleston or in cooler and healthier upcountry summer migration areas, but for the land speculator like Harper these laws must have been a phenomenal boon. In 1794 Harper left his residence in Charleston to run for Congress from Ninety-Six District in the western part of the state. Not only did he win this election, but he simultaneously won election to the state legislature from Spartanburg District. Moreover, one month later he was elected to fill the vacant congressional seat of recently deceased Gillon of Orangeburg District.[28] Here, obviously, was a man who could not possibly feel special loyalty to a particular election district, nor could those who elected him have wanted someone with allegiances only to their district. Here, also, was a practice that made the equal representation of equally populated electoral districts seem irrelevant. Harper and his constituents cared so little about residence as a requirement for representation that he continued to represent his district in Congress even after he moved to Maryland in 1799. He exchanged letters with his constituents in South Carolina as late as 1801.[29]

Harper's elections in 1794 are probably the most spectacular examples of nonresident representation, but the practice continued throughout the antebellum period. Even elections to the nullification convention of 1832, the place where one would expect the most concerted effort to elect resident representatives, give striking evidence of the insignificance of loyalty to a single district. Henry Middleton became a delegate to the convention from Greenville just after he lost election to the legislature in Charleston; Horry sent Daniel Elliott Huger after he had been defeated for the legislature in Charleston; St. Bartholomew elected Franklin H. Elmore of Laurens District.[30]

The migration patterns of South Carolina's leading families during the antebellum period further reinforced the attitude that representation did not require loyalty to a local body of electors. Such prominent low-country leaders as Thomas Pinckney, Jr., Francis K. Huger, and William A. Bull had moved into leadership positions in upcountry areas by the 1830s. The prominent low-country DeSaussure and Preston families moved west to Columbia and remained influential in politics. Similarly, some of the low country's most prominent political figures had migrated from upcountry areas. James Petigru, Ker Boyce, and Langdon Cheves of Charleston as well as John L. Wilson of Georgetown and Elmore of Colleton all had been born in the western part of the state. Others such as Benjamin F. Perry, James Henry Hammond, George McDuffie, and John C. Calhoun had left the upcountry and married wealthy low-country women. Such a pattern of movement, often leaving single families scattered across many districts, prevented the development of exclusively local loyalties among the political leaders of the state. Moreover, since the wealthiest men often owned several plantations throughout South Carolina, as well as townhouses in Charleston and a summer migration home in the upcountry, attachment to a single district proved impossible for the most influential people in the state.[31]

There are other reasons why the assumptions and practices of virtual representation remained alive in South Carolina. Most important, since virtual representation required a representative to speak for the interests of all, it made most sense in states that actually had a single united interest and where local and class differences seemed insignificant. South Carolina from the latter part of the colonial period through 1860 was bound by a unity of real interests felt by no other part of the country; or, to state the issue more clearly, in no other state of the Union did the planter class enjoy such unchallenged hegemony. This is not to suggest that blacks, poor whites, and others did not wish to challenge the power of the planter class. After all, the planters did experience a revolt of the poor whites during the Regulator movement of the 1760s. Furthermore, as the slave insurrectionist Denmark Vesey clearly recognized, the interests of black and white obviously did not coincide under the institution of slavery. The point is not that conflicting interests did not exist in the society but only that the planter interest successfully ignored other interests, remained united within itself, and formally dominated the politics, economy, and social structure of the state to an extent unequaled elsewhere.

Colonial South Carolina, unlike such New England colonies as Massachusetts, never developed numerous towns and counties with strong local governments. Charleston, the only real city in the colony, never had a local interest distinguishable from other local interests since, for all practical purposes, the colony was Charleston. The most careful recent student of South Carolina politics before the Revolution finds little overt conflict within the colony during the generation before 1776.[32]

During the years just after the Revolution, the state did develop a rather severe upcountry–low-country split. These years witnessed the only real movement toward actual representation ever undertaken by South Carolina. But this division became increasingly muted as the state found new external enemies to help fuse internal unity. In 1812 South Carolina spoke with a nearly unanimous voice in favor of the new war with England.[33] After North-South sectional issues began to develop in the 1820s, until 1865 disagreement within the state involved tactical decisions. Although the internal disputes over nullification in 1832 and secession in

1851 were severe, often involving to a certain extent the old upcountry–low-country split, these disagreements were universally recognized to be temporary. John C. Calhoun quite correctly understood the nature of political division in South Carolina. "Did not I believe, that the state was radically sound in feelings," Calhoun wrote Hammond with reference to the nullification crisis, "and that our divisions sprang from accidental circumstances, I would despair." After the "accidental circumstance" of nullification subsided, he informed Robert M. T. Hunter with a sense of satisfaction: "Our state is profoundly quiet. Publick sentiment approaches to something like unanimity on all the great questions of the day." In 1838 he wrote A. H. Pendleton in the same vein: "The tendency of our state Government, as it now stands, is to Union among ourselves, as experience amply proves. We are almost entirely free from party politicks, as far as our State Legislation is concerned." In 1840 Calhoun again affirmed his belief to Hammond: "Our natural political condition is the absence of local parties, and . . . past experience for the last thirty years proves it."[34] It was a profound insight into the nature of the state's antebellum politics.

After Calhoun's death, during the secession crisis of 1851, Carolina politicians pleaded for internal unity. "If we expect to go through the present controversy successfully," Francis W. Pickens begged the citizens of Edgefield District, "the very first thing to be done, is to produce union, concert of action, cordial and kind feelings at home, in every citizen of the State and between all classes and parties." W. F. Colcock explained to the Southern Rights Association of Charleston that "with us there has always been a 'unity of sentiment' which has emphatically constituted us one people." In the years after 1851 such politicians as these overcame all signs of internal division, and by December 1860 South Carolinians almost unanimously adopted secession.[35]

The peculiar social makeup of the state also contributed to the remarkable homogeneity of interest in South Carolina. During the colonial period the heavy concentration of slaves in low-country parishes operated to prevent serious open conflict among whites aware of their vulnerability to slave revolt. During the antebellum period upcountry areas became increasingly black as plantation agriculture extended deeper into the state's interior. By 1860, two-thirds of South Carolina's counties had black majorities. Under the impact of the abolitionist threat the state subdued all internal divisions and eventually assumed a united position against the North on the slavery issue, pushed by what one historian has labeled "The Fear."[36]

Other influences also operated to promote unity in antebellum South Carolina. The state remained dominated by a planter elite that intermarried extensively and, as has already been indicated, freely moved between tidewater and piedmont.[37] Moreover, as Carolinians began to retreat from a world increasingly hostile to their peculiar institution, many of the leaders of the state were educated at the South Carolina College in Columbia. Hence, it is little wonder that, united by a common education, a common economic position as planters, a common threat in the form of slaves and antislavery enemies, and bound by ties of marriage, the political leaders of South Carolina maintained that the state had a common interest. It was not any one of these factors alone that gave the state's white leadership a homogeneity enjoyed by no other part of the nation, but it was the overwhelming impact of them all combined.[38]

The centralization of power within the lower house of the legislature also gave virtual representation greater strength in South Carolina than in states where power rested in localities. Local government barely existed in colonial Carolina. After the lower House of Assembly completed the "quest for power" common to all colonial legislatures, after it had whittled away the royal authority and the authority of governor and council, no other power center but the legislature existed within the colony. Between 1776 and 1790, with the exception of the enormous wartime powers given the governor between 1776 and 1778, power in South Carolina did not flow back to the governor or to the new federal government. The constitutions of 1778 and 1790 limited the governor's term to two years, denied him the veto power, and required him to be elected by the legislature. Through the Civil War the governor remained a figurehead in South Carolina. Congressmen, of course, had to be elected directly by the people, but the legislature during the antebellum period kept control of the election of senators, of presidential electors, and even of such minor appointees as tax collectors. Moreover, the route to power always lay through a career in the legislature. According to one study of twenty-one Carolinians who served as either United States senators, representatives, or state governors between 1851 and 1860, seventeen had once held a position in the state legislature.[39] Since power in South Carolina remained at the center, few local groups were strong enough to demand and obtain the overriding loyalty of their representative. The real power relations in South Carolina were more like those of late-eighteenth-century England, where authority was centralized in Parliament and virtual representation flourished, than like those of medieval England or colonial Massachusetts, where decentralized power encouraged actual representation. In a society with no power at the periphery, and in which decisions made at the center determined an individual's political success, virtual representation could be expected to flourish.

The most rigorous statement of political thought in the state during the antebellum period, Calhoun's *Disquisition on Government* adheres to the virtual representation ideal of eighteenth-century England. As I have indicated in chapter 3, although Calhoun's vision of the concurrent majority (a system under which every major interest in the society has a veto on all legislation) may seem to create a government based on the actual representation of partial interests, it most definitely does not. As Calhoun describes it, under the concurrent majority, "each portion, in order to advance its own peculiar interests, would have to conciliate all others, by showing a disposition to advance theirs; and, for this purpose, each would select those to represent it, whose wisdom, patriotism, and weight of character, would command the confidence of the others. Under its influence,—and with representatives so well qualified to accomplish the object for which they were selected,—the prevailing desire would be, to promote the common interests of the whole."[40] Paradoxically, in other words, representation under the concurrent majority, a system that would seem to give each partial interest extraordinary power, actually encourages the election of men who could best use their reason to determine the good of the whole—the election of virtual representatives.[41]

Antebellum South Carolina's peculiar devotion to an older conception of representation had a number of interesting consequences. As we will see in chapter 5, among other things, it permitted Carolinians to find convincing that portion of the proslavery argument that emphasized that blacks consented to their condition—a portion of the argument that many Northerners found patently absurd.[42] A system of virtual representation does not require explicit consent since it is not the desires of people that are represented but their real interests. The assumption is that what appears good from the selfish viewpoint of individuals and localities may in reality be detrimental to the society as a whole and hence, by implication, detrimental to all its parts. The virtual representative, in other words, must use his reason to guard the interests of the whole society and in so doing he will invariably guard the interest of each part of it even though the parts may not initially recognize this. This idea is at the very heart of the proslavery argument.

When the poetic defender of slavery, William J. Grayson, described slavery as "the only condition of society, in which capital and labor are associated on a large scale—in which their interests are combined and not in conflict," and Calhoun portrayed the plantation as "a little community, with the master at its head, who concentrates in himself the united interests of capital and labor, of which he is the common representative," they pictured the plantation as a homogeneous society in which the parts had a single real interest—a conception logically parallel to the single real interest the state's politicians believed linked all white Carolinians.[43] Given this assumption and their belief in the legitimacy of virtual representation, white Carolinians had to perform no great leap of logic to argue that blacks were represented in government and hence, by implication, consented to their condition. This idea gives meaning to William Gilmore Simms's statement: "I took the ground, in my pamphlet on the Morals of Slavery, that our Institution was not slavery at all, in the usual acceptation of the term which implies some wrong done to the party, but that the negro in the South was a minor, under guardianship—forfeited no right—was recognized in all his attributes of humanity—was distinctly individualized, and protected in all his rights and privileges, through a representative master."[44] No English pamphleteer in 1765 more wholly accepted the assumptions of virtual representation than Simms in his proslavery argument. More important, these assumptions had long guided the behavior of white politicians in South Carolina, and it was no strain to extend them to cover the institution of slavery.

II

TO LABEL SOUTH CAROLINA'S adherence to virtual representation as unique in the South would be an error, but a great deal of evidence points in that direction. For example, other Southern states did have greater internal conflict, and they consequently moved more strongly toward actual representation during the antebellum period. They had greater socioeconomic diversity and a less powerful, less united ruling elite. The greater the diversity and conflict, it seems, the greater the cry for actual representation—at least from unrepresented groups and sections.

Consider, for example, the conflict between wealthier, often longer settled, large slave owner–dominated regions and yeoman farmer areas—the division between upcountry and low country that South Carolinians had successfully contained. The conflict in various states often took the form of an east-west split or a north-south split. From the time of the American Revolution, people living in the western portions of the South Atlantic states, for example, complained about their lack of actual representation in legislatures, governor's chairs, and other elected positions. They protested against the poor legal services, roads, and schools offered to the west by the virtual representatives from the east. Divergent interests, they argued, required actual representation. Easterners, in turn, maintained that if westerners were actually represented they might impose taxes on slaves in order to support internal improvements. Some even feared that westerners might abolish slavery.[45]

These kinds of conflicts, often coinciding with party antagonisms, generated a spate of state constitutional conventions and moved the South heavily in the direction of actual representation. Each of the Southern states outside South Carolina—some with more hesitation than others—

formally moved to extend the suffrage by abolishing religious tests and property qualifications; to reduce the age, property, and religious requirements for officeholding; to limit the reeligibility of elected officials for office; to increase the number of offices subject to popular election; and to reapportion districts in favor of a more equal representation of the white population. These reforms were all part of a more general movement toward the "democratization" of political institutions in the South during and after the Jacksonian period.[46]

Once again, as is quite obvious to any student of the American South, the experience of South Carolina was not the experience of the region as a whole. The South was simply too diverse. No single Southern state can stand as a model for all. But South Carolina does reveal a basic connection between slavery and virtual representation—a connection that was often reduplicated in the slave owner–dominated portions of other states.

Of course, the precise link between slavery and virtual representation is clouded by several factors. First of all, particular local circumstances led many masters to develop inconsistent, sometimes immediately self-serving arguments that did not fit into any logical pattern. Moreover, the concepts of "representation" and "slavery" are not single, simple, variables that can be isolated for analysis and clearly correlated. Finally, arguments about representation varied in the thought of individuals depending upon the unit under discussion—the family, the farm, the plantation, the county, the state, the region, or the nation. Still, there does seem to be a general connection between slavery and virtual representation. There are hints of it everywhere. The connection is evident in the way the slaveholding elites in Virginia, North Carolina, and Louisiana resisted for so long the formal constitutional changes that would allow all adult white males to vote. It is evident in the way so many Southern political leaders emphasized the ideals of statesmanship—the vision of the political leader as a wise and virtuous man devoted to the good of all. One can see the connection in Georgia during the final secession crisis: in order to "discard the narrrow unworthy notion that a member of the Legislature is the representative of a county" and to adopt the idea that a legislator "should be the representative of the honor and interests of the State," the secession convention decreased by two-thirds the number of elected state senators. It is also evident in Maryland where a traditional slave-owner elite quietly dominated the eastern shore, but areas with fewer slaves had greater political conflict and greater "democratization."[47]

There are several reasons why slavery and virtual representation should be so often associated. On the level of ideas, I have already noted (and will discuss in greater detail in chapter 5) the compatibility of the proslavery and virtual representation arguments. Both depended on a vision of an idealized society without internal conflict; both depended on a union of disinterested rulers—masters or statesmen—guided by a commitment to the common good; both sets of ideas reinforced each other. The proslavery writers Henry Hughes and George Fitzhugh repeatedly drew the analogy between representative governmental institutions and the relationship of slaves to masters.[48] They dared make explicit what was implicit in the thought of such men as John C. Calhoun.

Furthermore, the institution of slavery provided a social setting that encouraged the growth of virtual representation. In the states where slavery and slave owners dominated in the South, internal conflict among masters became muted during the antebellum period.[49] Real threats increasingly tended to appear from outside the society rather than from within. The more conflict became externalized the more virtual representation could flourish internally.

Slavery dulled internal conflict in several ways. For one thing, the South did not attract the kind of diverse foreign immigrant population that flooded Northern society. The Irish Catholics, Germans, and Dutch—the kinds of groups that formed the basis of the "ethnocultural" political divisions of the North—never existed in large numbers in the South. It was not simply that Southern attitudes toward manual labor discouraged immigration, even though work done by slaves became degraded and was considered debasing for whites. But foreign settlers could not have felt the full impact of these attitudes until they had already immigrated. Probably more important in discouraging immigration were the economic forces noted by historian-economist Gavin Wright. Slave society did not create the demand for an immigrant population characteristic of free society. Employers in the North, for example, welcomed new immigrants because they could be used to break strikes or keep wages low. In the South slaves performed these functions. Moreover, other economic groups in the North—landowners, town builders, railroad promoters—all stood to gain from an influx of foreign labor. Anyone with an interest in seeing the value of land rise welcomed the flood of new immigrants. Hence, in a struggle to attract the new population, Northern towns spent heavily for public improvements such as schools, roads, bridges, railroads, and commercial centers. But in states where slaves rather than land were the major capital investment, the same desire to attract immigrants did not prevail. New free laborers simply lowered the value of slaves since immigrants offered competing labor; and their alien ideas, some feared, might serve to "stir up" an otherwise contented slave population. Whereas Northern towns fought among themselves to attract the new immigrants, Southern towns remained quiescent.[50]

Related to the relative absence of foreign immigration into the

South—in part, as both cause and consequence—was the relative absence of towns and cities. The South was overwhelmingly rural. Historians Stanley Elkins and Eric McKitrick have compared the growth of antebellum towns in Mississippi and Alabama with the growth of towns in Ohio, Indiana, and Illinois. They discovered that, on the whole, "there were five to six times as many such towns per capita . . . [in Ohio, Indiana, and Illinois] as in Alabama or Mississippi." For example, when Indiana and Alabama reached comparable levels of population during the antebellum period, Indiana had 156 towns of 200 or more people whereas Alabama had only 34.[51]

Several aspects of slave society may have contributed to the relative absence of cities and towns in the South. It may be that masters found it difficult to control slave populations in large, urban concentrations (although this would not explain the relative absence of small towns). It may be that slavery reduced the rural market for urban growth. Slaves, after all, could never be conspicuous consumers of industrial goods. It may be that because masters owned slaves and found it in their economic interests to utilize their labor throughout the year they diversified their plantations, grew their own food, and removed the need for small towns as centers of local trade. It may be that because masters tried to use slave labor so completely on the plantation there was never an excess labor supply to fuel urban development. It may have been all of these factors together—and others as well—which stunted urbanization in the South. But one point seems likely. Slavery played a significant role in discouraging Southern town and city growth.[52]

The relative absence of Southern towns and cities deadened several aspects of potential political conflict. First of all, the South had a great deal less of the kind of town boosterism and its consequent interurban rivalry so common in the antebellum North. Not only did towns not compete to attract immigrants, but they also did not scramble so wildly for the county seat or for internal improvements.[53] Moreover, political districts were more likely to contain relatively homogeneous populations in both ethnic and occupational terms. Southern districts might have some diversity—the diversity of large slave owner, small slave owner, and non-slave owner. But these men often grew the same crops, and they lacked the range of occupational and ethnic identities characteristic of Northern urban areas. Moreover, given the absence of economic diversification, the South was full of districts that did not have an identifiable local economic interest to make them different from nearby districts. Southern attachment to one's own residence did not translate into conflict with neighboring localities. The sense of being in a locality surrounded by hostile and competing immediate neighbors—a central feature of New England town life since the colonial period—was never pervasive in the South.

Slavery even provided the social condition that muted open conflict between large and small farmers living in close proximity. It was not simply that small farmers, even non-slave owners, accepted the ideals of honor and sought to emulate rather than destroy their wealthy neighbors.[54] It was also that slavery provided the wealthy neighbors with many techniques to reduce conflict. Consider, for example, the impact of the comparatively low voter density in many Southern districts. Given the absence of towns throughout the South, the county was the primary unit of local politics. Many counties in the South, especially in areas with heavy concentrations of slaves, contained remarkably few white voters. The pattern can be seen in the 1852 presidential voting returns. Some of the states of the lower South, such as Texas and Florida, averaged under 250 votes per county. Other lower Southern states averaged 600 to 800 votes per county. Such Northern states as Massachusetts, New York, and Connecticut averaged 8,000 votes per county. Even newer states such as Michigan, Indiana, and Ohio averaged from 2,000 to 4,000 votes per county.[55] Moreover, in congressional elections Southern voter density was reduced by the constitutional clause requiring slaves to be counted as three-fifths of a person for the purposes of apportionment. Even on the state level, Georgia and Florida used the three-fifths formula in their own legislative apportionment, and Louisiana, at various times, counted slaves as whole people for the purpose of legislative apportionment.[56]

Low voter density meant that in many districts it was possible for social and political leaders to have a personal acquaintance with a large percentage of the voting population, making it difficult for small farmers to revolt openly against their wealthy neighbors. They might be wooed by the flattery of personal conversation or an invitation to a barbecue at the great plantation house.[57] Or wealthy planters might own a local grocery and extend generous credit to their political "friends." For example, one Georgia politician complained that his enemies "controlled the two groceries in this county and through that means caught *every* floater."[58] In fact it was quite customary in the South for wealthy men to be involved in an elaborate system of borrowing and lending among themselves and their poorer neighbors. These webs of owing enhanced planter control. As Bertram Wyatt-Brown has noted: "A man of wealth gained authority as well as accrued interest by allowing the number of those owing him to increase." Moreover, men of power also borrowed from social inferiors and then held off payment for long periods of time. This practice created obligations on the part of tradesmen-creditors because they sought to please the planter-debtor of higher social standing in hopes of both enhancing their own prestige and eventually receiving payment.[59]

Land may also have influenced political persuasion as is evidenced by a contemporary analysis of a Georgia voter who deserted the Democrats in 1848: "He is a poor man, and is living on land free of rent, belonging to a strong Whig, and this possibly explains the heresy."[60] Wealthy planters might also help and thereby influence their poorer friends with loans of equipment or slaves and assistance in marketing their crop. Low voter density, in other words, reduced the political anonymity of the common man so essential in modern democratic societies. It left poor men vulnerable to the subtle and not so subtle persuasions of their "wealthy" friends.[61] If one adds the general fear of slave revolts and changes in race relations, one should not be surprised to see a muting of much potential political conflict between rich and poor Southern whites living as neighbors in the same county.

To suggest that slavery created a society with no political conflict among whites would be a distortion. The point here is only that slavery eliminated many of the kinds of conflicts common in Northern society. It created enough homogeneity so that men could adhere to virtual representation arguments without seeming utterly ridiculous. Just as the proslavery argument would have been undercut had slaves revolted on a massive scale every day, so virtual representation would have been impossible to defend if free people openly fought each other at all levels most of the time. Slavery provided the social setting that permitted the imagination of a "community," both for masters and for slaves.

Of course, the virtual representation argument could never unequivocally triumph at all levels. When it seemed as if there was really no common interest—as between North and South on the eve of the Civil War—then the assumptions of virtual representation succumbed to the belief that no representation at all was possible. Just as proslavery theorists condemned the slavery of Northern wage workers to capitalists—a slavery involving dependence on unrestricted power, so virtual representation advocates condemned the slavery of the South to Northern political leaders. Even within the South, as the battles between upcountry and low country illustrate, the ideals of virtual representation could quickly be undercut by the first signs of real conflict. Those who portrayed themselves as the virtual representatives of the people sometimes found themselves attacked as their enslavers.

CHAPTER 5

The Proslavery Argument as an Antislavery Argument

THE PROSLAVERY ARGUMENT, the antebellum Southern defense of slavery as a positive good, was the product of a relatively small number of thinkers.[1] But they were an influential group. Their ideas were widely disseminated in speeches and articles, and by the eve of the Civil War many other Southern political leaders and writers had adopted and popularized large portions of their work. Hence, the proslavery argument was less the musing of a few isolated intellectuals than the thought of a large mass of Southern society. To expose the underlying structure of that thought is to understand some of the central ideals and aspirations of that society.

The proslavery argument was really an antislavery argument that remarkably resembled the virtual representation position of Southern political leaders. Both defended hierarchy, but neither defended slavery. Such a proposition may at first seem impossible and self-contradictory, but only because of the ambiguity associated with the concept of "slavery." Once the word is defined and the ambiguity is removed the real meaning of the contention will become clear. Just as the logic of Southern thought began to close the gap between the master and the statesman, it also began to close the gap between the slave and the free. Of course, these gaps could never entirely be eliminated. Thinkers alone could never resolve the fundamental tensions and contradictions of Southern social life. But they kept making the attempt.

I

FROM THE TIME OF THE American Revolution through the Civil War, large numbers of Southerners repeatedly condemned "slavery." They expressed themselves through words and through weapons. For example, during the years before 1776, Southerners frequently spoke out against the intentions and actions of the British government toward the colonies.

They compiled lists of grievances, noting such oppressions as excessive and unlawful taxation, inadequate representation, "illegal" proroguing of local assemblies, officeholding by placemen, and the inadequacy of trials by vice-admiralty courts. That pleas for relief, especially when the final break with England neared, so often assumed the form of a list indicates that the colonists perceived common forces and common purposes operating behind these instances of maltreatment. It was not so much the severity of individual acts that moved Southerners toward the decision for independence as their recognition of a pattern of oppression.[2] Those who believed in republican ideology feared the pattern of power that corrupted government and threatened the liberty of the people.

To many, the intention that gave form to this pattern seemed obvious. English ministers were conspiring to enslave the American colonies. "I hope every one of us," wrote Christopher Gadsden, leader of Charleston's Sons of Liberty, "will be ready at all Hazards to avert by every means in our Power the abject Slavery intended for us and our Posterity." The Reverend William Tennent explained in a 1774 sermon to the citizens of Charleston that "the Question is of no less Magnitude than whether we shall continue to enjoy the Privileges of Men and *Britons*, or whether we shall be reduced to a State of the most abject Slavery." George Washington used similar language: "The crisis is arrived when we must assert our rights, or submit to every imposition, that can be heaped upon us, till custom and use shall make us as tame and abject slaves, as the blacks we rule over with such arbitrary sway."[3]

The dread of enslavement (and the obvious disgust with such a condition) was a common concern of nineteenth-century Southerners as well. It was invoked during South Carolina's nullification crisis. Southerners who split away from Andrew Jackson during the 1830s used the language of enslavement to describe their fears. Within many Southern states, opposing political groupings frequently accused their enemies of trying to enslave them. Moreover, just as revolutionary Southerners cried out about enslavement in 1776, Southerners of the 1850s repeatedly voiced the same fear. The South Carolinian Lawrence M. Keitt, for example, echoed the words of his ancestors when he exclaimed in 1856: "I would rather my state should be the graveyard of martyred patriots than the slave of northern abolitionists." The Virginian George Fitzhugh complained that the South's own form of "Negro Slavery" was "not half so humiliating and disgraceful as the slavery of the South to the North." An Alabaman warned that unless his state resisted it would become "the inferior, the Bondsman in fact, of the North." One secessionist Georgia editor described the alternatives available to the state on the day of Abraham Lincoln's inauguration: "We are either *slaves in the Union or freemen out of it*."[4] All that seemed to have changed between 1776 and 1860 was the name of the enemy. The threat—enslavement—was the same.

What, exactly, did these Southern political leaders mean when they voiced their fear of becoming slaves? Obviously, they were not worried about literally falling into the same condition in which they held their own black slaves. Southerners feared the intentions of the British in 1776 and the Republicans in 1860, but they never really believed that these enemies planned to turn them into personal property to be bought and sold. Rather, what they had in mind was a condition of submission—a situation in which they would be subject to unrestricted power, a situation in which they would be absolutely defenseless and at the will of a master. Their fear of enslavement was simply another form of their fear of power. And it was unrestrained governmental power that they most dreaded—British ministers in 1776 and the Republican party in 1860.

Slavery, they believed, resulted from exposure to unchecked power. Power, they argued, inevitably tended to corrupt those who possessed it. John C. Calhoun expressed the idea most clearly, but he was echoed by generations of Southerners before and after he lived. "The powers which it is necessary for government to possess, in order to repress violence and preserve order, cannot execute themselves," he wrote in his *Disquisition on Government.* "They must be administered by men in whom, like others, the individual are stronger than the social feelings. And hence, the powers vested in them to prevent injustice and oppression on the part of others, will, if left unguarded, be by them converted into instruments to oppress the rest of the community." Calhoun then proceeded to assert that "power can only be resisted by power . . . [and that] those who exercise power and those subject to its exercise,—the rulers and the ruled,—stand in antagonistic relations to each other." The only way to ensure that the ruled should have sufficient guards against the abuse of power, Calhoun argued, was to establish government according to a constitution, or, as he termed it, "organism," that "will furnish the means by which resistance may be systematically and peaceably made on the part of the ruled, to oppression and abuse of power on the part of the rulers."[5] Slavery resulted from the ruled having no means to resist the power of the rulers.

The condition of slavery, in this way of thinking, was the opposite of the condition most cherished by Southerners—liberty. Liberty, as one revolutionary South Carolinian phrased it, was "the Right every man has to pursue the natural, reasonable and religious dictates of his own mind; to enjoy the fruits of his own labour, art and industry; to work for his own profit and pleasures and not for others." The essential characteristic of a free man was his independence. It was only through personal independence that a man could avoid subjection to the power and passion of others and could really act in conformity with reason. The slave, on the other hand, was a nonconsenting dependent who, in the words of Christopher Gadsden, was "at the will of his master."[6]

It is one of the most striking ironies of American history that the owners of black slaves should also have been among the most vigorous defenders of the ideal of liberty. But the connection between the institution of slavery and the love of liberty is no mere historical accident. There were good reasons why slavery and liberty should have developed in tandem. Black slavery, of course, was the essential economic underpinning for the condition of white liberty. The poorest group in American society, by its very exclusion from civil life and its relegation to a form of property, provided the economic and social base that allowed the ideal of liberty to flourish. Moreover, constant exposure to the conditions of black slaves made Southern whites peculiarly sensitive to any loss of freedom that might begin to place them in a similar condition. The heady experience of domination bred a devout commitment to freedom—at least to the freedom of masters.[7]

At one level, then, it is easy to see how black slavery and white liberty complemented each other in their historical development. But it is also quite clear that the coexistence of these two opposites in a single society was a source of tension. The tension, of course, was most obvious to outsiders, for outsiders are always quicker to see contradictions. Samuel Johnson, the English critic of the American Revolution, exposed the problem for all who cared to take note by posing the annoying rhetorical question: "How is it that we hear the loudest yelps for liberty among the drivers of negroes?"[8] It was a devastating question that served to uncover the inconsistency that Southerners would have preferred to ignore; it was a question that many other outsiders repeatedly asked as they watched Southerners defend their liberties throughout the eighteenth and nineteenth centuries. If Southerners were so devoted to liberty, so fearful of the human potential to abuse power, then how could they justify their enslavement of blacks?

Before 1820, aside from a few moments during the Constitutional Convention and the later controversies over the African slave trade, Southerners were not really pressed to face the apparent contradiction and to justify slavery. The institution simply existed without question because the challenges were too feeble to merit serious retort. But, beginning in 1820, in response to such events as the debate over the admission of Missouri as a slave state, the Denmark Vesey slave conspiracy in South Carolina and the Nat Turner insurrection in Virginia, the controversy generated by South Carolina's nullification movement, and the rise of a vocal abolitionist movement in the North, Southerners were forced to develop a formal, logical defense of slavery and hence to confront directly the problem of its tension with their devotion to liberty.[9] The proslavery argument was the attempt to resolve in thought the contradiction embedded in Southern social life.

The easiest solution to the contradiction, and one that proved attractive to some Southerners, was to rely on a racial defense of slavery. If blacks were inherently different from whites, then it would be possible to justify slavery for blacks while proclaiming liberty for whites. Some of the best minds of the age gave Southerners the prestige of scientific analysis as an underpinning to such a defense. Louis Agassiz, writing from that great citadel of learning Harvard University, gave respectability to theories of black inferiority and separate creation of the races. Black and white, he argued, were not ultimately brothers connected through a common ancestry to Adam and Eve. From Philadelphia, Samuel George Morton, the proud owner of one of the nineteenth century's greatest collections of human heads, placed blacks well below whites in intelligence in a ranking system based on skull volume. In the South, Dr. Josiah Nott of Mobile, Alabama popularized these ideas and used them in defense of slavery.[10]

Others picked up and gave further attention to the racial defense of slavery. It received eloquent treatment in the South Carolinian James Henry Hammond's 1858 "mud-sill" speech in the United States Senate. Hammond, using a broad definition of slavery as all labor and arguing that all societies required a "mud-sill" class of laborers, noted: "We do not think that whites should be slaves, either by law or necessity. Our slaves are black, of another and inferior race." The South Carolina diplomat William Henry Trescot boasted in a similar vein: "The great mass of coarse and unintellectual labor, which the necessities of the country require, is performed by a race not only especially fitted for its performance, but especially unfitted and disqualified for that mental improvement which is generally understood by the term education."[11]

It is difficult to determine just how many Southerners became fully committed to the racial defense of slavery. One of the central problems of such a defense—especially as it assumed the form of polygenesis (separate creation of the races)—was that it appeared to contradict the biblical account of the unity of the human race. The Bible, it seemed to many Southerners, described only a single creation of man. Of course, some Southerners, such as the Louisiana physician Samuel Cartwright, sought to reconcile the Bible with polygenesis; even Jefferson Davis believed in a version of polygenesis that he thought was consistent with the Bible. Still, the tension between religion and science on this issue seems at least to have dampened enthusiasm for the doctrine. Neither polygenesis nor the "scientific" evidence of black inferiority ever dominated the proslavery argument in public speeches, journals, or in E. N. Elliott's great compendium of proslavery thought published on the eve of the Civil War.[12]

In fact, there was something problematical about the racial defense of slavery even beyond its conflict with the Bible. After all, even if many Southerners could not accept polygenesis, they certainly had little trouble with the idea of permanent or relatively permanent black inferiority. Whether the inferiority came before or after the creation of man, few Southerners doubted the fact of inferiority. So why did the proslavery argument not rest exclusively, or at least primarily, on the idea that blacks were peculiarly suited to be slaves, that blacks were peculiarly suited to be at the will of the passions of an unrestrained master? Since the racial defense of slavery could so nicely, even neatly, resolve the tension between slavery and liberty, why did proslavery thinkers feel compelled to stray from it so often?

In a way, the racial defense of slavery was a bit beside the point. Whether or not one believed that blacks were inferior humans or wild beasts, a full defense of "slavery"—the kind of slavery Southerners repeatedly condemned when it threatened to consume them in 1776 and 1860—would have had to embrace the virtues of unrestrained power. That is the kind of proslavery argument which the racial defense did not and could not address. A real proslavery argument, an argument that defined slavery the way Southerners constantly used the term in their battles against government, would have had to maintain that subservience to the irrational will of a human was a desirable condition, even for inferiors. The racial defense of slavery never directly confronted that problem. When Southerners did confront the problem they found themselves unable to acclaim the virtues of unrestrained power; they found themselves unable to defend the kind of slavery for blacks they so feared for whites. These were men who dearly loved liberty. Instead, they denied that their own institution was really slavery, and they spent a great deal of time and effort condemning the real slavery they saw festering in Northern and in European society. In other words, the proslavery argument, the direct defense of the institution of slavery, was really framed as an antislavery argument.

II

UNCLE TOM'S CABIN, Harriet Beecher Stowe's novel condemning slavery, posed the problem in a way that proved disturbing to many Southerners and made the racial defense of slavery irrelevant. It was not simply that Stowe peopled her plantations with light-skinned mulattoes. That was not the central troubling element in *Uncle Tom's Cabin.* Most other tracts critical of slavery seemed to involve gross distortion and caricature of what

Southerners believed to be the real nature of plantation life. But here was a work that, although obviously overdramatized, readily conceded that the master-slave relationship could be benevolent; what proved troubling, however, was the contention that, since slaves were at the mercy of masters, the institution could just as easily prove tyrannical.

Uncle Tom's Cabin seemed so shocking to Southerners precisely because it did not contend that all slaveholders were Simon Legree. Such a charge would not have been so disturbing because it would have conflicted with the common experience of many masters. Stowe simply suggested that slavery, because it provided no check on power, permitted some masters to become Legree. The South Carolinian Edward J. Pringle understood that the novel depicted "the evils of the complete dependence of one man upon the arbitrary will of another." Mary Boykin Chesnut, wife of the antebellum senator and Confederate leader from South Carolina, had a fascination with the novel and fully understood its implications. She tried to read the book at least three times and in her diary repeatedly described a sense of disturbance. At one point she wrote that "[I] tried to read 'Uncle Tom.' Could not. Too sickening. A man send his little son to beat a human being tied to a tree?"[13]

Mary Boykin Chesnut knew that she, and most people she knew, had never mistreated a slave in the ways described by Harriet Beecher Stowe. Yet *Uncle Tom's Cabin* never contended that she had. It only said that Simon Legree did it and challenged her to defend Legree. Chesnut, of course, could not bring herself to do so, nor could any of her contemporaries. Perhaps Anne Middleton, wife of a president of the College of Charleston, just after reading *Uncle Tom's Cabin* best described the problem in a letter to her husband: "I do not after all shrink from the *suffering* as from them [slaves] being crushed down to involuntary sin—and then the probable confusion of moral perceptions which we have all ourselves been trying to raise.—I cannot see what is to prevent the possibility [of such cruelty]."[14] It was the possibility of abuse in a situation in which power had no restraint that proved most disturbing to Southerners.

George Frederick Holmes, the English-born Virginian who wrote several proslavery essays in *DeBow's Review*, the *Southern Literary Messenger*, and the *Southern Quarterly Review*, also clearly understood the nature of the challenge posed by *Uncle Tom's Cabin.* In a review essay he noted how the various Southern attempts to write similar books with a vision of happy slaves—such works as *Aunt Phyllis's Cabin*—missed the point. "[T]he argument of the work is," Holmes wrote, "in plain and precise terms, that any organization of society—any social institution, which can by possibility result in such instances of individual misery, or generate such examples of individual cruelty as are exhibited in this fiction, must be criminal in itself."[15] Holmes, like Mary Boykin Chesnut and Anne Middleton, also understood that Harriet Beecher Stowe had aimed at the possibility of abuse of unrestrained power. How could a society so fearful of power answer such a challenge?

Because antebellum Southerners distrusted power so intensely, proslavery thinkers had little basis to deny that Simon Legree could and did exist (or even, as a matter of fact, that all masters were in danger of becoming Legree themselves). Did not the master have a power over his slave that was unrestrained? Why should men with this kind of power not abuse it?

Yet, precisely because Legree was the embodiment of the kind of unrestrained, abusive power they so hated, Southern defenders of slavery could never concede that he was in any sense an inevitable product of the institution or that slaves had no security against him. Ironically, the very ideas that should have forced Southerners to agree that abuses of power occurred in slavery prevented them from admitting it. Thus, the course of their argument took an interesting turn. Unable to drop the idea that unrestrained power tends to corrupt, Southerners denied that masters had such power.

Southerners, in effect, argued that slavery contained, in Calhoun's phrase, "an organism," or constitution that limited the power of masters. The organism envisioned by the defenders of slavery was not the kind of formal, governmental structure elaborated by the American revolutionaries or by John C. Calhoun, although it did contain some formal elements. Nonetheless, the constitution for government, and the constitution for slavery did perform the same function. They were both ways of preventing the abuse of power. No white Southerner would have felt safe from abuse if protected by such an informal constitution, but the white defenders of slavery were undoubtedly concerned not so much with the actual protection of blacks or with a description of how slavery really operated as with discovering a way to resolve the tension between their ideals and their "peculiar" institution. The point here is to demonstrate not to what degree informal constraints actually protected blacks but only to what extent white Southerners felt compelled to believe they protected them.

It is striking how often the defenders of slavery argued that masters did not possess total power over their slaves. William Sumner Jenkins, author of the only comprehensive history of the proslavery argument, notes the tendency of the slaveholder to deny "that his power over the slave was absolute as in the case of the Roman master." Jenkins pointed out that many Southerners argued that "the slave of the South was held for specific purposes only, and the power of the master was limited to certain property rights that he held in the services of the slave."[16]

Many defenders of slavery in the South denied the charge that they held property in all of a man. Instead, they usually emphasized the limited nature of the master-slave relationship. James Henley Thornwell, Charleston's conservative Presbyterian minister, explained the nature of slave ownership: "The right which a master has is a right, not to the *man*, but to his labour." His more secular contemporaries agreed. Edward B. Bryan described slave property in similar terms: "With us this property does not consist in human 'flesh.' . . . Our property in man is a right and title to human labor. . . . *Our slave property lies only incidentally in the person of the slave but essentially in his labor.* . . . The proprietorship of his person extends only so far as the derivation of a fair amount of labor. . . . *In fact we own our slaves for their labor. We govern them as men.*"[17]

Corollary to the idea that masters held property only in a man's labor and not in a man himself was the denial that slaves in the South were treated as "things." To recognize the limited nature of slave ownership was to concede that slaves existed in a capacity other than as objects of the master's power. "The slave is not a tool, a mere instrument," noted the Reverend Ferdinand Jacobs, a colleague of Thornwell in the Second Presbyterian Church in Charleston, "but is capable of a high sense of responsibility to God and man, and may as conscientiously discharge his obligations in his relations as any other man." One defender of slavery, sighing with relief in 1844, stated: "The disposition to regard slaves as chattels for any object, had been very much overcome throughout the South, and precautions were taken to secure in many cases to them the essential rights of social beings." Edward J. Pringle, in his response to *Uncle Tom's Cabin*, pointed out that "the position of the slave does not necessarily make him the 'chattel' that our northern friends call him."[18]

Henry Hughes, the Mississippi proslavery writer, devoted a great deal of his *Treatise on Sociology* to a description of the powers that a master did *not* have over a slave. "The fundamental power of warrantors [masters]," he wrote, "is therefore just so much as is sufficient to execute economic, hygienic and political order in their warranties [slaves]. It is no more. That is the limit." Although Hughes did concede great powers to a master within these limits, he was much obsessed with carefully describing restraints on power. Among other things, he argued, masters did not have the power to deny subsistence to slaves; they could not resign from their responsible position as masters; they could not separate families, "except such separation as is essential to the subsistence of all"; they had no power at all to "separate mothers and children under the age of ten years"; they had very limited judicial powers; they could not punish "except after trial or fair hearing"; and they could not employ "cruel or unusual" punishment or "endanger life or limb."[19]

The conception of slaves as moral beings rather than amoral objects often was accompanied by the recognition that even the master's relatively limited power over the slave could not be claimed without the simultaneous assumption of certain obligations. Hence, slavery was frequently pictured as a kind of unwritten contractual relationship in which masters exercised power over the slave's labor but in exchange had to supply "his bodily wants, feeding, clothing, housing him, taking care of him when sick, preventing wrongs and injuries from being done to him, and supplying him with the means of moral and religious instruction, which are necessary to his soul's health."[20] The South Carolinian James Henry Hammond explicitly used contractual language to describe the relation:

> *If we travel back with the philosophers who refer all human institutions to an original compact, I will still engage to find a place for slavery there. Let it be regarded as a compact between the master and the slave, and I assert that no saner or more just agreement was ever made working to the mutual benefit of both and charitably inclined in favor of the weaker party. The master exacts of the slave obedience, fidelity, and industry; and places him under just so much restraint as insures compliance with his regulations. The slave in return has far more certainly insured to him* peace, plenty, security, *and the proper indulgence of his social propensities—freed from all care for the present, or anxiety for the future with regard either to himself or his family.*[21]

Even when Southerners did not employ contractual language to describe the master-slave relationship, they still repeatedly described the duties—the obligations—of men who owned slaves. No proslavery treatise was ever complete without a full discussion of the burdens that fell upon masters. Henry Hughes, for example, discussed three categories of master's duties: "economic, political, and hygienic." Economic duties included the obligations to regulate the productive labor of blacks, prevent idleness and vagrancy, prevent waste, provide "wages," act as the agents for slaves in the buying and selling of all goods, and provide consumable goods. Hygienic duties included disease prevention, the imposition of quarantines when necessary, the enforcement of "such needful regularity of rest, labor, and amusements, as are sanitary," maintenance of the safety of workers, and the obligation to care for the sick. In the area of the political duties of masters, Hughes suggested that "the warrantor [the master] is the political servant of the warrantee [the slave]." Masters must act in the interest of slaves "against legislative injustice"; they must "keep the peace of the warranty"; they must prevent crime, and they must act to adjudicate the matters over which they have jurisdiction.[22] Sometimes, as one reads such statements, it becomes hard to know whether the writer is discussing the obligations of masters or of statesmen.

The Virginian George Fitzhugh clearly stated the implications of the burdens of masters. "Slaves," he wrote in his *Sociology for the South*, "have a valuable property in their masters. Infant negroes, sick, helpless, aged and infirm negroes, are simply a charge to their master; he has no property in them in the common sense of the term, for they are of no value for the time, but they have the most invaluable property in him. He is bound to support them, to supply all their wants, and relieve them of all care for the present or future."[23]

Not only did many proslavery essays describe the limited powers as well as the obligations of masters, but they also tried to explain the mechanisms that would ensure that those powers would remain limited and that those obligations would be fulfilled. Such mechanisms had to ensure that the master's power over the labor of the slave did not extend into forbidden areas (the breakup of families, sexual abuse, excessive cruelty). Moreover, the master had to be compelled to provide shelter, food, and clothing to the slave. Some proslavery thinkers turned to the law. Edward C. Holland, author of one of the earliest defenses of slavery in South Carolina, pointed the way: "It is not true that the authority of the master over his slave is without limitation or restriction; but, on the contrary, we affirm that it is watched and guarded by some very jealous statutory provisions. He is protected by the humanity of our laws, both in his life and his limbs, and from any brutal attack on either." Holland then noted that masters could neither kill nor maim their slaves without facing the death penalty themselves. William Gilmore Simms also used slave law to justify the institution, indicating that slaves were "as effectually secured against wrong and murder as the white man, and his securities are as unfrequently outraged." "Grand juries," he argued, "closely watched brutal masters." Henry Hughes noted that law required that masters perform their responsibilities. "This responsibility," he wrote, "is civilly enforced. It is nothing other than punishment for breach of political laws. Such punishments are fines, confiscations, imprisonment, or any other personal or property penalty. The political responsibility of warrantors [masters] specially differs in nothing, from the responsibility of other magistrates, for misfeasance or nonfeasance in office."[24]

Although proslavery writers believed that law, like custom, humanitarianism, and social pressure of neighbors, offered slaves some protection from abuse of power, they generally recognized it alone was not adequate.[25] It extended only to certain very specific aspects of master-slave relations, mostly offering some minimal protections to life and limb. Moreover, these restraints relied too heavily on the good will of the master alone for their proper operation. If the rulers became corrupted by their excessive power these safeguards would be of little use. Masters were supposed to be like statesmen, men of good character and intelligence. But, like statesmen, they also needed to be restricted by the limits of a "constitution."

To Southerners the most convincing solution to corruption emphasized the operation of impersonal, natural forces rather than the good will of masters. Some proslavery writers used a portion of the racial defense of slavery. They pointed to the physical nature of blacks to argue that they could never feel the impact of the abuse of power. One writer likened blacks to mules who would always stop work before it became too burdensome. Thus, he argued, to extort more work than a "moderate service" was an impossibility. This kind of argument was akin to those that contended that blacks could better stand the heat of Southern climates, that they were immune to certain diseases, or that they had skulls so thick a white man could not break it without first breaking his fist. George Frederick Holmes resorted to such an argument in his critique of *Uncle Tom's Cabin.* He contended that the book erroneously assumed that blacks and whites were equally sensitive to misery. "It takes advantage of this presumption," he wrote, "so suspiciously credited where slavery is unknown, to arouse sympathies for what might be grievous misery to the white man, but is none to the differently tempered black."[26]

But this aspect of the racial defense could never prove entirely satisfactory. It still left an image of an abusive master, even if the slave could not sense the abuse. To Southerners, the most convincing explanation of why masters would not abuse their power rested on the nature of the master-slave relationship. Masters would not kill, maim, overwork, or otherwise mistreat slaves because to do so would be against the powerful impetus of their economic self-interest. Hence, George Frederick Holmes moved away from the racial defense of slavery to argue that, because masters owned slaves, "the interests of the labourer and the employer of labour are absolutely identical. . . . The consequence is that both interest and inclination, the desire of profit and the sense or sentiment of duty concur to render the salve-owner considerate and kind toward the slaves." Slavery, William John Grayson, famous for his poetic defense of the institution, contended, "is the only condition of society in which labor and capital are associated on a large scale—in which their interests are combined, and not in conflict." John C. Calhoun described the same communal atmosphere of the plantation. "Every plantation," he wrote, "is a little community, with the master at its head, who concentrates in himself the united interests of capital and labor, of which he is the common representative."[27]

Henry Hughes also saw the primary obstacle to abuse of power in the common interest of master and slave. "Damage to the warrantee [slave]," he wrote, "is . . . damage to the warrantor [master]. . . . The warrantor is economically enforced therefore to warrant health, strength, and justice, to the warrantee. . . . The wrongs by their consequences right themselves. They find the wronger, and are self-executing."[28] In other words, masters who beat their slaves brutally, diminished their value and hence hurt themselves as property owners.

Many slaveholders cited the idea of an identity of interest of master and slave when they offered advice on the proper care and management of slaves. One Mississippi planter wrote in an 1847 issue of the *Southern Cultivator* that "humanity and interest need not be separated" in the management of slaves; another planter wrote in 1851 that "the master's interest and the Negro's comfort are the most intimately blended." An 1853 Georgia committee in charge of selecting the best essay on slave management noted that all the essays submitted agreed that "the pecuniary interests of the master are best consulted by a humane and liberal treatment of the slave."[29]

Perhaps no other part of the proslavery argument resolved so completely and satisfactorily the problem of power in the master-slave relationship—the problem of the possibility of Simon Legree—as did the idea of an identity of interest of ruler and ruled. It made Simon Legree virtually impossible. In one stroke, it resolved the antagonism between "the individual and social feelings," as Calhoun called them, by making the individual into the social feelings. It was the best of all possible "organisms"—an organic organism or community, one that operated naturally and required no one to oversee its functioning. Little wonder that nearly all proslavery writers relied heavily on this argument.[30] Often, they coupled it with or emphasized in its place vague references to the "natural" love of men for someone totally dependent on them, or they wrote about the humanitarian inclinations of masters. But such arguments performed the same function—they satisfactorily resolved the problem of power in slavery by abolishing antagonistic interests.

The common proslavery description of the master-slave relation as "familial" was simply another way of expressing these ideas. The Baptist minister Dr. Richard Furman wrote that slaves "become part of his [master's] family, (the whole, forming under him a little community) and the care of ordering it, and of providing for its welfare, devolves on him. The children, the aged, the sick, the disabled, and the unruly, as well as those, who are capable of service and orderly, are the objects of his care: the labour of these, is applied to the benefit of those, and to their own suppport, as well as that of the master. . . . Cruelty, is, certainly, inadmissable." Henry Hughes, using his peculiar brand of sociological jargon, expressed the same basic idea: "By the essence of warranteeism [slavery], the interests of warrantors are affamiliated; they are syntagonistic; they are family interests. Grievance to warrantees, is grievance to warrantors; as grievance to wife is grievance to husband. Warrantors and warrantees are wedded in interest. The sovereign warrantor is therefore, the petitioner for redress of all grievances by others than himself."[31]

Noteworthy in these descriptions, as in all other proslavery characterizations of slaves as dependent parts of the master's family, is the emphasis on the obligations of the master and the protections such a relationship afforded blacks from abuse of power. The family, in proslavery thought, was not the one once described by Sir Robert Filmer as analagous to absolute monarchy, in which the father "governs by no other law than by his own will, not by the laws or wills of his sons or servants." It was much more akin to that described by John Locke, in which the failure of a father to perform certain necessary obligations to his children and to respect their rights would, presumably (and this was a point left implicit by Southerners fearful of legitimizing slave revolts), eliminate his right to claim obedience from them. It was a family that established the permissible limits of power rather than one that justified absolute power.[32]

Proof, according to slavery's defenders, that these various mechanisms actually operated to protect Southern blacks was that slaves consented to their condition as dependents—perhaps not explicitly but tacitly. "There are few people," wrote William Gilmore Simms, "so very well satisfied with their condition as the negroes,—so happy of mood, so jocund, and so generally healthy and cheerful." Another South Carolinian, Edward Thomas Heriot, offered a similar analysis of slave attitudes: "I will say as far as I have seen and know, that there is no class of people . . . of the same grade, where there is so much real happiness, where the wants of nature are so abundantly supplied, where the requirements of labour are as little, and where the guaranty against poverty, and distress from all the conditions of existence is so great."[33]

The notion of slave contentment was simply a part of the widely accepted conception of the black as a "Sambo"—a perpetual child who was loyal, lazy, docile, irresponsible, and, most important for defenders of slavery, gloriously happy and satisfied with his condition. Historians have long recognized that whether or not Sambos existed Southern whites found it useful to believe in them. They have usually emphasized, however, that the image allayed fears of slave rebellion. Just as important, though, is that it indicated tacit consent. "*Involuntary servitude*," wrote one defender of slavery, "is not a definition of slavery, though forced upon us, that we accept." James Henley Thornwell agreed: "This view of the subject exposes the confusion, which obtains in most popular treatises of morals, of slavery with involuntary servitude. The service, in so far as it consists in the motions of the limbs or organs of the body, must be voluntary, or it could not exist at all. If by voluntary be meant, however, that which results from hearty consent, and is accordingly rendered with cheerfulness, it is precisely the service which the law of God enjoins."[34]

Repeatedly, proslavery thinkers asserted that, if given the choice, blacks would select slavery over freedom. "There are few slaves, we believe," one writer noted, "in the Southern country who would change their present condition, which is one of dependence, for all the advantages which freedom would bring." Another described with pleasure how "many a poor fugitive to the land of freedom . . . has wept to return to the indulgent master and the well filled corncrib."[35]

Proslavery writers even explained slave rebellion in such a way as to preserve the illusion that blacks consented. Insurrection, they believed, never came in response to abuses inherent in the institution but rather in response to "external" agitation.[36] The slave uprising in Santo Domingo was the "work of the French people." "The Assembly," James Henry Hammond explained, "*decreed* the massacres of St. Domingo as an appropriate underplot to the awful tragedy it was enacting then in France itself." He then warned prophetically: "And if ever danger or suffering occur to us from our slave system, it will spring from a similar source. Left to ourselves we have nothing to fear and everything to gain from it." South Carolinians blamed the influences of Santo Domingo and Northern agitation during the Missouri crisis for the Denmark Vesey conspiracy of 1822. William Gilmore Simms carefully pointed out that the Nat Turner insurrection erupted not before abolitionism developed but only before abolitionists were detected. Edward B. Bryan announced conclusively in 1858 that every Southern slave rebellion "has been directly traced to outside influence." Harpers Ferry reconfirmed the suspicion.[37]

Hence, much of the so-called defense of slavery was no defense of slavery at all. At least in this context, Southerners had repeatedly defined a slave as a nonconsenting dependent "at the will" of his master. To argue that black slaves were protected from abuse of power and that they consented to their condition was to suggest that they were not slaves in this sense of the term. Many proslavery writers recognized this implication of their argument. Some contrasted the condition of blacks in the South with other possible conditions that seemed more "slavish." Edward B. Bryan, for example, conjured a yeomanlike image of the Virginia slave "plying his frugal hoe on the banks of the Rappahannock or the Roanoke" in juxtaposition to the African barbarian "inured to the most abject slavery it has ever been the lot of man to witness . . . reveling in all the vices known to his savage condition."[38] The image here is that "freedom" might produce slavery to sin. Others pointed out that, if freed, blacks would be more subject to abuse of power, and hence, paradoxically, would be by implication less free. Edward J. Pringle described the various circumstantial forces that would press down on free blacks. "As long as this force of circumstances," he wrote, "has no conscience, is out of view, has no duty or responsibility, it is a more dangerous power than the slaveowners. In a word, it is mere short-sightedness to talk of the power of the white man over the black in slavery, when the alternative is between that and competition between the races. The one is at least a degree of protection, the other would be extermination, to the weaker." The reference here was to the part of scientific racism that suggested that "inferior" races, if free, would be exterminated. Proslavery writers who made this argument often pointed to the "empirical" evidence available in the disappearance of Indians and the disappearance of blacks in the North to prove that two races could not live together without one or the other, the "weaker," being exterminated unless protected by slavery.[39]

Southerners frequently contrasted "wage slavery" with their own form of slavery in such a way as to imply that their slaves had more real "freedom." One writer described the complete vulnerability of "free" laborers, or wage workers, to abuse of power, noting that they were totally "dependent on the wealthy employer" and were "liable to have that employment determine [terminate] at any moment, either by caprice, ill health, or the state of trade." This condition, he continued, was "the most intolerable slavery that men can suffer—a slavery which throws them into a state where wealth and power exercise the worst oppressions." This vulnerability appeared to him as a far more slavish condition than that faced by Southern blacks, secure from abuse. The writer was more disturbed by the greater vulnerability of the wage slave to possible abuse than by the difference in material circumstances. Edward J. Pringle spelled out the distinction between the wage worker and the slave: "The slave is at the mercy of a master, who must feel more or less the responsibility of his position. The freeman, who is weighed down by the inevitable ill[s] that society is subject to, has no tyrant but the hard laws of demand and supply, stern and unchangeable. The one depends upon a master, whose interest it is to raise him up; the other can look only to capital, whose interest is antagonistic to labor." Henry Hughes offered a long critique of free labor and described the vulnerability of workers who were paid wages. "The capitalist," he explained, "has no preservation-interest in the laborer. Loss of a laborer is not the capitalist's loss." In other words, in a free society, the interests of the capitalist and the laborer were antagonistic. A capitalist can exploit his workers—perhaps even starve them—and he would feel no pecuniary loss because they were not his property. James Henry Hammond made the point most bluntly: If Great Britain were to elevate its working class to the condition of Southern slaves, he noted, "it would be . . . a most glorious act of *emancipation*."[40]

Southerners could not easily drop the word "slavery" as the name of their institution since it had been associated with it for so long. Yet, since so much of their defense of the institution was not really a defense of the kind of real slavery they abhorred, it should occasion little surprise to discover that a number of proslavery thinkers decided to discard the old name. "They [Northern abolitionists] need not regard the South as in any wise apologists for, but defenders of, slavery, or as it should be termed African servitude," wrote George A. Gordon, an assistant editor of Robert Barnwell Rhett's *Charleston Mercury*. One South Carolina writer, utilizing the "mud-sill" idea, noted: "*Here*, [in the South] he is not a *slave* in the odious sense, but a *servant*, under the form of force, controll, government, and protection of law and order." Another used a similar argument to maintain that "what is called slavery is so suited to the condition of the negro, that we might call it civil liberty; for it is for him 'being restrained by no law which does not contribute in a greater degree to the public good.' " A writer in the *Southern Quarterly Review* refused to be called a defender of slavery because the institution existed only in Europe. He rather wished to write in defense of "patriarchal" government, "the same form of government to which the abolitionists subject their wives and children." Another writer argued that black slaves were really freemen in comparison to the abolitionists: "Under the protection of that law and justice which sanctifies the natural rights of every class, [the black slave] is more of a freeman than the mad slaves of fanaticism and ignorance, who would violate his [the black's] natural condition, and make him tenfold more the devilish bondsman of iniquity and lawlessness than themselves." Henry Hughes announced simply that slavery did not exist in the South. "In the United States South," he wrote, "warrantees are persons who have all their rights. They are not slaves; they are not persons who have no rights. Their slavery is nominal only; and the name, a wrong to the warrantee states." Hughes even referred to his "warrantee" laborers as "Liberty Laborers" in contrast to "free" workers who were paid wages.[41] That Southerners groped for new terms—"patriarchalism," "servitude," "peculiar institution," "warranteeism"—testifies to their discomfort with attempting to justify "slavery."

Even those who used the term "slavery" in a positive way redefined the word to mean something entirely different from being "at the will" of a master. A number of Southerners, for example, contended that slavery was simply any relationship of power between people. In this sense, it was defined as the principle of law, or the principle of the family. Edward J. Pringle suggested: "The power that slavery gives to one man over another is met with everywhere in society." Claiming to disagree with such "utopians" as Saint-Simon, Charles Fourier, and Robert Owen, Pringle maintained that any relation of ruler to ruled was slavery and that it existed in all places at all times—even in the power of parents over children.[42] A writer in the *Southern Quarterly Review* carried this peculiar meaning of slavery to its absurd conclusion: "Every individual, subjected to the laws of any society, must be more or less the subject or slave of those laws, in so far as he is, to certain extent, in a state of bondage to them."[43] George Fitzhugh, describing the mutual obligations of masters and slaves, suggested that "each in a broad sense [is] equally slaves, for the superior is as much bound by law, natural feeling, self-interest, and custom, to take care of, govern, and provide for inferiors or dependents, as they to labor for him."[44]

III

THE PROSLAVERY ARGUMENT was not—nor could it have been—entirely successful in resolving the tension between slavery and liberty in Southern life. For one thing, in denying that real slavery existed in the South, the argument also moved far toward denying that real liberty existed there. The more proslavery writers described blacks as protected by a caring master, the more the master became tied to his slaves; the more he became enmeshed in a web of duties and responsibilities, the more he lost his independence. The underlying logic of the proslavery argument "abolished" slavery by abolishing abusive power; it also abolished liberty by eliminating real independence. What it left behind was a world of mutual dependency. For Southerners, the denial of slavery was far easier to accept than the denial of liberty.

If Southern society had no history; if it had only a master class and no bourgeoisie; if it had no political, social, economic, and intellectual connections with Northern society; if it was not enmeshed in a competitive system of world trade; if it did not have to justify a revolution in 1860; if Southerners could have abandoned their love of liberty and independence; if all slaves were really content and loved their masters; if there were no differences between the dependence of masters and the dependence of slaves; if all these things and a great deal more were true—then, perhaps, for a brief while, the proslavery argument could have fully resolved in intellectual form the contradictions of Southern social life. But masters were never left alone to dream their dreams in peaceful slumber. Their social world kept intruding.

Still, the proslavery argument indicates, as does the virtual representation argument, a central tendency of Southern thought. This central tendency would have probably become even more widely accepted had Southern masters really succeeded in isolating themselves from the world. Southern thought had to deal with the central contradiction of slave society. These men, after all, hated power and yet they also sought the power necessary to bring them honor. Both virtual representation and the proslavery argument tried to resolve the tension generated by this double longing by defining the government of free people and the government of slaves as rooted in an organic community. Such a community could be ruled by men of power and honor who would never abuse their privileged position. Leaders in such a world could be both powerful and honored and yet powerless and dependent on their community at the same time.

PART III

THE LOGIC OF SECESSION

CHAPTER 6

From Anglophobia to New Anglophobia

AS SOUTHERNERS LOOKED OUT from their statehouses and plantations, as they surveyed the organic communities they imagined all around them, they sensed the fragility of their world. Both their republican values and their search for honor directed them to be careful. As republican theorists had argued for several hundred years, Southerners believed that their governments were fragile structures that could quickly and permanently succumb to abusive power unless the citizens carefully guarded their liberties. Moreover, the man in search of honor had to be ever watchful of slights and insults. Not one insult, not one statement that implied dependence or inferiority, could be allowed to pass without permanently damaging a man's status and reputation. In an attempt to understand the logic of secession, this chapter and the next explore these Southern fears of corruption and loss of honor. First, I examine Southern attitudes toward England and New England, Southerners' perception of the threats to their world, and the origins of their sense of separate nationality. Then, in the last chapter, I carefully describe both the form and the logic of secession in relation to the larger political culture of slavery.

I

NATIONS ARE CONCEIVED in love and hate. The sense of identity that holds a nation together is a mixture of shared faiths, ideals, and customs as well as of common fears and enemies. Often, at the moment of birth fear of a common enemy is the dominant unifying force—fear of the corrupt, old regime or of the foreign oppressor. The United States has been no exception. Despite the similar customs and beliefs that might have bound the colonies together before 1776, fear of English oppression precipitated the final union. Eighty-five years later a similar fear pushed the Southern states into a new Confederate nation.

What is most striking about America's two experiences with nation-creation—in 1776 and in 1861—is not the existence of a fear of oppression but rather the remarkable historical connection between the objects of that fear. During the antebellum period traditional Southern anxieties about England, inherited from the republican ideology of the revolutionary period and reinforced by later events, underwent a slow transformation into a fear of New England and the North. The nature of this Anglophobia and its change into "New" Anglophobia must be closely analyzed if we are to understand the full dimensions of Confederate nationhood.

One must begin, of course, by recognizing that Anglophobia and Anglophilia—the hatred and love of England and things English—peacefully coexisted in the minds of many Americans, Northern and Southern, throughout the nineteenth century. This ambivalent response to the old colonial mother country is precisely what one should expect from a relatively young nation struggling for a distinct identity despite its largely derivative cultural heritage. Young American writers both imitated and tried to reject the models offered by English authors; Americans demanded a uniquely American literature even as they continued to read and copy the works of great English writers; American travelers found themselves drawn to and repulsed by their experience of English society.[1] Even one of the central myths accepted by many nineteenth-century Americans, a myth embedded in numerous antebellum writings, depended on a double image of English society. The North, so the myth explains, had been settled by Puritan Roundheads, whereas the South was peopled by Cavaliers—the supporters of the monarchy in the English Civil War. "Under the stimulus of this divided heritage," suggests historian William R. Taylor in his elaboration of this set of ideas, "the North had developed a leveling, go-getting utilitarian society and the South had developed a society based on the values of the English gentry."[2] This way of describing English society and its extension into America necessarily stimulated ambivalent responses. England could be conceived of as the cause of either of two opposite societies.

Yet to recognize that Americans had ambivalent attitudes toward England is not to denigrate the importance or power of these ideas. It would be improper to conclude that all Americans simultaneously loved and hated England, and hence the attitudes had no real significance because they canceled each other out. As is often true with ambivalent attitudes, different circumstances cause a people to emphasize one side of the ambivalence or the other in specific contexts. For example, it seems clear that certain portions of Southern society, especially the large planters of the coast, developed aristocratic pretensions that pushed them to imitate the English gentry. Many wealthy Southerners sent their sons to be educated at Eton, Oxford, and the Middle Temple. Two hundred and twenty-five of the

350 Americans who were admitted to the Inns of Court in London before 1860 came from Southern states, including 89 from South Carolina and 76 from Virginia. Similarly, some wealthy planters delighted in tracing their ancestry to the English upper classes; some built their houses after English models; and some bought their books in England.[3] Yet, as we will see, it was often these same men, as well as many other less wealthy Southerners, who used Anglophobic images and ideas to explain a variety of critical problems faced by their society.

The Revolution stimulated a host of negative attitudes toward England in every section of the emerging new nation. In the style of traditional republican thought, Americans repeatedly wrote not only of specific grievances, but of a subversive conspiracy of power-hungry men, as well as of a more general moral decline of an increasingly corrupt English society. Southerners shared the general fear that the tax acts and other British oppressions leading up to 1776 resulted from a conspiracy of power-hungry British ministers who threatened England's delicate mixed government. Many Southerners gradually came to feel that within the structure of English government they could not protect themselves against the abuses of these powerful men. They frequently described their situation as approaching slavery.[4] Others came to see this conspiracy as symptomatic of a more general moral corruption eating away at English society. Henry Laurens, Edmund Jennings, and Landon Carter advised Americans to avoid English schools for fear that colonial youth might become tainted with the corruption. William Lee described Englishmen as "immersed in riches, luxury and dissipation." Henry Laurens bemoaned "the wretched state of female virtue in this kingdom [England]!" Thomas Jefferson and James Madison placed England in the general category of decadent, artificial, urban, hierarchical Europe, in contrast to a more egalitarian, rural, and natural America.[5] Even if few Southerners understood the full logic of such arguments, the general image of powerful conspirators in control of a decadent, corrupt English society threatening to enslave Americans probably achieved wide acceptance.

The experience of the revolutionary war in the South added another dimension to the images of a power-hungry and corrupt English society. Many Southern states witnessed some of the most bitter fighting of the Revolution. The British occupation of Charleston and Savannah and the fighting in the Carolina back country left memories of brutality that would not easily fade. The South Carolinians John C. Calhoun, Andrew Pickens Butler, Preston Brooks, and Wade Hampton all grew up on stories of English butchery. Calhoun's 1843 campaign biography proudly noted that he had been named after his maternal uncle "whom the Tories had murdered in cold blood, and in his own yard, after destroying his house by fire." As a boy, John Randolph of Virginia wore an "ABRACADABRA" around his neck "to keep off the Ague and the British."[6]

After the Revolution, in the 1790s, anti-British feeling continued to smolder in the South. The Democratic-Republicans under the guidance of the Virginians Thomas Jefferson and James Madison strongly advocated a pro-French and anti-British foreign policy. Opposition to the pro-British Jay Treaty and to the undeclared war with France were cornerstones of Republican policy in the 1790s. Even more revealing, Southern Federalists never seem to have become as Anglophile as their Northern counterparts. Perhaps because of heavy debts to British merchants, annoyance at English interference with American foreign policy, or fears of British merchant influence in the politics of such cities as Charleston, Federalists in South Carolina, North Carolina, Georgia, and Virginia registered strong protests against the Jay Treaty. Moreover, the Southern Federalist party press exploded in a rage of Anglophobia when the British warship *Leander* fired at an American ship and killed an American sailor off the coast of Virginia in 1806. Similarly, in 1807 when the United States frigate *Chesapeake* was attacked and boarded by the crew of the British *Leopard* in search of deserters, Southern Federalists joined with Republicans in a burst of Anglophobia. At least for a while, party politics virtually ended in a rush of anti-British hysteria.[7] Although Southern Federalists may have spent much of their time explaining that France was a greater threat than England, even they were not immune to periodic Anglophobic outbursts.

The Anglophobia of other Southerners, of course, was even more intense than the hysteria of the Federalists. The citizens of Baltimore met in a giant public meeting to consider the *Chesapeake-Leopard* affair, and they urged the president to "enforce satisfaction for the outrage so daring and injurious to the honor and dignity of our country." Similar public meetings of indignation spread throughout the South. Georgia armed its citizens in preparation for war. In fact, it was because of this very issue that John C. Calhoun first entered public life, authoring a resolution for the citizens of Abbeville, South Carolina. Calhoun called for the end of all trade with England. He promised that Carolinians, "emulating the glorious example of '76 and relying confidently on the resources of our country . . . will readily renounce as mere luxuries, all articles of foreign importation." Calhoun's career began in the heat of Anglophobia, and his initial public statement aired the Anglophobic themes that reappeared throughout his life—annoyance at a specific British grievance, a call to emulate the "glorious example of '76," and a hint of American virtue and innocence being challenged by English power and decadence. Calhoun soon even evoked the old images of British conspiracy when, in 1812, he uncovered evidence of a British "plot" to divide the American states over the embargo issue. It was only the first of many "conspiracies" he "discovered"—conspiracies emanating from England.[8]

America entered the War of 1812 in a burst of Anglophobic hatred—outrage at the humiliation of seeing American ships boarded and its sailors impressed, annoyance at English interference with American trade, a desire for territorial conquest at the expense of the British, and a revival of the old fears of English power, brutality, and decadence. The South played a uniquely important role in pushing the nation to war in 1812. The membership of the small but influential "war hawk" group in Congress included John C. Calhoun as well as South Carolinians William Lowndes and Langdon Cheves. The only states that cast unanimous votes in favor of war were South Carolina, Georgia, Kentucky, and Tennessee.[9]

Almost from the beginning, the English threat against American slavery had been an important component of Anglophobia in the South. As Lord Dunmore hovered off the Virginia coast in 1775, encouraging slaves to revolt against their American masters, Southerners knew that England could attack their liberty by attacking their slavery. When Quakers presented the first petitions to Congress in 1790 urging the end of the slave trade, some Southerners questioned their motives as unpatriotic by noting their connection to English abolitionists as well as their nonparticipation in the Revolution. One of the Southern grievances against the Jay Treaty involved its failure to win compensation for American slaves lost during the Revolution. Once Britain and America had abolished the slave trade in 1808 England kept pressing for the right to search American vessels for violators, just as they had demanded the right to search for deserters. In fact, one of the many instances of British "violation" of American shipping included the capture of the slave ship *Amedie* in 1810. Even those who did not want to continue the slave trade reacted with suspicion when antislavery Northerners supported the English right to search American slave ships. As Southerners perceived it, English power and its threat to American liberty often seemed simultaneously to threaten American slavery.[10]

Although the English threat to American slavery had always been a part of Southern Anglophobia, it became increasingly important beginning in the 1820s, especially as the abolition movements in England and then in America began to win wider popular attention. As early as the 1820 congressional debate over the extension of slavery into Missouri, William Smith of South Carolina charged that the North and Great Britain were involved in a conspiracy to abolish slavery. Smith maintained that the attack on the extension of slavery was only part of a larger and more insidious plot to destroy the institution.[11] Such an idea seemed to win additional confirmation by events that followed in the wake of the discovery of the 1822 Denmark Vesey slave conspiracy.

Denmark Vesey had been accused of organizing an elaborate slave rebellion in Charleston. The rebellion, in fact, never took place but South Carolinians reacted to the discovery of the plot with considerable panic. Confronted with evidence of their vulnerability to secret conspiracy, Carolinians embarked on a series of measures to strengthen their security. Among other things, the Vesey plot seemed to reveal that slave contact with free black sailors—especially those who could bring word of the successful slave rebellion in Santo Domingo—had been a source of insurrectionary inspiration. One of the conspirators even admitted that he gave letters to black sailors in an attempt to win support for the rebellion from the Santo Domingo government. In response to such information the state legislature passed a law requiring free black employees on board a vessel entering Carolina ports to be imprisoned until the vessel departed. If the ship's captain failed to pay for the detention and ultimately failed to remove the prisoner, the black would become a slave. It was the first of many so-called Negro Seamen laws enacted in the South throughout the antebellum period. Georgia passed a similar law in 1829, North Carolina in 1830–31, Florida in 1832, Louisiana in 1842, and Alabama in 1839.[12]

What is interesting about the Negro Seamen laws is that they placed England and the Northern states together in the position of attacking slavery. Free black sailors in Southern ports generally came from Great Britain or other American states where slavery had been abolished. Hence, soon after the South Carolina law went into effect, the owners of a Northern vessel assailed the statute in court. Simultaneously, England challenged the law through diplomatic channels. English diplomacy first took the form of a protest note from Ambassador Stratford Canning to Secretary of State John Quincy Adams. Adams, recognizing the merits of the English case, first worked quietly through Carolina congressmen, but failing to win satisfaction, he submitted the English protests directly to Governer John L. Wilson. The South Carolina Senate framed a defiant reply for Wilson: "The duty of the state to guard against insubordination or insurrection . . . is paramount to all *laws*, all *treaties*, all *constitutions*."[13] These words captured the spirit of South Carolina's reaction to English and Northern interference, even though the language proved too harsh to win the concurrence of both houses of the legislature.

The Negro Seamen controversy illustrates interesting connections among Anglophobia, New Anglophobia, republicanism, and the defense of slavery. First of all, the controversy was not a simple, insignificant, or isolated event in Southern history. Even when it first exploded, the dispute touched a raw nerve in Carolina society. Because of its connection with its fear of slave insurrection, the dispute became a major obsession of the South Carolina Association, a self-created, extralegal organization founded by the wealthiest and most influential members of the planter gentry in the wake of the Vesey insurrection. In fact, this private organization single-handedly undertook the defense of the laws in the courts and successfully lobbied for their enforcement in practice. The Negro Seamen acts provided the first opportunity for a large portion of the Carolina planter gentry openly to defy the federal government.[14] The lesson of their success did not go unnoticed. But beyond this, the controversy continued to fester throughout the antebellum period as other states adopted these measures of "self-defense" and defied pressures from the courts and federal government. The Carolina example of resistance spread through the South.

Even more significant for the development of Southern nationalism, the Negro Seamen controversy presented Southerners with their first clear example of a Northern and English alliance to subvert slavery. They had always looked with suspicion at the Anglophilia of some in the North, but here was evidence of clear cooperation—a cooperation directed at undermining slavery. Here, for the first time, just ten years after the War of 1812, they confronted New Englander John Quincy Adams in alliance with England against the South's vital institution. He must have known immediately that he had hit a sensitive spot. Adams noted that, when the subject came up in a dinner conversation, Carolina Senator Robert Y. Hayne showed "so much excitement and temper that it became painful and necessary to change the topic." But it was a sensitive spot that Adams would repeatedly touch during his political career. Nearly twenty years later, in 1842, Adams as a congressman sponsored resolutions requesting the State Department to furnish documents related to the Seamen acts. The request for information was part of his continuing battle against these laws. Carolina Congressman Isaac E. Holmes denounced the resolution and accused Adams of "throwing a firebrand . . . which was to create a conflagration that might endanger the Republic, . . . he was calling on this union . . . to trample upon those rights which the states deemed most essential, and which they would not yield."[15] Adams's antislavery agitation only seemed to threaten the Union and to benefit England.

The significance of the apparent association between the New Englander Adams and old England can be seen in South Carolina's reaction to the abortive attempt by Adams's home state, Massachusetts, to destroy the Negro Seamen acts. In 1844 Massachusetts sent a representative, Samuel Hoar, to Charleston in order to test once again in court the legality of the controversial legislation. The Carolina legislature, fully aware of the connection among England, Adams, and Massachusetts, simply labeled Hoar "the emissary of a foreign government" and asked Governor James Henry Hammond to expel him from the state. Even before the governor could act, however, Hoar was driven back to Massachusetts by the threat of mob violence—no doubt the work of the South Carolina Association. Louisiana treated its own "visitor" from Massachusetts with similar ceremony. When Southern states expelled Massachusetts emissaries as foreign agents their citizens had moved far down the road to a new national identity. By 1850, William Henry Trescot simply lumped together England and Massachusetts as opponents of the Negro Seamen acts. "England and Massachusetts," he wrote, "Lord Palmerston and Governor Briggs—both think the law of South Carolina imprisoning colored seamen a very unfeeling measure." The only difference between the two, he concluded with obvious implication, was that England, being a foreign power, could not so easily send an ambassador to the state to challenge its laws.[16]

Throughout the antebellum period some Southerners continually uncovered "evidence" that England was the major source of antislavery and abolitionist agitation, that to the extent New England and the North attacked slavery they did so as the tools of a foreign nation. Anglophobia, fears of the fragility of republican government as it came under attack from abusive power, the defense of slavery, and New Anglophobia, all mixed together into a brew that never failed to stimulate strong Southern emotion. Aside from the continuing agitation over the Negro Seamen controversy and English attempts to suppress the slave trade, new incidents kept England and antislavery continuously before the Southern public, creating a pool of hostility that could easily be redirected at the North and New England. Consider the Southern reaction to the 1833 English abolition of slavery in the West Indies. By the late 1820s emancipation seemed inevitable, and many in the South carefully analyzed the events to determine how it had come to pass. They wanted to glean lessons from the English experience that would be useful in fending off the threat of American abolition. They concluded that abolition operated by stealth, that the English example proved that the earlier, apparently innocuous, movements against the slave trade or for the African colonization of free blacks inevitably led to ultimate abolition. The lesson that at least some Southerners learned from the West Indies was that attacks on slavery must be met at the frontier—at the point at which they did not seem clearly to threaten abolition. One needed to maintain a careful watch. Ironically, of course, these were the very terms in which traditional republican thought warned about the dangers to liberty. It was also the way gentlemen thought about threats to their honor.

As early as 1827, when the American Colonization Society petitioned Congress for federal aid to transport free blacks to Africa, many planters in the South Carolina low country thought they recognized the action as analogous to the course English abolitionists had once pursued. Robert Turnbull, in his pamphlet on the crisis that threatened American slavery, argued that the English experience demonstrated that abolition operated in a series of steps, that when Wilberforce first approached the Parliament with the idea of ending the slave trade, he was "even *more cautious* than the Colonization society. He took special care not to profess that the abolition of the slave trade was but the *first* step towards an object which he then had most deeply at heart."[17] For Turnbull, the progress of English abolition exposed the real meaning of the apparently harmless Colonization Society's antislavery activity in the United States: it would set the nation down the road to abolition. It was no surprise to many that a few years later the radical abolitionist William Lloyd Garrison should emerge in America. He had been expected. That his arrival coincided with English emancipation only heightened concern.[18]

The close cooperation between American and British abolitionists constantly reconfirmed Southern fears. "[W]hen Garrison was in England," explained one proslavery pamphleteer in 1836, "an arrangement was made with individuals in that country to obtain for their designs English cooperation. It will be seen hereafter," he warned, "that English funds and English influence are at work to disturb and distract this country." Similarly, in the midst of the controversy surrounding the acceptance of abolitionist petitions in Congress, Georgia Senator Alfred Cuthbert simply declared that abolition was un-American; "it originated on the foreign soil of England." In an 1844 letter published in the *Charleston Mercury* and later republished in pamphlet form, Langdon Cheves, old "war hawk" of the War of 1812, also noted the links between English and American abolition: "These Foreign Societies have their agents and orators, with whom they correspond, on the floor of Congress." Cheves even believed that the threat extended to the Whig party. He predicted that if a Whig was elected president "it will be through the aid of these 'Foreign Societies.' "[19]

Some Southerners sketched out the course of the English abolitionist plot in considerable detail. South Carolina Congressman Daniel Wallace explained in an 1850 circular letter to his constituents:

> *[The Englishman] Wilberforce was the propagandist of the idea which resulted in the ordinance of 1787 [preventing the extension of slavery in the Northwest Territories], and the article in our Constitution for the abolition of the slave trade in 1808. The abolition idea, with all its attendant train of heresies, was thus transplanted into the American mind. The abolition policy became active in England and America in the same year, that is in the year 1787. England, unable to subdue America by her arms resorted to a far deeper and more dangerous policy. . . . The disciples of Wilberforce crossed over into America and brought with them their disorganizing ideas, and engrafted them on the Northern portion of the American mind.*

Wallace even suggested, in a way that was right out of the republican tradition, that the "Abolition Party," a party of greedy, power-hungry office seekers, was in control of the "American Parliament." Others argued that it was not simply the "American Parliament" that England had successfully subverted. One writer in the *Southern Quarterly Review* maintained that Northern churches had also become objects of English manipulation. "In the late Conference of the Methodist Church," he wrote, "it was stated more than once, that every arrival from abroad stimulated the congregations of the Northern churches to repudiate the connection with the bishops and ministers who were arraigned before them 'stained with the crime of slavery.' "[20]

One of the most disturbing evidences of American-English abolitionist cooperation was the 1840 World's Antislavery Convention in London. As Southerners watched in horror, to London flocked much of the leadership of American abolition—William Lloyd Garrison, James G. Birney, William Jay, Wendell Phillips, Lucretia Mott, Lydia Child, and dozens of others. There they fought among themselves on strategy and there they paid homage to the venerable leaders of the successful English abolitionist movement. As they rose in united silent tribute to British abolitionist Thomas Clarkson, expressing a unity they evidenced on few other issues, they helped dispel any lingering Southern doubts of the close connections between English and American abolitionism. James G. Birney, 1840 Liberty party candidate for president of the United States, provided additional evidence, spending the entire period of his campaign and election at the London conference. When the conference published an address that was delivered to the governors of all the slaveholding states under the frank of United States Congressman Seth M. Gates, Southerners gave voice to a flood of abolitionist and Anglophobic criticism. Governor James K. Polk of Tennessee singled out Gates for special condemnation. One wealthy slaveholder in Georgia offered to pay $500 to anyone who would deliver Gates to Savannah. There they knew how to deal with traitors.[21]

Virginia Senator Henry Wise delivered a two-day speech in the Senate in which he voiced all the fears stimulated by the World's Antislavery Covention. He was prompted to speak in response to a resolution that censured John Quincy Adams for introducing abolitionist petitions seeking the dissolution of the Union. Wise labeled the petitions British-inspired. He warned of a British-trained black army in Jamaica, poised to attack Cuba and the United States. He spoke ominously of "English influence abroad . . . in league with the same English influence at home." Wise even told of an interchange of "emissaries" between British and American abolitionists. He believed that Joseph Sturge, a "British monarchist," had come to the United States to destroy the Union. Similarly, Wise argued, James G.

Birney's speech at the World's Antislavery Convention offered proof that "American emissaries" had gone to England "to beg for British influence, British prayers, and, if need be, for British gold."[22]

Stirring further Southern Anglophobia were the host of slavery-related issues surrounding the negotiations that resulted in the Webster-Ashburton Treaty of 1842. These issues had long stimulated Southern Anglophobia and would continue to do so even after the treaty had been signed. One set of problems had to do with American coastal vessels containing slaves that, by weather or some other mishap, ended up in the British Bahamas. English policy was to free the slaves, and many in the South saw this policy as an open encouragement to slave revolt. In fact, in October 1841, the American ship *Creole* set sail from Hampton Roads, Virginia, with a few whites and 135 slaves. Several days into the voyage the slaves mutinied and brought the vessel into Nassau where they were given their freedom. The incident seemed to embody all that Southerners had feared. The Virginian John Tyler was president at the time, and his reactions typified the response of many in the South. As Lord Ashburton described it: "The President as a Virginian, has a strong opinion about [the] Creole case, and is not a little disposed to be obstinate on the subject." Tyler, he wrote at another time, "is very sore and testy about the Creole."[23]

Another issue raised by the *Creole* case, but with implications far beyond it, was the problem of extradition. The blacks on the *Creole* had killed some of the white crew, but they could not be tried for their crime because no extradition agreement then existed between England and America. This issue was connected to the continuing problem of fugitive slaves who escaped to Canada. Southerners demanded some provision for their extradition because they had "stolen themselves" or the personal property they brought with them. They had also committed a murder in the act of freeing themselves. England, of course, did not want to enter the business of returning fugitive slaves.

The continuing British attempt to suppress the African slave trade also arose during the Webster-Ashburton negotiations and stirred Southern Anglophobia. England wanted the right to "visit" American ships suspected of carrying slaves. But, as had long been the case, even those who did not support the slave trade could not bring themselves to allow the English to board American vessels. It conjured up the same images that had led to the War of 1812—the images associated with English naval officers boarding American ships to search for deserters and to impress sailors.[24]

Of course, those who favored the slave trade even more readily resorted to Anglophobic arguments. When, for example, Edward B. Bryan attempted to convince Southerners to reopen the trade during the 1850s, he elaborated a full English conspiracy theory. "This alliance [between

Britain and Northerners to stop the slave trade]," he contended, "was originally proposed by the British Government, and, as it now stands, there is not an American feature in it." He charged, among other things, that the 1820 American law declaring slave traders pirates had been a British invention and that the antislave trade provisions of the Webster Ashburton Treaty (authorizing English and American squadrons to suppress the trade) had been agreed to because "the British [abolition] societies established branches in New England, and sent preachers to expound their doctrines."[25]

Southern Anglophobia also received periodic support from foreign policy clashes over such objects of American expansion as Texas and Cuba. The Anglophobic Texas hysteria reached severe proportions in the early 1840s. Texas had fought for independence from Mexico and presented itself as a candidate for annexation to the United States. In 1843 President Tyler, already aware that abolitionist forces in America opposed annexation because it meant the extension of slavery, received indications from Duff Green in London that England also had abolition plans. Green reported that Great Britain planned to offer financial aid to an independent Texas in exchange for the abolition of slavery. Green apparently misunderstood British intentions, but given his own Anglophobic fears as well as those of Tyler, one can understand why the idea of an English abolitionist conspiracy proved so attractive. John C. Calhoun and Secretary of State Abel P. Upshur also received news of the plot from Green and they tried to spread the word in Southern newspapers.[26] Southerners responded with pro-annexation meetings and numerous articles warning of the danger to the South if Texas should fall under the influence of English abolition.[27]

The Anglophobic Cuba hysteria reached its peak during the 1850s. The United States, especially expansionists in the slave states, had long hoped to steal Cuba from Spain and extend the American empire into the Caribbean. But the cries of the expansionists became more insistent as England put pressure on both Spain and Cuba to abolish slavery. Cuban planters added their voices to the chorus as they began to lobby for annexation to the United States as a way of avoiding English-inspired abolition. By 1853 the "Africanization" of Cuba scare won wide attention in the South. For many, the horrible image of "Cuba as a free colony but a few leagues distant from our most populous Slave States" was too terrifying to contemplate. These kinds of fears helped win widespread Southern support for John A. Quitman's ill-fated filibustering expedition to conquer Cuba for the South. That Senator Salmon P. Chase of Ohio, a founder of the emerging Republican party in the North, expressed his "sympathy" and "best wishes" to the emancipation movement in Cuba, whether inspired by the English or the French, only reconfirmed old Southern fears of an Anglo-American abolitionist conspiracy.[28]

Given these issues involving Britain it should occasion no surprise that England often was the villain in the proslavery literature of the South. When proslavery writers sought to contrast a decadent free society with their virtuous slave society, they turned to England for negative examples. In fact, they did exactly what American republican thinkers had always done. Since the time of the Revolution Americans had viewed British labor as degraded and dependent.[29] Proslavery writers loved nothing better than to draw on this old tradition and to dwell on the horrors of English poverty. "[T]he two most frequently used [words] in English politics, are distress and pauperism," explained Chancellor Harper, quoting James Boardman. "After these," he continued, "of expressions applied to the . . . poor, the most common are vice and misery, wretchedness, sufferings, ignorance, degradation, discontent, depravity, drunkenness, and the increase of crime; with many more of the like nature." James Henry Hammond specifically addressed his most famous proslavery work to the English abolitionist Thomas Clarkson, the man to whom American abolitionists had offered their united silent tribute at the World's Antislavery Convention. Hammond, like Harper, lingered on the terrible condition of the English laborer. "Now I affirm," he wrote, "that in Great Britain the poor and laboring classes of your own race and color . . . are more miserable and degraded, morally and physically, than our slaves." George Fitzhugh of Virginia offered the most searching critique of English society, condemning the rise of capitalism in England as producing a society of "Slaves Without Masters." "Thirty thousand men own the lands of England," he wrote, "three thousand those of Scotland, and fewer still those of Ireland. The great mass of the people are cut off from the soil, have no certain means of subsistence, and are trespassers upon the earth, without a single valuable or available right." The abolition of "slavery" or "serfdom" in England had produced real slavery.[30]

Some proslavery writers also sought to understand English abolitionist motives and, not surprisingly, they found them far from altruistic. In fact, they saw the prime motivating forces as material greed and a lust for power. English abolition, they believed, sought the enslavement of the world, just as corrupt English ministers sought the enslavement of America according to the republicans of 1776. In an 1836 tract, William Drayton described how British greed once forced slavery on the colonies, but now that it was unprofitable Britain hoped to abolish it. John C. Calhoun gave further elaboration to this idea in an 1842 letter to his friend Duff Green. "It is surprising to me," he wrote, "that the Statesmen of the continent do not see, that the policy of England is to get control of the commerce of the world, by controlling the labor, which produces the articles by which it is principally put in motion." Later, he wrote that "the abolition of slavery would transfer the production of cotton, rice and sugar, etc., etc. to her

[England's] colonial possessions, and would consummate the system of commercial monopoly, which she has been so long and systematically pursuing." A writer in the *Southern Quarterly Review* described English abolition motives with perhaps the greatest clarity: "The extreme zeal which now animates the British Government for the emancipation of half a million of slaves in Cuba, is prompted, in part at least, we trust not entirely, by the same spirit which has led them to rivet the fetters of a more galling slavery upon the limbs of a hundred million Hindoos, and which is urging them to the slaughter and subjugation of three hundred million Chinese—the lust for universal dominion."[31]

The movement for Southern literary nationalism also had roots in Anglophobia. In fact, Anglophobia was the central obsession of one of the antebellum South's greatest literary figures, William Gilmore Simms. Like many other South Carolinians, as a child he had been exposed to stories of British revolutionary violence. Simms's grandmother had told him about his great-great-grandfather who fought the English in Charleston and about his great-grandfather who rode with Francis Marion and helped liberate Charleston. Many of Simms's novels were patriotic stories of the Revolution. As editor of one of the most influential Southern publications, the *Southern Quarterly Review*, he gave a great deal of space to articles that aired many of the central themes of Anglophobia, including everything from the World's Antislavery Conference, to the *Creole* affair, to the English plot against Texas slavery. Like Hammond, he even addressed his own major proslavery work to an English abolitionist. Meanwhile, he kept up a steady stream of writing calling for a distinctive Southern literature that would be independent of England. Later, he would advocate a Southern literature independent of New England as well. Simms's Anglophobia moved smoothly into New Anglophobia. The movement for Southern literary nationalism pursued precisely this path.[32]

Anglophobia was an essential, perhaps the central, ingredient in the movement for Southern nationalism. Consider how it worked. It was by no means a single coherent set of ideas but a series of arguments and images with considerable emotional power. Southern Anglophobia conjured up memories of the American Revolution and the War of 1812—republican battles for liberty against tyranny. When slavery became a central object of English assault, it was added to the older set of images, becoming just another part of the attack on American liberty. When circumstances placed New England and the North on the side of England during a long series of conflicts over such events as the Negro Seamen acts, the World's Antislavery Convention, the *Creole*, Texas, and Cuba, the South transferred its entire stock of Anglophobic and republican fears and images onto New England and the North. Northerners just seemed to copy everything that England had already done—encourage slave revolts, fail to return fugitive slaves, prevent the extension of slavery, develop an abolitionist movement, exploit labor, and threaten liberty with power. Southern nationalism drew much of its power from the fact that it was a variant of an extant American nationalism. Both nationalisms could trace their roots to a fear of enslavement by the English. Both nationalisms could point to England as the symbol of evil—a symbol that tied together otherwise inconsistent ideas and images. When Southerners were told by the South Carolina secession convention that "the Southern states now stand exactly in the same position towards the Northern States that the Colonies did toward Great Britain," and that "the people of the Southern states are compelled to meet the very despotism their fathers threw off in the Revolution of 1776," the analogy evoked a series of images and ideas rooted in the close connection of republicanism, Anglophobia, and New Anglophobia.[33] An American patriotism had become a Southern patriotism.

II

ANGLOPHOBIA AND SOUTHERN nationalism were intimately connected with elements of the political culture of slavery already considered in other sections of this work. It is not correct to emphasize causal links here—that slavery in any sense caused Anglophobia. But slavery did create certain conditions that helped shape and nurture Anglophobic thought. It did so in several different ways.

First, consider the relationship of Southern ethnicity, Anglophobia, and slavery. Recent studies indicate that by 1790 the Southern states had already developed a peculiar disproportion of non-English peoples in their population. The bulk of this non-English population consisted of Celtic groups such as the Welsh, Scots, and Irish. These groups had long been the objects of English conquest and domination and they probably came to America with a long history of Anglophobic memories.[34] South Carolina and North Carolina were over 50 percent Celtic whereas in contrast Massachusetts and Connecticut were approximately 80 percent English. Already, by 1790, it seems clear that the South offered a better breeding ground for Anglophobia.[35]

Slavery probably had little to do with the ethnic makeup of the Southern population in 1790. But, as I have already noted, there is some evidence that slavery may have helped preserve the ethnic homogeneity of the South in the nineteenth century. Nineteenth-century slaveholders simply did not try to attract new immigrant labor that might compete with slave labor. Moreover, slave owners distrusted the new arrivals as potential threats to slavery. Hence, the newer immigrants flocked to the North, and with their multiple ethnic identities they tended to compete with one another. But the dominant Celtic ethnic identity in the South tended to focus on an external enemy—the English. Moreover, traditional honor-related and republican concerns caused Southerners to be watchful against the advance of power and to fight it at the frontier. Perhaps for a while they looked at the ethnic English groups that accumulated in Southern coastal areas as enemies, but whenever these groups joined in the general Anglophobia, they all seemed to redirect their focus outward.

Slavery was compatible with other elements of Anglophobia. Masters in the South, like masters in all slave societies, found that they could never fully control their slaves. Slaves ran away; they plotted insurrections; when disgruntled they set fires; and they sometimes resisted work schedules and routines. They even murdered their masters. The masters' fears of danger from their slaves are evident in their tendency to overreact to the first overt signs of resistance. When Nat Turner killed a handful of whites in Southampton, Virginia, a wave of panic flooded the South. Everywhere, masters thought they had uncovered evidence of slave conspiracies. Slave revolt or the rumor of slave revolt in the South frequently generated hysteria.[36]

The fears and panics that periodically swept the South during the years before 1860 seem an essential part of slave society, for they were firmly rooted in reality. Slaves in fact did resist, and masters were quite vulnerable to secret conspiracy—to a match tossed into a wooden town or to ground glass put in their oatmeal. In such an atmosphere, Anglophobia and later New Anglophobia served an essential function. The message of Anglophobia was that the real threat to masters came from outside the society rather than from within. Hence all a master had to do was to put up a good fence—to close the seaport to abolitionist emissaries or to close the mails to their literature. This approach was useful on several levels. On a political level it could support the pleas for internal unity that masters hoped to achieve for their society. On a psychological level it allowed masters to sleep at night. As long as the fences were up one need not fear external instigation of internal treachery. Slaves would never, on their own initiative, slit a master's throat. It was England or New England that would provoke throat slittings, and they, at least, could be kept at a safe distance. On the level of the proslavery argument, Anglophobia also proved useful. Southerners liked to believe that their institution was based on consent, that slaves were happy and content with their condition. The logic of Anglophobia and New Anglophobia allowed Southerners to continue belief in this fiction in the face of slave resistance. Slaves never willfully rebelled; they were tricked into rebelling only by the activities of outside emissaries. The problems of slave society were not the problems of slavery, but came from interference by free society.

Anglophobia also performed another service that coincided with the demands of the proslavery argument. It provided a series of experiences that seemed to demonstrate that those who defended slavery really defended liberty. This idea, as we have argued, was at the core of the defense of slavery. Anglophobia intertwined the defense of slavery with resistance to a nation that had always tried to enslave Americans, with the rights of American ships freely to plow the seas, and with the right of America to expand and spread republican institutions in the new world. The events that seemed to reconfirm Anglophobia, that reconfirmed the Southern image of themselves as opponents of tyrannical power and defenders of liberty in the old republican tradition, simultaneously reconfirmed the proslavery argument. Anglophobia fit well into the larger political culture of slavery.

CHAPTER 7

Sectional Conflict

SLAVERY IN THE ANTEBELLUM South was an important element of an intimately related, interdependent group of political values, institutions, and practices. In the political culture of slavery the ideals and rhythms of statesmanship and honor flourished, the proslavery argument became an antislavery argument, virtual representation and antiparty thought and practice continued to survive, and political leaders fought duels among themselves and tended to look outside their society for subversive threats. But the insight that slavery was deeply intertwined with Southern political culture must be carefully circumscribed and qualified. For one thing, no single element of the political culture of slavery was a unique product of slave society. Duels, statesmanship, antiparty, and virtual representation flourished at various times and among various groups during the eighteenth and nineteenth centuries in the North and in England; many in the antebellum North also had visions of external subversion; and the Southern fear of unrestrained power had a long history in Western political thought. If there was anything unique in the political culture of slavery it was not in any one of its elements but in their combination in a particular context. Furthermore, the political culture of slavery never fully triumphed in the South. Not everyone in the region shared the values and practices of the dominant group. Actually, the values and practices were not so clear, simple, uncontradictory, or static that they could possibly have achieved a commanding position in any complete sense. As we will see, a political life rooted in the master-slave relationship could never entirely be free of tension and contradiction. Moreover, the South did not develop as an isolated political entity. Southerners were deeply involved in a world market and hence could not help but absorb some of the ideals of free labor societies. They also were involved in a network of national political institutions stretching beyond their own borders. The political culture of slavery was never left alone to grow and mature in quiet isolation.

To recognize the limitations of the political culture of slavery is not to deny its existence altogether. In fact, even if the political culture of slavery was neither unique to the South nor totally triumphant there, it was still the central element shaping the form and content of Southern conflict with the North during the antebellum period.

I

DISAGREEMENT NEED NOT lead to war. Any modern nation-state consists of economic, ethnic, religious, and social groups with widely divergent values and interests. Yet these groups often can live together in an uneasy peace, working within a common political structure even as they disagree. South and North lived together in this way for all of the antebellum period. Despite the divergent ideals, despite the divergent labor systems, despite the bitter disputes over the tariff, the territorial expansion of slavery, fugitive slaves, and a host of other issues, South and North remained for a long time in a single political system. Why the system broke down, why the standard methods of dispute resolution ultimately failed, why sectional disagreement ended in secession and civil war, is one of the most profound historical puzzles. The breakdown must be understood as the failure of a political structure. A careful analysis of the political culture of slavery can help us understand that failure.[1]

The success of secession depended on a widely shared Southern view that political leaders and political parties had become corrupt, that the existing political structures could no longer resolve disputes because they had become hopelessly perverted. In fact, what largely differentiated radicals from moderates throughout the various sectional crises was this sense of political corruption. Radicals saw no hope of redress within the existing structures; moderates held on longer to the possibility of redress, but they too eventually became disillusioned. By the eve of the Civil War the vision of a corrupt American politics had triumphed in the South. Let us first examine evidence of this attitude and then seek its origins.

The sense of political corruption reached its peak earliest in the most radical Southern state, South Carolina. The South Carolina vision of corruption is worth describing in some detail because it was later reduplicated in many other states. John C. Calhoun had warned of the danger as early as the 1832 nullification crisis. Drawing on the tradition of seventeenth- and eighteenth-century republican thought, Calhoun repeatedly argued that the nation needed disinterested statesmen who could resist such temptations as executive patronage and the desire for spoils.[2] A great danger to the Republic lay in the nation falling into the hands of corrupt spoilsmen, men who sought money and power in politics. By the late antebellum period many in South Carolina, as they looked at political life in Washington and the North, thought that Calhoun's fear had become reality. Langdon Cheves saw in Washington "men known to the nation by no distinction of talent or public service, the Hales, the Giddings, the Sewards." He feared "the ambition of low-minded politicians who are determined to govern and to crush all power in the Southern states." Lewis M. Ayer in 1855 conceded that the government might have been pure under the hands of the virtuous stateman Washington, but "it was too purely artificial to withstand the selfish passions, wicked prejudices, and lustful appetites for ruthless rule, of the degenerate and fanatical brood who have succeeded to the control of its powers, and who have extracted from 'its page sublime,' a breed of lust, hate, and crime." Isaac Hayne wrote Charles Cotesworth Pinckney, Jr., in 1860, offering his sarcastic analysis of the state of American politics: "Who would live under a Government where a man had to be honest to obtain office, or really great to be thought so? How much more preferable it is to attain distinction by a little dextrous wire-pulling."[3]

Many Carolinians associated the general decline in political virtue with party activity. As one writer in the *Southern Quarterly Review* dramatically phrased it, party "blasts where it is excited, and virtue, withering, shrinks from its presence." H. W. Connor wrote Calhoun from Charleston in 1845 that he hoped that political parties would soon disintegrate. "There is no principle of cohesion amongst them," he informed Calhoun, "except the common love of plunder and so corrupt have the politicians of both parties become that they dare not confide long enough in each other to commit an act of party pillage." Connor fervently hoped for a reorganization of party on the basis of principle, and Calhoun thereby catapulted into the presidency. It was a hope that never became a reality.[4]

By the 1850s, party behavior and the decline of political virtue were closely correlated in the minds of Carolinians. One newspaper from Due West in Abbeville District, for example, in an 1850 editorial complained about "the Dignity Departing" from Congress. The senators had become obsessed with "long details of personalities and party matters" and the House was full of "Buncombe speeches, and party squabbles." W. Allston Pringle told the citizens of Charleston about the evils of party behavior. "Politics," he argued, "whose ends should be the general welfare, have become a game, and a means of livelihood. Party tactics, through which the public voice should be fairly heard, have so disfigured and deformed the government, that public service rather debases than elevates. The Constitution itself which was thought so comprehensive and noble in its aspirations, is regarded as the charter of a private corporation to be used and employed for the promotion of private views." In other words, Pringle believed that party spoilsmen had come to control the government. Their desire for plunder would force them to advocate strengthening government power. "These adventurers," Pringle maintained, "who live upon the abuses which they create, and whose only object is the plunder of the treasury, and a share of the power of the general government, find their ends best attained by every measure which tends to strengthen that government." One year later, Henry L. Pinckney, Jr., reaffirmed these ideas in another oration to Charlestonians. In national politics, he saw only "avarice and ambition." "The pride of party and the greed of gain," he declaimed, "the lust of power and the love of self, that mark the conduct of the North, have driven a faithful and loyal people to the last refuge of despair."[5]

The same message reached Carolinians over and over again in the years just before the Civil War. The Reverend J. C. Coit, in his address to the people of Chesterfield District, analyzed the two motives that competed to guide the behavior of "our civil rulers at Washington." "First; moral: those resulting from their official obligation to the Constitution and liberties of the people. Second; personal: those that spring from their obligations to party, and from their love of money, power and fame." Coit believed that the second motive now dominated. "Under such temptations," he argued, "our federal rulers have proved too frail a depository, for such a trust as the civil government of a people politically free. The Constitution has proved an ineffectual barrier to their encroachments. Fortified by military power and party combinations, the central government has now assumed a position, which, if maintained, will be fatal to the political liberties of the people."[6]

The belief in party as a correlate of corruption clearly affected the Carolinian attitude toward participation in the national party conventions. Just before the 1856 Democratic Convention, for example, the *Unionville Journal* warned Carolinians to remain aloof from party activity. "[L]et other states," admonished an editorial, "if they choose, continue to countenance these self-constituted bodies of politicians, whose object is power, for the sake of plunder, but let her [South Carolina] wash her hands of them." Carolinian experience with party conventions did little to change this belief. One Spartanburg newspaper, after the 1860 Charleston Democratic Convention, reported the impressions of J. P. Reed who watched Stephen Douglas struggle for the nomination and split the party. "Instead of meeting with statesmen like those of old who had so much distinguished and illustrated our country's name, he found that our political leaders had become corrupt, and like petty spoilsmen were anxious for the loaves and fishes of office."[7]

Even a Carolinian who had cooperated with the national Democratic party, Francis W. Pickens, was troubled by the sense that virtue in national politics seemed in jeopardy. Just before the 1856 election, for example, he wrote privately to Armistead Burt, expressing his deepest fears of political corruption: "If Buchanan is defeated we will be near the beginning of the end and we must solemnly prepare to meet great events. If he is elected and the selfish and designing get control of him and bring into power the camp followers who have pressed as to their plunder of victory, then there will be still great confusion, and his Administration will lead the country into inextricable difficulties." He hoped Buchanan would be a statesman, but he remained uncertain.[8]

Gradually during the antebellum period Carolinians became convinced that only men who had no principles could be elected in the Northern states, and that only unprincipled men could possibly become president. The presidency seemed the great prize of the most skilled plunderer. Claudian B. Northrop, probably with the difficulty of Calhoun becoming president in mind, complained bitterly in 1843 about the scramble for presidential office: "What has become of the dignity of our free empire, when its republican throne, which Washington with modesty reluctantly filled, has been the prize of dishonest bribery and popular delusion; and is no more regarded as the free-will offering of the country's approbation to high public merit, but as the rightful prey of the robber bands which may seize the state." Calhoun's inability even to win the Democratic nomination also greatly disturbed James Hamilton who, in 1844, complained of a Democratic party in a condition "which compels it to pass over the *first* of its Men and to rally on those scarcely above mediocrity." By 1846 Hamilton had become so disillusioned he suggested the White House be inscribed with the label: "*The Temple of Demagogism inscribed to the Genius of Mediocrity dulness Ignorance and Deceit.*"[9]

James Henry Hammond also believed that the presidential race had become a bitter battle for spoils and that only the most unscrupulous could hope to win. At one point in his career he even suggested both limiting the president's patronage power and choosing him randomly. "Draw a President by lot from the Senate annually," he advised in a letter to W. B. Hodgson, "and limit his power to filling vacancies or allow removals only with the concurrence of the Senate and we shall soon be at peace at home and abroad." By 1858 Hammond was thoroughly convinced that "only callous, thoroughly trained politicians, who know every view and every man, and are a short mile for all business and very little trouble about right and wrong, can tenant the White House long."[10]

Countless other Carolinians echoed these same themes during the decade before the outbreak of the Civil War. Paul Johnston lamented the passage of an age when statesmen held the highest office in the land. "Then," he recalled with nostalgia, "eminent ability alone was esteemed worthy of the high place of the American Executive; now no party dares hope that any candidate will succeed who has so far escaped mediocrity as to have made enemies." William John Grayson glanced back over the history of politics during the years before 1860 from his vantage point in the midst of the Civil War and reached an identical conclusion. "According to the theory of republics," he reasoned, "the highest places in the Commonwealth are the rewards of the most distinguished virtue and ability. It was so at first in our practice. But now the most exalted station is the prize of the man who is most plastic in the hands of political managers and demagogues."[11]

By the late antebellum period, Carolinians believed that national politics inevitably involved such corruption that the best men no longer even wished to enter the political arena. John L. Manning described for Charlestonians in 1848 those "moderate and excellent men" who were "unwilling to leave their calm pursuits and temperate mode of thinking and acting, to be rudely jostled by jarring factions, where their motives may be prejudged and condemned on the one side, and blindly advocated to subserve bad and factious ends on the other." An 1853 article in the *Southern Quarterly Review* noted: "Good men shrink from a contest, where the prizes belong to those who pander best to low passion and most unscrupulously employ the basest acts." John Belton O'Neal wrote privately to Armistead Burt in 1856 expressing pleasure "to hear you say you will have nothing to do with politics—it is a poor business. For it has become a mere affair of faction."[12] *Russell's Magazine* echoed the same theme in an 1857 plea to get Southern gentlemen to pay less attention to the patronage of politics and more to the patronage of the arts:

> *Politics as conducted at present, is merely a game—a game in which the winner is not always—not often, perhaps,—an honest man. At best, it has degenerated from a science into a trade. Its purpose is no longer the direction of free government, the elucidation of national right, but the promotion of selfish, sectional, personal interest. Now why should gentlemen who have leisure, opportunity, talent, and property, defile themselves with the inevitable pitch from which scarcely a single phase of political labor is free.*[13]

The idea that Northern spoilsmen had gradually come to dominate the political offices of the nation coincided with and was reinforced by a prevailing Southern stereotype of Northern society: the "Yankee" as a man of insatiable greed who measured worth only by wealth. "It is a melancholy fact," one *Southern Quarterly Review* article reasoned, "and a subject of common observation, that *public* spirit is at its lowest ebb among us, whilst the commercial and political are evidently in the ascendant. Our councils no longer, as in former days, are governed by that noble self-sacrificing patriotism, which can recognize nothing but country, and legislate for no interest which embraces anything short of the general welfare."[14] Political corruption, in other words, had risen with the commercial market.

If Carolinians sensed the spread of political corruption in general in the North they believed the antislavery politician was the most corrupt of all. John Townsend, for example, warned in 1850 that it was impossible to compromise with antislavery political leaders. "Fanatics in religion," he wrote of his enemies, "fanatics in politics, the ravening demagogue, hunting after office, and the spoils of party. And when, from the beginning of time, to the present hour, have *such* men been satisfied with concessions." By the time the Republicans came to power in 1860, Carolinians knew precisely what kind of men had finally taken control of the nation. "Well, we have a Republican speaker," Susanna Sparks Keitt wrote in February. "I expect the old United States Treasury was pulled at today and tonight feels quite exhausted." James Henry Hammond still believed in 1860 that if only the abolitionists, whom he equated with Republicans, could be defeated for the presidency in one or two more elections, "the politicians would give it up because it could not gain them Spoils and Power." The Reverend William O. Prentiss, after the election of Lincoln, told Charlestonians in unequivocal terms precisely what kind of administration had just taken control: "That party [the Republicans] has sold its offices to the highest bidder; its Justices have dispensed justice for reward; its Governors have shared in embezzlements and peculations; its Representatives have been expelled from Congress for bribery." Carolinians simply despised these new politicians. It even offended their honor. "I care nothing for the 'Peculiar Institution,' " R. N. Hemphill wrote W. R. Hemphill just one week before secession in December 1860, "but I can't stand the idea of being domineered by [a pack] of Hypocritical Scoundrels, such as Sumner, Seward, Wilson, Hale, etc., etc."[15]

That Abraham Lincoln himself did not initially seem the most malevolent or most cunning Republican political leader failed to blunt the feeling among Carolinians that statesmen no longer had control of the government, the feeling that spoilsmen were ascendant. The very features which made Lincoln so attractive to many Northerners—his "man of the people" quality and poor upbringing, his earthy sense of humor—made him seem the epitome of the low and vulgar politician Carolinians had been watching with trepidation for years. As Susanna Sparks Keitt wrote with amazement to a Philadelphia friend at the time of Lincoln's inauguration: "Did you think the people of the South, the Lords Proprietors of the land, would let this low fellow rule for them? No. His vulgar facetiousness may suit the race of clock makers and wooden nutmeg venders—even Wall Street brokers may accept him, since they do not protest—but never will he receive the homage of southern gentlemen." The whole Lincoln style of politics offended many Carolinians. Susanna Sparks Keitt could never submit to rule by a man who "exhibits himself at railway depots, bandies jokes with the populace, kisses bold women from promiscuous crowds." If Abraham Lincoln was not the most skillful of the new Republican spoilsmen, in the minds of Carolinians he was at best an unskilled spoilsman and at worst the foolish tool of the most malevolent, far from the kind of statesman needed to control the impending Republican search for plunder. Of course, when war finally broke out, Carolinians quickly realized that Lincoln was no buffoon, that he was as skilled in the unrestrained use of power as any of the most hated Republican leaders.[16]

During the decades before the Civil War many Carolinians believed that Southern and South Carolinian politicians remained relatively immune from the kind of political corruption that had seeped into the deepest recesses of the North and the national government. "Our statesmen have been notoriously superior—," boasted one 1849 article comparing the virtues of Southern statesmen to Northern politicians, "their equal, and often their superiors in talents, and much their superior in disinterested patriotism, in faithfulness to the great constitutional principles of their Government—in the spirit of liberty and hatred of tyranny, and unconstitutional, partial and class legislation." One 1851 newspaper editorial still argued that South Carolina remained insulated from the spreading political disease: "To break the spirit of the people of South Carolina, and to make them pliant instruments in the hands of parties, it is necessary to destroy these guards which the Constitution has thrown around their rights, for as it now stands, it presents an unsurmountable difficulty in the way of political demagogues, and is an effectual protection against the streams of corruption which are flowing in every direction from the Federal government." Many in South Carolina, it should be remembered, believed that the absence of national political parties within the state for most of the antebellum period was a sign that political virtue still remained intact.[17]

Nonetheless, Carolinians always worried that Southern representatives might succumb to the strong temptations of power. A friend warned Armistead Burt in 1848 about Southern representatives who might betray the cause of liberty "for the sake of office and emolument." Henry L. Pinckney, Jr., advised Charlestonians in 1851: "We have been fortunate, so far, in the faithfulness of our sentinels, but is it not their interest to deceive us? They are utterly unprized at Washington, and will ever be so, 'till they learn to betray! We all know the charm of office and honor, and will Government neglect to apply its fascinations?" William H. Barnwell, rector of St. Peter's Church in Charleston, told his congregation about his fear that even South Carolina politicians might be tempted by executive patronage. "The patronage of Government," he explained, "has seduced but too many whose virtue seemed immaculate, and I tremble for our commonwealth [South Carolina] lest she too may encounter the blighting smiles of Executive favor, and shame, burning shame—the shame of having sold herself for money, be smirched upon her brow, and that of her sons." John Townsend warned Carolinians that, once the spoilsmen gained control of the national government "we shall be betrayed and weakened by desertion from all ranks, through the *bribes* which shall be held out to the ambitious or the needy." Christopher Memminger reiterated the same theme in his 1860 plea for Virginia to join with South Carolina in cooperation against federal aggression. After describing the hostility and strength of Northern power in the Union, he noted: "The immense patronage and spoils of the government, and the large interests involved in the public expenditures, and the discriminatory tariffs, bring to the aid of the dominant party every selfish interest, and enable it to rivet its fetters upon the South, while the hope held out to southern aspirants for office is used to corrupt our leaders and confound our people."[18]

The charge that corruption had begun to spread from North to South was obviously a self-serving argument for the most radical secessionists. They could characterize every sign of hesitation on the part of Unionists or cooperationists as another example of the growing cancer. But many radicals sincerely believed what they charged, and they slowly won converts among the moderates. It was no propaganda maneuver when Robert Barnwell Rhett privately wrote to James Henry Hammond describing his fears of the national Democratic movement in South Carolina in 1858. "During the last few years," he told Hammond, "in the stagnation that has followed the failure of the secession movement, a spoils party has sprung up here."[19] Moreover, since so many of the moderates believed that large numbers of federal politicians were corrupt, they struggled to throw off the taint of having compromised with spoilsmen. Thus, for example, during the 1850–52 secession crisis Armistead Burt had to begin his defense of a nonradical position by noting: "I have never sought office—I have never seen the day when I would have held an office under the Federal Government. I could not do so, at this time, without a feeling of personal degradation."[20]

It was precisely because everyone in South Carolina feared the disease of political corruption that secession could be viewed as an act of purification, an operation that cleanly removed the spreading cancer. W. Alston Pringle told Charlestonians in 1850: "If you wish the government to be venerated and respected, you must purge it of its impurities,—you must rescue it from the thraldom of party—you must restore it to the people, its rightful owners—you must shape its measures to its proper ends." Pringle advised either the transformation of public opinion in the North or secession. W. F. Colcock told the assembled Carolina Southern Rights Associations that they could "be assured that the secession of a single state of this union will bring up for judgment the mightiest questions of a modern age. Statesmen, sir, not venal politicians, not hireling presses, not pensioned libelers, but statesmen will find materials for the exercise of their highest intelligences, their profoundest wisdom."[21]

The imagery of purification dominated the final secession crisis. "We cannot coalesce," explained the Reverend William O. Prentiss to Charlestonians in late 1860, "with men whose society will eventually corrupt our own, and bring down upon us the awful doom which awaits them." Susanna Sparks Keitt in 1861 tried to convey to one of her Northern friends the reasons for South Carolina's secession and conjured a similar image of purification. She recalled a sight they had once seen together in Europe—the "bright and limpid" waters of the Rhone, "fresh from the cold purity of the glacier's bosom" as it mingled with the "turbid Arno." "Frantically," she remembered, "it resisted the muddy impurity of its embraces; for miles and leagues waged the war between Dark and Bright; but finally the struggle ceased. Together in the same current bed they must run; so, mingled waters—the turbid sullying the clear and securing back nought of its purity—together they quietly flowed into the sea." The secession of South Carolina, for Susanna Sparks Keitt, would isolate political pollution, just as the sundering of the two rivers might keep the Rhone forever "fresh from the cold purity of the glacier's bosom."[22]

Finally, with secession many Carolinians felt that statesmen rather than low politicians once again might control the government. James Henley Thornwell described with obvious pride the kind of men who populated the secession convention:

> *It was not a conclave of defeated place hunters, who sought to avenge their disappointment by the ruin of their country. . . . There were men in that convention utterly incapable of low and selfish schemes, who, in the calm serenity of their judgments, were as unmoved by the waves of popular passion and excitement, as the everlasting gravity by the billows that roll against it. There were men there who would listen to no voices but the voice of reason; and would bow to no authority but what they believed to be the authority of God. . . . They deliberated without passion, and concluded without rashness.*

Francis W. Pickens, governor of South Carolina in 1861, wanted to be certain that this kind of purity would permeate the new Confederacy as well. He wrote Jefferson Davis early in the year, noting that he did not care who in particular held the highest positions in the new government, "only that they should be high toned gentlemen of exemplary purity, and firmness of character with full and thorough statesmanship, and no demagogism. We must start *our Government*," he wrote, "free from the vulgar influences that have debauched and demoralized the Government at Washington."[23]

The full purity that some Carolinians sought seemed to elude them even in the new government. Probably no human government could have totally satisfied William John Grayson. "The greediness for office and pay is prevalent everywhere at the South as well as the North," he wrote during the Confederacy. Mary Boykin Chesnut, even more cynical than Grayson, sensed that politics in the new government was not much more elevated than in the old. "Everywhere," she wrote while at Montgomery in February 1861, "political intrigue is as rife as in Washington."[24]

Nonetheless, whether or not some Carolinians ultimately became disillusioned with the new order, most originally seceded with the intention of keeping their politics from becoming polluted by a corrupting Republican administration. When the war finally ended in defeat and the "carpetbaggers" (those malevolent Northerners who came South for plunder) arrived, Carolinians had long been expecting them. Modern historians have had a much more difficult time discovering evidence of the greed of these Northern carpetbaggers; the assumption is a tribute to the shaping force of prewar fears on postwar Carolina perceptions. According to the logic of their expectations, when government threatened liberty, corrupt politicians always lurked in the background—placemen during the Revolution, spoilsmen during nullification and secession, and carpetbaggers during reconstruction.

South Carolinians may have been the earliest and most vocal proponents of the danger of political corruption, but the same disillusionment spread to other Southern states as they edged closer to secession. The states of the lower South seemed most susceptible to the fear. The distrust of parties and political leaders took several different forms in Alabama. Voters became increasingly cynical about their elected representatives, calling them "tricksters" and throwing them out of office in increasing numbers during the late 1850s. The fire-eaters kept up a steady barrage of warnings about the corruptions of parties and politicians. They warned that Southern men who sought federal office became "traitor[s] to the South, bought with the hope of conciliating Northern favor"; they complained of Southern politicians who "as soon as they get in sight of the Presidential mansion and Treasury office are at once transformed into the most national beings in the world"; they spoke of the danger of "the trammels of party," of the "demoralizing influence of party spirit," of "the hot party agitations which has [*sic*] for years past stirred up and floated into Congress some of the very drugs [*sic*] of society, too light and too filthy to comprehend any duty save that of obedience to party leaders."[25]

In Georgia speakers warned citizens of "old and effete political parties," of "basely corrupt" leaders. They explained: "We have but little virtue, heroic virtue or patriotism now amongst our public men." If Lincoln were elected he would use "patronage for the purpose of organizing in the South a band of apologists." The governor guessed: "So soon as the Government shall have passed into Black Republican hands, a portion of our citizens, must, if possible, be bribed into treachery to their own section by the allurements of office." Georgians hoped that secession would "sweep away the past corruptions of the Government."[26]

Perhaps at no other time in American history have so many people expressed disillusionment with political leaders and parties as in the South on the eve of secession. They feared the corruption emanating from the federal government and the North, but they also saw it eating away at the integrity of their own political structures. Secession became the vehicle of purification.

II

THE SENSE OF POLITICAL corruption—the fear of a degeneration emanating from the North but capable of rotting the South as well—had deep roots in the political culture of slavery. There was, first of all, a real difference between Northern and Southern political life. What Southerners repeatedly thought they saw, at least in part, they actually saw. As I have argued throughout this book, the ideals of statesmanship, honor, antiparty, and virtual representation—all had greater vitality in slave society. When Southerners ranted about "party hacks," "vulgar politicians," and "managers" in the North, it was because they saw, at least by their own definition, "party hacks," "vulgar politicians," and "managers." Their fears had some basis in reality. Consequently Southerners who went to Washington often wrote about their experience as if they had just entered an alien world, a metropolitan world of political intrigue that contrasted sharply with the simple pleasures of country life. For example, Howell Cobb wrote his wife in 1850 about dining with the attorney general, mingling with guests such as the judges of the Supreme Court, the British ambassador, Daniel Webster, and the vice-president. "This part of my business," he confessed, "is the most unpleasant to me. . . . I could pass my time far more agreeably with my little boys at a circus or monkey show by way of variety than to be seated up wine bibbing with swell heads of the metropolis." Similarly, in an 1839 letter to George W. Jones, Jefferson Davis charged that Martin Van Buren had "sowed indecision, a plant not suited to the deep furroughs plowed by his predecessor." Realizing that he had just resorted to a metaphor of farm life, Davis quickly added: "[Y]ou perceive that when I write of Politics I am out of my element and naturally slip back to seeding and ploughing about which I hope to talk with you next summer."[27] Southerners, after all, were just country boys (or so they liked to think of themselves), and they felt ill at ease in the Northern-dominated metropolitan centers of the nation. The nation's capital offered intrigue and calculation rather than a good, wholesome monkey show.

Regardless of the real overall difference between Southern and Northern political life, Southerners eagerly pounced on any incident that illustrated or emphasized the difference. They especially loved to focus on instances of corrupt Republican party behavior. In 1857 Virginian Edmund Ruffin wrote in his diary, with a kind of glee, that he had just heard about the early career of John C. Fremont, 1856 Republican candidate for president. John Bachman of Charleston had told him of Fremont's "swindling of his creditors, & other rascally acts." Moreover, "[t]hese acts were far exceeded in his subsequent swindlings of the government, when an officer in trust—& by his duplicity & lying." "What a character," Ruffin concluded, "does it give of his supporters, that, notwithstanding the exposure of all these acts, this man barely missed being elected President of the United States." When, in 1857, Congress expelled four of its members for taking bribes—members closely identified with antislavery—many in the South used this incident as further proof of what they already knew about antislavery political practices. Ruffin wrote in his diary: "Four members, all abolitionists & northern men (3 of N. Y., & 1 of Con.) are proved guilty of receiving enormous bribes, for their acts to enrich private interests. . . . We have enough of immoral men in the south, & enough of such representatives in Congress. Nevertheless, not a member from any slaveholding state has been suspected of sharing in this base conduct, of receiving bribes, which, though only now proved, has existed for a long time." The South Carolina newspaper the *Sumter Watchman* concluded in a similar vein: "It is a striking fact, but certainly in keeping with the deeds, history and principles of that party, that *all* these money seekers should have come from the ranks of the Black Republicans." That one of the accused congressmen, a close associate of Thurlow Weed in New York, resigned in order to avoid expulsion and then won immediate reelection only reconfirmed the worst Southern fears. Vulgar politicians had triumphed in the North. However much Southerners may have singled out for special emphasis instances of Republican and Northern corruption, Republicans and Northerners supplied a plentiful amount of material for selection.[28]

Another dimension to Southern fear of corruption requires careful analysis. After all, it was not simply that Southerners thought that Northern political leaders and practices had become corrupt but also that they believed that the corruption had begun to undermine their own political virtue. Aside from the traditional republican fear of the fragility of republics and the corrupting influence of power, why were Southerners so ready to doubt themselves? Why did they think they were so vulnerable to the evil temptations of the newer political values and practices?

Part of the fear of subversion derives from the inability of Southern political leaders to cut themselves off from developments transforming political life in the rest of the nation. They could not shape their practice to conform to their ideals. For a Southerner to enter Congress was invariably to enter a world of political intrigue that made statesmanship virtually impossible. To be in politics was to enter a world dominated by political parties. Management had even entered into Southern political life. Despite their claims, men like John C. Calhoun did engage in political manipulation; they did solicit patronage for their friends. To do otherwise would have been to abandon politics. But the actions that clashed with their values must have left a residue of guilt. They must have been aware of their own vulnerability. If even they could sin, then they had every reason to believe that others were equally vulnerable.

But the core problem of Southern political life lay at an even deeper level. It was a political life rooted in the master-slave relationship. Such roots prevented the development of a stable and consistent set of political values and practices, prevented the development of a political culture free of contradiction. Let us look once again at the way masters justified their power over slaves. But this time let us focus not on the logic of the argument but rather on its illogic. Masters, like any ruling group, wanted to think well of themselves and wanted others to think well of them. The ideal master was a man of good character and virtue, a man who was independent and could follow the dictates of his own reason. Such a man always sought to resist the attempts of others to reduce him to slavery—a condition in which he would be subject to the unrestricted power of another man. At the same time, these masters had to justify their own power over the people they owned. The main technique of justification was an elaborate description of the bonds of mutual affection and interest that united masters with their property. The problem with this concept of legitimation was that the more the master conceived of himself as dependent on his slaves, the less he could conceive of himself as an independent man of virtue. Here then was the irresolvable problem of the master-slave relationship: in order to legitimize their position masters had to be both independent and dependent at the same time.[29]

The problem of authority on the plantation repeated itself in the statehouse. On the one hand, the values and rhythms of statesmanship and honor demonstrate an obsession with the independence of political leaders. Statesmen had to be free of party, free of instructions, free of bargains, and free of institutional strictures of any kind. On the other hand, Southern constituents were jealous of their own independence and honor, and many could never completely trust their lives to such free and unrestrained leaders. Thus the independent statesman tended to deprive others of their independence. In yet another, completely contradictory way, some constituents wanted their leaders to be dependent on the people they represented. A statesman had to share the values of his community in order to be elected. If there was any doubt that he did, his constituents might get rid of him. The statesman, in other words, was really quite dependent on his community. But the statesman would despise himself if he really did become totally dependent and, ironically, his constituents would have agreed. The statesman, like the master, had to be both dependent and independent in order to legitimize his position in power. If he became too independent he might be accused of being an enslaver of his constituents; if he became too dependent he might be considered a political hack, a slave of his constituents or of his party. He might lose his honored position in the community.[30]

As one would expect, the same tension repeated itself in the duel, the ritual that embodied the central values of political life in slave society. A duelist did everything he could to establish his credentials as a statesman and master—as a man of good character and independence. He stood alone and faced death on the dueling ground; he resented insults that implied greedy, selfish motives, or that suggested that he was the tool or instrument of any man or group. Yet at the same time not only did the duel bind all the participants into a united group, but it also demonstrated the duelist's utter dependence on popular opinion. These men of independence needed to be thought independent by the public witnesses of the duel. The total detachment from the world exhibited by the man who shot into the air while giving his opponent a chance to kill him was not really detachment; he expected that either he or his friends would later describe it all in the newspapers. This action would gain him the approval of others. Just as independent masters had to depend on slaves, just as independent statesmen had to depend on constituents, the duelist had to depend on public opinion. The search for independence could easily result in its opposite.

Many Southern leaders may have aspired to be perfect masters and statesmen, but the fundamental tension at the core of the ideal meant that they had to fail. Consequently Southerners had the sense that their political leaders, indeed the very structures of their politics, seemed vulnerable to corruption. The injunction to be both independent and yet dependent meant that it was easy to perceive leaders as leaning excessively in one or the other direction. Either way, a political leader might be accused of advancing slavery in the world. It was easy for any leader to slip into the pose of excessive independence and to be seen as arrogant, ill-tempered, rootless, untrustworthy, or aristocratic. In the eyes of some, such a man might be seen as an enslaver of free men.[31] Moreover, some leaders tried to remain so far above the combat of political life, tried to assert their independence with such extreme passivity, that they simply faded out of the public life of the society. Hence, a common lamentation was that true virtue often never received its just reward in Southern political life.[32] It was equally easy for any leader to slip into the pose of excessive dependence—so emphasizing his identity with the people, or his love of the people, that he might be described as their servant. This pose too seemed outside the ideal of statesmanship. The point, of course, is that the ideal leader had to be both independent and dependent; anyone who leaned in one direction or the other (and it was almost impossible not to lean in one direction or the other) left himself open to the accusation of corruption—to be labeled either an enslaver or a slave. If accusations could be leveled against those who sincerely tried to live up to the statesman ideal, imagine the possible charges against those who abandoned it altogether.

Little wonder that so many in the South thought their political leaders would easily succumb to the temptations of Northern political life. Of course, even though many would have liked to think so, secession could never have solved the crisis of legitimacy in slave society, a crisis rooted in the master-slave relationship. The cries of corruption would continue unabated in the Confederacy.

III

THE POLITICAL CULTURE of slavery also helped shape the form of sectional conflict. It provided the framework for perceiving threats from the North and helped structure the responses to those threats. The point can best be understood if we recognize just how often the style and language of sectional conflict resembled a dueling encounter, the ritual that embodied the values of the political culture of slavery. Recall the essentials of a duel. Gentlemen fought each other to assert their equality. They would not submit to an insult and hence admit their inferiority. The same ideas reappear over and over again in the language of Southern rights activists. Antislavery action insulted them and denied their equality.

The language of the duel, for example, is evident in the private letters of South Carolina militant Robert W. Barnwell. In 1841 he wrote Robert Barnwell Rhett on the subject of New York's refusal to extradite blacks accused of helping a slave escape. "If no Southern convention meets upon this matter," he concluded, "we are gone, for it is not easy to conceive of anything more injurious and degrading than the treatment which the South will thus have patiently, no not *patiently* but *basely*, submitted to. For she has proved that she understood and felt the wrong and succumbs." In 1844 he wrote: "The impudent contempt with which we are now treated and the timid acquiescence with which we receive it are certainly very ominous prognostics of our coming fate." When John C. Calhoun rejoined the Democratic party in 1844 and divided South Carolina between radicals and moderates, Barnwell decided, in words that might have been used to describe a cowardly duelist, that the state "has decidedly flinched and nothing but the election of Polk can veil her disgrace."[33]

Robert J. Turnbull resorted to dueling language in his early protest against colonization, the tariff, and internal improvements as threats to slavery. "To talk" he explained, "of resistance to the tariff, by all *constitutional* means, is to talk to no purpose. . . . Let us say distinctly to Congress, 'HANDS OFF'—mind your *own* business. . . . It is not a case for reasoning or for negotiation. It must be a *word* and a *blow*."[34] "Words and blows," of course, lay at the heart of any dueling encounter.

Southerners always understood the problem of slavery in the territories in a way that would have been familiar to any duelist. Whatever else Northern attempts to exclude slavery from the territories might have meant, it primarily signified a denial of Southern equality. One Virginia Supreme Court justice, for example, denounced the Wilmot Proviso because it "pretends to an insulting exclusiveness or superiority on the one hand, and denounces a degrading inequality or inferiority on the other: which says in effect to the Southern man, Avaunt! You are not my equal, and hence are to be excluded as carrying a moral taint with you." Georgian Alexander Stephens explained in a public letter: "Any legislation by Congress or by any territorial legislatures which would exclude slavery would be in direct violation of the rights of the Southern people to an equal participation in them and in open derogation of the equality between the states of the South and North which should never be surrendered by the South." In 1849 John C. Calhoun tried to rally support behind his "Address of the Southern Delegates in Congress to Their Constituents." It was a statement that objected to any attempt to exclude slavery from the territories because it would push the South "from being equals, into a subordinate and dependent condition." An 1851 Alabama newspaper argued that to prevent the expansion of slavery was to declare "that a free citizen of Massachusetts was a better man and entitled to more privileges than a free citizen of Alabama."[35]

In language that recalled both republican fears of enslavement as well as a loss of honor, Southern rights activists repeatedly warned of the danger of submitting to Northern insults, warned of the danger of submitting to a condition of inequality. "Let her only *will* that she will *not submit* to the tariff," emphasized Robert Turnbull in 1827, "and the business is three-fourths finished." Thomas Cooper exhorted that "every year of submission rivets the chains upon us. . . . The question, however, is fast approaching the alternative, of submission or separation." Mississippian John A. Quitman explained in 1850: "The South has long submitted to grievous wrongs. Dishonor, degradation, and ruin await her if she submits further." On the eve of the Civil War in 1861, Jacob Thompson, Buchanan's secretary of war, understood the alternatives available to the South as "naked submission or secession."[36]

Of course, in the context of Southern political meanings, submission to a condition of inequality really meant submission to a condition of slavery. In the end, the threat from the North always seemed to be slavery. Over and over again during the years before 1860 Southerners stated and restated their fear of becoming subject to unrestrained and unprincipled power emanating from Northern society. The cries could be heard clearly as early as the nullification crisis: "It is a question of liberty on the one hand, and slavery on the other"; "are we Russian serfs, or slaves of a Divan?"; "the controversy is one between power and liberty."[37] The same images kept reappearing throughout the 1840s and 1850s: "Everywhere, liberty is surrounded by open and secret enemies"; "though other people submit to slavery we would have South Carolina contend for liberty"; "Southerners must refuse to be bridled and saddled and rode under whip and spur"; they should not submit to the "humiliating and disgraceful slavery of the South to the North"; if the Republicans assumed power they would "produce the most complete subjection and political bondage, and ruin of the South"; "we are either slaves in the union or freemen out of it."[38] The fire-eaters most frequently resorted to the vision of impending enslavement from the North, yet by 1860 such a vision had acquired wide acceptance all over the South. Just as duelists fought each other to avoid falling into a condition of subservience, so the political movement to defend the institution of slavery had become an antislavery movement.

It is also possible to detect the style of the duel in the strategy and actions associated with sectional conflict. Consider the issue of compromise. If real compromise involves overt concessions from both sides in a conflict, each giving up something desirable in order to preserve the peace, then proper duels never involved explicit recognitions of compromise. When duelists exchanged shots they clearly resolved their dispute without a compromise. But even when seconds reached an agreement, they never did so with the explicit recognition that either side had conceded anything.

The careful phrasing of a dueling agreement allowed both sides to feel their positions had triumphed. For either side to have made a concession would have been an acknowledgment of a willingness to abandon principles. It would have even acknowledged inferiority. Outsiders might later decide that someone had made a concession, but participants intended no compromise. The Cilley-Graves duel, remember, was over a small issue, a "mere point of honor," but neither side would modify its demands.

This negative attitude toward compromise appears over and over again in Southern public life. It was an attitude parallel to the way men spoke about the "compromise" of a woman's virtue. Similarly, in Southern legislatures the conventional morality objected to the "swapping of votes"—the practice by which legislators supported each other's special, local projects. Such activity involved mutual concessions for a mutual gain that Southerners branded corrupt. As one careful student of Alabama's legislature described it: "The negotiation and compromise almost necessarily incident to the enactment of legislation, then, appeared *per se* corrupt in the eyes of many antebellum Alabamans."[39]

A good illustration of how the negative attitude toward compromise affected conflict in the South, an illustration of how it generated situations that paralleled duels, is offered by the Test Oath controversy during nullification in South Carolina. The nullifiers, in order to ensure the allegiance of officers in the state militia in case of attack by federal troops, wanted to impose a loyalty oath that read, in part, "that I will be faithful and true allegiance bear to the State of South Carolina." Although this statement certainly contained ambiguity, Unionists understood the meaning intended by nullifiers: in any confrontation with the federal government, the oath commanded primary loyalty to the state. If Unionists took such an oath they would concede victory to the nullifiers. Similarly, nullifiers could not retreat from imposing the oath, especially after the Unionists had voiced their opposition. This impasse was a classic dueling encounter in which neither side could compromise and each side felt its honor and equality at stake. For a while an exchange of shots seemed inevitable. But the antagonists finally reached an agreement—not a compromise, but a mutually satisfactory agreement: the legislature adopted a report explaining that "the allegiance required by the oath . . . is the allegiance which every citizen owes to the state consistently with the constitution of the United States." Of course, since neither nullifiers nor Unionists believed that the allegiance they owed the state was inconsistent with the allegiance they owed to the nation, both sides could claim that their position had been totally vindicated. The agreement was no compromise. It was a standard dueling resolution. In fact, the entire nullification dispute with the federal government ended in a parallel way, with no exchange of shots but with nullifiers conceding nothing. Calhoun always maintained that nullification had worked, that the federal government had modified the tariff law.[40] As Calhoun intended it, nullification was not a method for developing compromises. It was the way a state could absolutely protect itself, could totally eliminate serious threats. Calhoun's "dual presidency" idea, his idea of a nation headed by presidents from the two sections, also had the same quality. In a sense, the dual presidents would duel.

The same pattern reappeared during the great sectional "compromise" over slavery in the territories. It is remarkable how few political leaders in the South acknowledged that they had compromised in any way. True, the Missouri Compromise of 1820 certainly won some Southern support, but because so many saw it as no compromise at all. As one student of the subject has put it: "the vote [on the Missouri bill] does *not* mean that Southern members of Congress were generally more reasonable and flexible than their Northern colleagues. It means only that in this particular compromise plan, formulated by proslavery leaders, the South got what it wanted most and the North did not."[41] But the Compromise of 1850 illustrates the point even more clearly. At stake were a large number of sectional issues including the admission of California without slavery, the problem of slavery in the other territories recently acquired from Mexico, the Texas boundary, slavery and the slave trade in Washington, D.C., a new fugitive slave law, as well as the right of Congress to act on the interstate slave trade. A true sectional compromise on all these issues would have required Southerners to vote against their interests and principles in one area in exchange for Northern support in another area. Henry Clay's famous omnibus bill placed in one package all the elements needed for such a true compromise, and yet the package won little Southern support. It was Stephen Douglas, fully aware of the anticompromise spirit [in both North and South], who manipulated the elements so that a "compromise" passed with almost no one agreeing to a compromise. He arranged for separate votes on each of the issues, and took advantage of absences, abstentions, and a few compromise votes in order to push the package through in pieces. But, as historian David M. Potter has put it, "there really was no compromise—a truce perhaps, an armistice, certainly a settlement, but not a true compromise."[42]

Of course, not every issue was equally uncompromisable, but slavery issues almost always had that quality since they struck at the heart of Southern power, honor, and values. Hence, the so-called moderates of the South never really sought to compromise on the slavery issue. Almost no Southerners openly embraced compromise with the antislavery North. The "cooperationists" in Southern politics opposed the secessionists on tactical matters. They wanted united Southern action as a way to intimidate the North. They never saw themselves as compromisers, although they were accused of it often. On the eve of secession, the Southern members of the moderate Constitutional Union party never suggested any compromise on slavery. In state after state recent studies have shown that these so-called moderates often condemned their political opponents for desiring "compromise" with the hated and corrupt Republican party.[43] If this was the attitude of Southern moderates, little wonder that the final, frantic efforts to avert hostilities on the eve of civil war should have met with such dismal failure.

Secession itself was an act that paralleled the duel. Just as an insulted gentleman withdrew from the world in a statement of independence, so did secessionists. The final acts of resignation from federal offices must have given Southerners the same feeling of exhilaration experienced by a duelist left alone to face his adversary. Consider the dueling language in Georgia Congressman Alfred Iverson's threat to resign his seat during the 1859 crisis over the election of a Speaker of the House of Representatives. "[T]he very moment you elect [Republican] John Sherman," he told the Congress, "thus giving the South the example of insult as well as injury, I would walk, every one of us, out of the Halls of this capitol, and I would never again enter until I was bade to do so by those who had the right to control me."[44] Here, Iverson suggested a course familiar to any duelist: an insulted man should withdraw and consult his "friends." This route, of course, is exactly what Southern politicians did by the score as they fled Washington after Lincoln's election.

Of course the duel between the sections was not like most Southern duels because it was not between social equals. Southerners, after all, regarded antislavery Northerners as corrupt, as carrying on an English tradition of enslavement. They could not assert their equality, exchange shots with such men, and then become reconciled. Nothing more strikingly illustrates this aspect of the sectional crisis than the 1856 confrontation between South Carolina Congressman Preston Brooks and Massachusetts Senator Charles Sumner. In this encounter, the sectional conflict which so often resembled a duel actually became a duel—but, at least in the Southern mind, a duel between a superior and an inferior. The incident originated in remarks contained in Sumner's "Crime against Kansas" speech delivered in the Senate on May 19 and 20, 1856. Speaking to a packed chamber, Sumner not only dealt with Kansas but delivered carefully prepared insults to, among others, Senator Andrew Pickens Butler and his native state of South Carolina. He called Butler the Don Quixote of slavery, who "has chosen a mistress to whom he has made his vows, and who, though ugly to others, is always lovely to him; though polluted in the sight of the world, is chaste in his sight . . . the harlot, slavery." During the second day of his speech, Sumner even made reference to an earlier Butler oration, unkindly referring to his slight facial paralysis, by noting that he "with incoherent phrases, discharged the loose expectoration of his speech" about Kansas. "There was no extravagance . . . which he did not repeat," Sumner charged, "nor was their any possible deviation from truth which he did not make." As for Butler's comparison of South Carolina to Kansas, Sumner simply dismissed it out of hand. South Carolina suffered from a "shameful imbecility from slavery." "Were the whole history of South Carolina blotted out of existence," Sumner continued, "civilization might lose—I do not say how little, but surely less than it has already gained by the example of Kansas, in its valiant struggle against oppression."[45]

The aged Senator Butler, home in South Carolina, was not present at the speech. But his cousin, Congressman Preston S. Brooks, had sat in the Senate gallery long enough to hear at least some of the insults. Brooks, after carefully reading the printed version of the speech, realized that the insult could not go unanswered and that Butler was too old to take any action himself. The speech had accused his cousin of lying; it had accused his native state of "imbecility" and inequality. It was reported afterward that a Carolinian in Washington "could not go into a parlor or drawing room, or to a dinner party, where he did not find an implied reproach that there was an unmanly submission to an insult to his State and to his countrymen."[46] In the Southern mind it was as if Sumner had verbally whipped Carolinians, reducing them to subservience. The abolitionist enslaver had enslaved. Brooks had to act.

The remedy was obvious. Brooks could not challenge Sumner to a regular duel. He was a corrupt Republican, and decidedly not a gentleman. Not only would Sumner have rejected a duel as a barbarous Southern relic alien to his own culture, but for Brooks to have challenged him would have been to have acknowledged his equality. A cane was the proper weapon to use in such a circumstance. As masters beat their slaves to remind them of their inferiority, so Brooks would beat Sumner. The effects of Sumner's verbal whipping would be obliterated by a nonverbal whipping. Waiting for the opportune moment, Brooks approached Sumner seated at his desk in the recently adjourned Senate, softly informed him that "I have read your speech twice over carefully. It is a libel on South Carolina, and Mr. Butler, who is a relative of mine," and proceeded to rain "about 30 first rate stripes" on Sumner's head. In the end, Sumner lay on the floor of the Senate, bloody and unconscious.

From the Southern point of view, the Charles Sumner caning embodied the entire sectional conflict. It reduced an abstract dueling encounter into a rather concrete dueling encounter. It captured the Southern fears of inequality and of submission to insult by corrupt enslavers like Sumner. The remedy won wide approval all over the South, although there was some quibbling over the time and place of the attack. "Every Southern man sustains me," Brooks wrote his brother.[47] The *Richmond Enquirer* summarized the sentiments of many in its conclusion: "We consider the act good in conception, better in execution, and best of all in consequences. The Vulgar Abolitionists in the Senate are getting above themselves. . . . They have grown saucy and dare to be impudent to gentlemen! . . . The truth is, they have been suffered to run too long without collars. They must be lashed into submission."[48] Here was the core of the Southern reaction. Sumner had been "lashed into submission." The abolitionist enslaver had become the enslaved.

IV

THE CENTRAL PROBLEM OF political life for antebellum Southerners was how to avoid becoming an enslaver or a slave. It was an insoluble problem for men who sought both republicanism and honor. Whereas republicanism demanded a renunciation of all forms of unrestrained power, honor demanded its accumulation. Still, they did repeatedly imagine one possible solution to this problem: the way to avoid becoming a master or a slave was to live in a true community. When abolitionists accused masters of slavery, proslavery writers denied the charge, noting the bonds of love, affection, and interest that united master and slave. When free citizens worried about unrestrained leaders they could be reminded of the homogeneity of interest that united rulers and ruled in slave society. Similarly, when duelists faced each other in the field each hoped to avoid falling into the condition of slavery; they shot at each other to reestablish equality and community.

From the Southern viewpoint, the problem of avoiding slavery also lay at the core of sectional conflict. Corrupt abolitionists carrying on an old English tradition threatened to enslave the South. Moreover, Southerners viewed the North as alien with its different labor system and foreign political culture. When community seemed impossible only two options remained: to become an enslaver or to separate forever.

Notes

PREFACE

1. Some of the best descriptions of this intellectual tradition can be found in Gordon Wood, *The Creation of the American Republic, 1776–1787*; J.G.A. Pocock, *The Machiavellian Moment: Florentine Political Thought and the Atlantic Republican Tradition*; Drew R. McCoy, *The Elusive Republic*; Lance Banning, *The Jeffersonian Persuasion.*
2. For a more complete discussion of the importance of honor in Southern life see Bertram Wyatt-Brown, *Southern Honor.*
3. For a fuller discussion of the Hobbes and Pitt-Rivers definitions see Orlando Patterson, *Slavery and Social Death*, 10, 79–81. See also Julian Pitt-Rivers, *Encyclopedia of the Social Sciences*, 2d ed., S.V. "Honor."

CHAPTER 1: THE RHYTHM OF SOUTHERN STATESMANSHIP

1. The masters were sometimes actually the fathers of their slave children.
2. Given their elaborate networks of intermarriage, masters were sometimes the fathers of their constituent children.
3. Richard Walsh, ed., *The Writings of Christopher Gadsden, 1746–1805* (Columbia: University of South Carolina Press, 1966), 277; Robert L. Meriwether, ed., *The Papers of John C. Calhoun, 1801–1817*, vol. 1 (Columbia: University of South Carolina Press, 1959), 72.
4. James Henry Hammond, "Thoughts, Gossip, Fancies, Facts," May 13, 1852, James Henry Hammond Papers, South Caroliniana Library; "Characteristics of the Statesman," *Southern Quarterly Review* 6 (1844): 107, 110, 114.
5. Walsh, *Writings of Christopher Gadsden*, 157.
6. Richard K. Crallé, ed., *The Works of John C. Calhoun*, vol. 4 (New York: D. Appleton and Co., 1857), 330. For other, more general statements about the importance of independence for Southerners see Bertram Wyatt-Brown, *Southern Honor*, 72; Catherine Clinton, *The Plantation Mistress*, 48.
7. "Characteristics of the Statesman," *Southern Quarterly Review* 6 (1844): 128;

Francis Wilkinson Pickens to Milledge Luke Bonham, October 14, 1859, Milledge Luke Bonham Papers, South Caroliniana Library.

8. Crallé, *Works of Calhoun*, 2: 180; Lawrence M. Keitt to Susanna Sparks, January 20, 1855, Lawrence M. Keitt Papers, Duke University; Hammond, "Thoughts, Gossip, Fancies, Facts," March 27, 1852; "Abuse of Suffrage," *Southern Quarterly Review*, n.s. 8 (1853): 533.
9. James Hamilton, Jr., and Daniel Huger quoted in William W. Freehling, *Prelude to Civil War*, 89, 241.
10. Raymond Starr, ed., "Letters from John Lewis Gervais to Henry Laurens, 1771–1778," *South Carolina Historical Magazine* 66 (1965): 28.
11. George C. Rogers, Jr., *Evolution of a Federalist*, 125; Walsh, *Writings of Christopher Gadsden*, 157, 205; George C. Rogers, Jr., ed., "The Letters of William Loughton Smith to Edward Rutledge, June 8, 1789 to April 28, 1794," *South Carolina Historical Magazine* 70 (1969): 39; Rogers, *Evolution of a Federalist*, 265–67.
12. Samuel Gaillard Stoney, ed., "The Memoirs of Frederick Adolphus Porcher," *South Carolina Historical and Genealogical Magazine* 46 (1945): 198; 47 (1946): 32; William J. Grayson, *James Louis Petigru*, 75, 121.
13. Francis W. Pickens to Milledge Luke Bonham, April 14, 1860, Francis W. Pickens Papers, South Caroliniana Library; David F. Jamison to John Jenkins, June 8, 1860, David F. Jamison Papers, William R. Perkins Library, Duke University; Hayne quoted in Harold S. Schultz, *Nationalism and Sectionalism in South Carolina, 1852–1860*, 218.
14. Mary C. Simms Oliphant, Alfred Taylor Odell, and T. C. Duncan Eaves, eds., *The Letters of William Gilmore Simms*, vol. 2: (Columbia: University of South Carolina Press, 1953), 214–15; vol. 4: 282; William Porcher Miles to Robert N. Gourdin, December 10, 1860, Robert N. Gourdin Papers, William R. Perkins Library, Duke University.
15. James Franklin Jameson, ed., "Calhoun Correspondence," *Annual Report of the American Historical Association for the Year 1899*, vol. 2, 1101; James Henry Hammond to George Wimberly Jones DeRenne, April 27, 1860, James Henry Hamond Papers, William R. Perkins Library, Duke University; I. W. Hearst to W. R. Hemphill, May 27, 1856, Hemphill Family Papers, William R. Perkins Library, Duke University.
16. William W. Freehling, "Spoilsmen and Interests in the Thought and Career of John C. Calhoun," 36.
17. Jameson, "Calhoun Correspondence," 375, 433, 512, 541. Other examples of Calhoun's public and private statements of passivity can be found in ibid., 574, 671, 674; Crallé, *Works of Calhoun*, 4: 330; W. Edwin Hemphill, ed., *The Papers of John C. Calhoun*, vol. 8 (Columbia: University of South Carolina Press, 1975), 59, 61, 203, 204, 208, 215, 311, 313, 354, 430; vol. 11 (1978), 152, 227, 457, 461, 480; vol. 12 (1979), 61, 336, 534; vol. 13 (1980), 262, 283, 526–27. Calhoun, of course, did not remain entirely passive. The causes and consequences of deviation from the ideal—both for Calhoun and others—are examined in chapter 7.
18. On Southern Whigs and statesmanship see Thomas Brown, "Southern Whigs and the Politics of Statesmanship, 1833–1841," 361–80.

19. Ulrich B. Phillips, ed., "The Correspondence of Robert Toombs, Alexander H. Stephens and Howell Cobb," 108, 180, 537.
20. Ibid., 147, 420, 492.
21. William Kauffman Scarborough, ed., *The Diary of Edmund Ruffin*, vol. 1 (Baton Rouge: Louisiana State University Press, 1972), 30–31, for example; Robert Gray Gunderson, *The Log-Cabin Campaign*, 63–64.
22. Haskell L. Monroe and James T. McIntosh, eds., *The Papers of Jefferson Davis*, vol. 1 (Baton Rouge: Louisiana State University Press, 1971), lxii.
23. As with the discussion of statesmanship, to suggest that the oration was at the core of Southern public speaking is not to suggest that speakers always delivered orations. One student of Southern oratory, Waldo W. Braden, has collected a series of essays on the subject and argues that there was no such thing as a Southern orator in terms of any consistent pattern of style and content. Braden is correct in one sense. There is a great deal of diversity. But, as with many other features of Southern life, the recognition of diversity should not prevent us from distinguishing the central from the peripheral. Orators seem to have been more prevalent in the South than in the North and they seem to have been a much more vital part of the culture. Braden's discussion of Southern oratorical diversity can be found in Waldo W. Braden, ed., *Oratory in the Old South, 1828–1860*, 17–18. On the importance of speech in an honor society such as the South see Wyatt-Brown, *Southern Honor*, 47.
24. Braden, *Oratory in the Old South*, 74–75.
25. Daniel P. Jordan, "John Randolph of Roanoke and the Art of Winning Elections in Jeffersonian Virginia," 390.
26. Examples of how public speaking in the South revealed a man's character can be found in Braden, *Oratory in the Old South*, 98, 99, 118, 140.
27. Quoted in ibid., 114. Some stump speeches almost became duels. The relationship between the duel and the statesman is examined in chapter 2.
28. Ibid., 170.
29. Richard N. Current, *Daniel Webster and the Rise of National Conservatism*, 26, 111; David Herbert Donald, *Charles Sumner and the Coming of the Civil War*, 278–311.
30. Frederick Law Olmsted, *A Journey in the Back Country*, 467.
31. Carl Schurz, *The Reminiscences of Carl Schurz, 1852–1863*, 2: 177.
32. Ibid., 198.
33. Southerners cultivated conversation as a way of conversing among social equals in private. See Braden, *Oratory in the Old South*, 89–90.
34. Schurz, *Reminiscences of Carl Schurz*, 2: 30–31, 34–37.
35. Charles G. Sellers, Jr., "Who Were the Southern Whigs?" 338, 339; Ulrich B. Phillips, "The Southern Whigs, 1834–1854," *Turner Essays in American History*, 210.
36. Michael F. Holt, *The Political Crisis of the 1850s*, 40; Jean E. Friedman, *The Revolt of the Conservative Democrats*, 103; Brown, "Southern Whigs and the Politics of Statesmanship," 370. Many Northerners among the Conservative Democrats sided with Taylor. As a matter of fact, many Northerners switched parties and resigned from office during these years of tumultuous party devel-

opment. But in the North, these reversals did not fit into a larger pattern of statesmanship.

37. Linda Rhea, *Hugh Swinton Legaré*, 175.
38. Daniel Walker Howe, *The Political Culture of the American Whigs*, 241–51.
39. Edward Pessen, *Jacksonian America*, 188; Daniel P. Jordan, "Mississippi's Antebellum Congressmen," 179. Pessen offers many examples of Northerners who also switched parties during these years but nobody seems to have approached "General Weathercock" of Mississippi.
40. Ralph A. Wooster, *The People in Power*, 41–42. Wooster also notes the same pattern in other state and county offices, 62, 67, 79, 92–94. The pattern of Southern office turnover does not appear at the congressional level. Although Southern congressmen switched positions and parties, they persisted longer than Northern congressmen. This persistence may have been due to another feature of the political culture of slavery—lower competition. Samuel Kernell, "Toward Understanding 19th Century Congressional Careers," 683.
41. Lawrence M. Keitt to Susanna Sparks, January 20, 1855, Lawrence M. Keitt Papers, William R. Perkins Library, Duke University.
42. Crallé, *Works of Calhoun*, 3: 271; Freehling, *Prelude to Civil War*, 91, also notes: "Popular men who dissented from popular policies frequently won high office."
43. Roy P. Basler, ed., *The Collected Works of Abraham Lincoln*, vol. 1 (New Brunswick, N.J.: Rutgers University Press, 1953), 431. For other examples see John C. Fitzpatrick, ed., "The Autobiography of Martin Van Buren," *Annual Report of the American Historical Association for the Year 1918*, vol. 2 Washington, D.C., 1918, 29–30; Robert F. Dalzell, Jr., *Daniel Webster and the Trial of American Nationalism 1843-1852*, 246.
44. Pessen, *Jacksonian America*, 188.
45. Wooster, *The People in Power*, 41, 117. For other evidence of the dominance of masters in the political leadership of the antebellum South see William L. Barney, *The Secessionist Impulse*, 88; J. Mills Thornton III, *Politics and Power in a Slave Society*, 299; Michael P. Johnson, *Toward a Patriarchal Republic*, 113, notes the importance of slave owners in the Georgia secession convention; Randolph B. Campbell, "Planters and Plain Folk," 389.
46. Eugene D. Genovese, *Roll, Jordan, Roll*, 75–86.
47. James O. Breeden, ed., *Advice among Masters*, 40, 79; Genovese, *Roll, Jordan, Roll*, 76, 81.
48. Genovese, *Roll, Jordan, Roll*, 7–25.
49. William Kauffman Scarborough, *The Overseer*, 95–97, 99, 104; Genovese, *Roll, Jordan, Roll*, 21.
50. Breeden, *Advice among Masters*, 85, 86, 45.

CHAPTER 2: THE DUEL AS SOCIAL DRAMA

1. On the concept of social drama see Victor Turner, *The Drums of Afflication*. See also Clifford Geertz's analysis of cockfighting as a social drama in Balinese culture in *The Interpretation of Cultures*, 412–53. For an application of the

concept of social drama to gambling and horse racing among seventeenth- and eighteenth-century Virginia gentry see T. H. Breen, "Horses and Gentlemen," 239–57.

2. John Hope Franklin, *The Militant South*, 61; Dickson D. Bruce, Jr., *Violence and Culture in the Antebellum South*, 28.
3. John Lyde Wilson, *The Code of Honor*, 8; Charles Oscar Paullin, *Duelling in the Old Navy*, 1156.
4. Daniel J. Boorstin, *The Americans*, 210.
5. James E. Moss, *Duelling in Missouri History*, 23.
6. Clifford Geertz, in his essay "Deep Play: Notes on the Balinese Cockfight," also recognizes that the single combat of the cockfight, a ritual that resembles the duel in many ways, is really an activity involving the competition of major social groupings in the community. Social divisions are often reflected in such "play" situations. Geertz, *Interpretation of Cultures*, 412–53.
7. Cited in H. E. Scudder, ed., *Men and Manners in America One Hundred Years Ago*, 307; Preston Brooks, "Preston S. Brooks on the Caning of Charles Sumner," ed. Robert L. Meriwether, 4; Franklin, *The Militant South*, 53.
8. [S. S. Prentiss], *A Memoir of S. S. Prentiss*, I: 134.
9. Clement Eaton, *Henry Clay and the Art of American Politics*, 142-44; Bruce, *Violence and Culture in the Antebellum South*, 26. Other examples of duels deriving from words spoken in debate can be found in Albert D. Kirwan, *John J. Crittendon*, 198; Seth Ames, ed., *Works of Fisher Ames*, vol. 1 (New York: DaCapo Press, 1969), 216n.; *Niles' Weekly Register*, June 18, 1836, 1.
10. Moss, *Duelling in Missouri History*, 19.
11. John Spencer Bassett, ed., *Correspondence of Andrew Jackson*, vol. 1 (Washington, D.C.: Carnegie Institution, 1926), 207; Charles M. Wiltse, ed., *The Papers of Daniel Webster, Correspondence*, vol. 1 (Hanover, N.H.: University of New England, for Dartmouth College, 1974), 243. Other examples of duels that involved the combat of political factions appear in William Omer Foster, Sr., *James Jackson*, 30; Bernard Mayo, *Henry Clay*, 338–42; Moss, *Duelling in Missouri History*, 20–21; David Hackett Fischer, *The Revolution of American Conservatism*, 186–87; Robert V. Remini, *The Election of Andrew Jackson*, 21–22.
12. Josiah Quincy, *The Journals of Major Samuel Shaw*, 55–56; "Preston S. Brooks on the Caning of Charles Sumner," ed. Meriwether, 2; Dunbar Rowland, ed., *Jefferson Davis, Constitutionalist: His Letters, Papers, and Speeches*, vol. 8 (Jackson: Mississippi Department of Archives and History, 1923), 475.
13. Franklin, *The Militant South*, 55–58.
14. Bruce, *Violence and Culture in the Antebellum South*, 30; Moss, *Duelling in Missouri History*, 16. Family involvement in duels sometimes led to family feuds. Alexander Keith McClung, known as "the black knight of the South," was reported to have killed seven members of a family in duels. Franklin, *The Militant South*, 39.
15. Quoted in Moss, *Duelling in Missouri History*, 4; William Cabell Bruce, *John Randolph of Roanoke, 1773-1833*, 1: 315. For other examples of posting see Marquis James, *Andrew Jackson*, 99; "When Knighthood Was in Flower," 367.

16. Bassett, *Correspondence of Andrew Jackson*, 1: 22, 127; quoted in John Carl Parish, *George Wallace Jones*, 170; Charles Oscar Paullin, *Commodore John Rodgers*, 182.
17. This account of the Cilley-Graves duel is derived from U.S. House of Representatives, 25th Cong. 2d sess., 1837–38, *Report of the Committee on the Late Duel*, April 25, 1838; *Funeral Oration Delivered at the Capitol in Washington over the Body of Hon. Jonathan Cilley* (New York: Wiley and Putnam, 1838); Lorenzo Sabine, *Notes on Duels and Duelling*, 89–108; *Niles' Weekly Register*, March 3, 1838, 5–6; March 10, 1838, 18–19; March 24, 1838, 52–54; March 30, 1839, 69; July 27, 1839, 345–56; Parish, *George Wallace Jones*, 157–70.
18. A good example of a duel whose primary purpose was to produce a death occurred in Mississippi. The parties "agreed to take four pistols each and a large Bowie knife, to commence walking up to each other, being placed *eighty yards* apart, and fire when they pleased; and in case neither should hit or kill with the pistols to close in with their knives." *Niles' Weekly Register*, September 6, 1834, 9.
19. David Duncan Wallace, *The Life of Henry Laurens*, 301; James, *Andrew Jackson*, 49; Bruce, *John Randolph of Roanoke*, 1: 523; *A Memoir of S. S. Prentiss*, 1: 133; Henry Thomas Shanks, ed., *The Papers of Willie Person Mangum*, vol. 4 (Raleigh: North Carolina State Department of Archives and History, 1955), 400–401. See also Bruce, *Violence and Culture in the Antebellum South*, 26.
20. Paullin, *Duelling in the Old Navy* 1155, 1157. These figures are in line with British dueling statistics. *Niles' Weekly Register*, June 5, 1841, 224.
21. Paullin, *Duelling in the Old Navy*, 1188, 1192.
22. *Niles' Weekly Register*, November 7, 1840, 153; General Dabney Herndon Maury, *Recollections of a Virginian in the Mexican, Indian, and Civil Wars*, 106; J. Winston Coleman, *The Trotter-Wickliffe Duel*, 20.
23. Bassett, *Correspondence of Andrew Jackson*, 1: 48; Harold C. Syrett, ed., *The Papers of Alexander Hamilton*, vol. 26 (New York: Columbia University Press, 1979), 253.
24. Bassett, ed., *Correspondence of Andrew Jackson*, 1: 88; Denis Tilden Lynch, *An Epoch and a Man*, 298.
25. Wilson, *Code of Honor*, 16, 15.
26. Moss, *Duelling in Missouri History*, 24; Paullin, *Duelling in the Old Navy*, 1171.
27. Wilson, *Code of Honor*, 10; Wilmuth S. Rutledge, "Dueling in Antebellum Mississippi," 187; Lillian Adele Kibler, *Benjamin F. Perry*, 145.
28. Wilson, *Code of Honor*, 12. For an example of a close duel see Moss, *Duelling in Missouri History*, 20.
29. Wilson, *Code of Honor*, 9, 10; Bassett, ed., *Correspondence of Andrew Jackson*, 1: 138.
30. Richard Walsh, ed., *The Writings of Christopher Gadsden* (Columbia: University of South Carolina Press, 1966) xxiv; Simms, William Gilmore, ed., *The Army Correspondence of Colonel John Laurens in the Years 1777–78* (New York, 1857), 123–24; Moss, *Duelling in Missouri History*, 15.
31. Foster, *James Jackson*, 132; Bruce, *John Randolph of Roanoke*, 2: 314–15.

32. Bassett, *Correspondence of Andrew Jackson*, 124, 126.
33. Evarts B. Greene, "The Code of Honor in Colonial and Revolutionary Times with Special Reference to New England," 383; Simeon E. Baldwin, *Life and Letters of Simeon Baldwin*, 347.
34. *A Memoir of S. S. Prentiss*, 134; Shanks, *The Papers of Willie Person Mangum*, 4: 269; Bruce, *Violence and Culture in the Antebellum South*, 28. See also Wilson, *Code of Honor*, 4.
35. George C. Rogers, Jr., *Evolution of a Federalist*, 128; Foster, *James Jackson*, 30; John Stockton Littell, ed., *Memoirs of His Own Time*, 323; Simms, *The Army Correspondence of Colonel John Laurens in the Years 1777–8*, 39. See also Boorstin, *The Americans*, 209.
36. Wilson, *Code of Honor*, 14.
37. Wallace, *The Life of Henry Laurens*, 217n.; Bruce, *John Randolph of Roanoke*, 1: 523; Eaton, *Henry Clay*, 61; Rutledge, "Dueling in Antebellum Mississippi," 186; *A Memoir of S. S. Prentiss*, 1: 133; John S. Kendall, "According to the Code," 149. See also Theodore D. Jervey, *Robert Y. Hayne and His Times*, 198; Paullin, *Duelling in the Old Navy*, 1195; *Niles' Weekly Register*, January 31, 1835, 370.
38. Paullin, *Duelling in the Old Navy*, 1183; David F. Long, *Nothing Too Daring*, 187; Robert Baldick, *The Duel*, 128. See also *Niles' Weekly Register*, September 17, 1831, 37.
39. Bruce, *Violence and Culture in the Antebellum South*, 22–23, 30; Scudder, *Men and Manners in America One Hundred Years Ago*, 307; Mayo, *Henry Clay*, 338; Moss, *Duelling in Missouri History*, 12.
40. Wilson, *Code of Honor*, 7, 13.
41. Orlando Patterson, *Slavery and Social Death*.

CHAPTER 3: PARTY AND ANTIPARTY

1. Ronald P. Formisano, "Deferential-Participant Politics," 473–87; Ronald P. Formisano, "Toward a Reorientation of Jacksonian Politics," 42–65.
2. William Nisbet Chambers, *Political Parties in a New Nation*, 44–48. See also Maurice Duverger, *Political Parties*.
3. William J. Cooper, Jr., *The South and the Politics of Slavery*, 38–42.
4. Thomas B. Alexander, "The Civil War as Institutional Fulfillment," 15. See also Jerome M. Clubb, William H. Flanigan, and Nancy H. Zingale, *Partisan Realignment*, 71.
5. Richard P. McCormick, *The Second American Party System*, Thomas B. Alexander, Peggy Duckworth Elmore, Frank M. Lowery, and Mary Jane Pickens Skinner, "The Basis of Alabama's Ante-Bellum Two-Party System," 243–76; J. Mills Thorton III, *Politics and Power in a Slave Society*, 140; Brian G. Walton, "Elections to the United States Senate in North Carolina, 1835–1861," 168–92; William L. Barney, *The Secessionist Impulse*, 54, 59, 64. For an interesting table demonstrating the close party rivalry in all sections of the country during the presidential contests from 1836 to 1856 see Paul Kleppner, *The Third Electoral System, 1853–1892*, 21.

6. William N. Chambers and Philip C. Davis, "Party, Competition, and Mass Participation: The Case of the Democratizing Party System, 1824–1852," in Joel H. Silbey, Allan G. Bogue, and William H. Flanigan, eds., *The History of American Electoral Behavior*, 174–97.
7. The states within each region are the same as in note *a* in table 1. The source for all elections is U.S. Congress, *Congressional Quarterly's Guide to U.S. Elections* (Washington, D.C., 1975).
8. McCormick, *The Second American Party System*, 177–254, 287–320; William N. Chambers and Philip C. Davis, "Party, Competition and Mass Participation," 176, 188.
9. Thornton, *Politics and Power in a Slave Society*, 38.
10. Holt, *Politics Crisis of the 1850s*, 92–93, 118–19, 231–35; Cooper, *The South and the Politics of Slavery, 1828-1856*, 304, 360.
11. McCormick, *The Second American Party System*, 246–54; Holt, *Political Crisis of the 1850s*, 101–38.
12. McCormick, *The Second American Party System*, 177.
13. Ralph A. Wooster, *The Secession Conventions of the South*, 29, 39; Barney, *The Secessionist Impulse*, 267–68, Holt, *Political Crisis of the 1850s*, 220; John V. Mering, "The Slave-State Constitutional Unionists and the Politics of Consensus," 407; Randolph Campbell, "Political Conflict within the Southern Consensus," 232.
14. Thomas B. Alexander and Richard E. Beringer, *The Anatomy of the Confederate Congress*, 35, 343–44; Richard E. Beringer, "The Unconscious 'Spirit of Party' in the Confederate Congress," in Robert P. Swierenga, ed., *Beyond the Civil War Synthesis*, 185–201; Wilfred Buck Yearns, *The Confederate Congress*, 42–59; Eric L. McKitrick, "Party Politics and the Union and Confederate War Efforts," in William Nisbet Chambers and Walter Dean Burnham, eds., *The American Party Systems*; Joel H. Silbey, *A Respectable Minority*, 151.
15. On the anti-organizational implications of the tradition of honor see Bertram Wyatt-Brown, *Southern Honor*, 71.
16. Thomas Brown, "Southern Whigs and the Politics of Statesmanship, 1833–1841," quotation on 368.
17. Quoted in Perry M. Goldman, "Political Virtue in the Age of Jackson," 48. Goldman concludes: "The new political morality posited the success and preservation of the party above all other considerations; the new ethic called for party loyalty, obedience, and a self-effacing attitude." See p. 50. See also McCormick, *The Second American Party System*, 30, 342, 344.
18. W. Edwin Hemphill, ed., *The Papers of John C. Calhoun, 1823-1824*, vol. 8 (Columbia: University of South Carolina Press, 1975), 312. See also pp. 33, 34, 39, 45, 72, 173, 203, 215, 311, 313, 354, 430. Thornton, *Politics and Power in a Slave Society*, 332. See also p. 337. Ulrich B. Phillips, ed., "The Correspondence of Robert Toombs, Alexander H. Stephens, and Howell Cobb," 2: 456. See also W. Alston Pringle, *An Oration Delivered before the Fourth of July Association*, 15–16; "The Danger and Safety of the Republic," *Southern Quarterly Review*, 14 (1848), 152; Thomas W. Hanckel, *Government and the Right of Revolution*, 11. For John C. Calhoun's ideas on the few who rule political parties see

William W. Freehling, "Spoilsmen and Interests in the Thought and Career of John C. Calhoun," 25–42.

19. Carl Schurz, *The Reminiscences of Carl Schurz, 1852-1863,* 2: 23.
20. James O. Breeden, ed., *Advice among Masters,* 8, 11, 16. See also 31, 32, 35, 38, 43.
21. There is some evidence that many masters resisted the idea of thinking of themselves as the "managers" of slaves because it seemed to imply the transformation of slaves into objects. Consequently they would attach an even greater negative association to the concept of management. On the reluctance to think of slaves as the objects of management see ibid., 7, 16, 32, 36, 38, 41–42.
22. David Herbert Donald, "Died of Democracy," in David Herbert Donald, ed., *Why the North Won the Civil War,* 79–90.
23. John C. Calhoun, *The Works of John C. Calhoun,* ed. Richard K. Crallé, 2: 461; [William Gilmore Simms], "The Southern Convention," *Southern Quarterly Review,* n.s. 2 (1850): 198; *Unionville Journal,* June 22, 1855; Daniel Wallace, *The Political Life and Services of the Hon. R. Barnwell Rhett of South Carolina,* 9.
24. On the antiparty ideas associated with the older tradition of statesmanship and republicanism see J.G.A. Pocock, *The Machiavellian Moment,* 407, 483–84.
25. "Characteristics of the Statesman," *Southern Quarterly Review* 6 (1844) 126; "Independent Voter" [Letter to Editor], *Lexington Flag,* October 7, 1858.
26. Calhoun, *Works,* ed. Crallé, 2: 100, 515; James Franklin Jameson, ed., "Calhoun Correspondence," *Annual Report of the American Historical Association for the Year 1899,* vol. 2 (Washington: Government Printing Office, 1900), 447; Calhoun, *Works,* ed. Crallé, 4: 328. See also Calhoun, *Works,* ed. Crallé, 2: 349; 4: 18, 329, 337; Jameson, ed., "Calhoun Correspondence," 2: 725.
27. Hugh Lawson White quoted in Brown, "Southern Whigs and the Politics of Statesmanship, 1833–1841," 367; Phillips, ed., "Correspondence of Robert Toombs, Alexander H. Stephens, and Howell Cobb," 146, 470; Thornton, *Politics and Power in a Slave Society,* 210, 228, 235–37, 366–67; Holt, *Political Crisis of the 1850s,* 37, 221–22; Alexander and Beringer, *Anatomy of the Confederate Congress,* 42, 43, 46–47, 50, 54, 56, 58.
28. "Letters on the Nullification Movement in South Carolina, 1830–1834," 738; Jameson, "Calhoun Correspondence," 281–82, 420, 483.
29. Francis W. Pickens, *Speech of the Hon. F. W. Pickens, Delivered before a Public Meeting,* 3, 4; [William D. Porter], *Separate State Secession,* 9; E. M. Seabrook to James J. Pettigrew, May 8, 1852, Pettigrew Family Papers, Southern Historical Collection, University of North Carolina.
30. Jameson, "Calhoun Correspondence," 452; W. F. Colcock, *Speech of the Hon. W. F. Colcock,* 15–16; J. C. Coit, *An Address Delivered to the Freemen of Chesterfield District,* 10; James Louis Petigru, *Oration Delivered on the Third Anniversary of the South Carolina Historical Society,* 16. See also Charles E. B. Flagg, *Oration Delivered before the '76 Association and the Society of the Cincinnati,* 22.
31. Iveson L. Brookes to Messrs. Greeve and Orne, March 20, 1849, Iveson L. Brookes Papers, Southern Historical Collection, University of North Carolina;

William Gilmore Simms, *The Letters of William Gilmore Simms*, ed. Oliphant, Odell, Eaves, 4: 300; 3: 160. See also Iveson L. Brookes, *A Defense of the South*, 48.

32. Hugh C. Holman, "William Gilmore Simms' Picture of the Revolution as a Civil Conflict," 441–62; William Gilmore Simms, *The History of South Carolina*, 323; also 149, 214. For Simms's condemnation of parties as divisive of Southern unity see Jon L. Wakelyn, *The Politics of a Literary Man*, 204.
33. William D. Porter, *Separate State Secession*, 6, 10. See also Calhoun, *Works*, ed. Crallé, 1: 15–16; 2: 251.
34. Calhoun, *Works*, 1: 1–107.
35. Ibid., 48.
36. Ibid., 49.
37. Michael P. Johnson, *Toward a Patriarchal Republic*, 42, 138; see also 39–43, 55–56, 122, 126–28, 181. Barney, *The Secessionist Impulse*, 310.
38. Goldman, "Political Virtue in the Age of Jackson," 58–59.
39. McCormick, *The Second American Party System.*
40. For a general discussion of the agitation over the direct election of presidential electors in South Carolina see Chauncey Samuel Boucher, "Sectionalism, Representation and the Electoral Question in Ante-Bellum South Carolina," 3–62. Boucher describes the problem largely in upcountry–low-country sectional terms.
41. James Henry Hammond, quoted in Boucher, "Sectionalism and Representation," 24; Lewis Malone Ayer, Jr., *An Address on the Question of Separate State Secession, to the People of Barnwell District*, 9.
42. Johnston, *The Electoral Question Discussed*, 11, 29, 32; Boucher, "Sectionalism, Representation and the Electoral Question in Ante-Bellum South Carolina," 15–16.
43. Holt, *Political Crisis of the 1850s*, and Thornton, *Politics and Power in a Slave Society*, both describe the anti-organizational style of political organization, although their interpretations differ from mine.
44. William N. Chambers, "Parties and Nation-Building in America" in Joseph LaPalombara and Myron Weiner, eds., *Political Parties and Political Development*, 83–84. For good descriptions of the relationship between economic and social homogeneity and stunted party development in the South see Randolph Campbell, "Political Conflict within the Southern Consensus," 238–39; Whitman H. Ridgway, *Community Leadership in Maryland, 1790–1840.*
45. Leonard D. White, *The Jacksonians*, 13.
46. See, for example, Phillips, "Correspondence of Robert Toombs, Alexander H. Stephens, and Howell Cobb," 69. For a good indication of reluctance to use federal appointees as party workers see pp. 398–99. See also Barney, *The Secessionist Impulse*, 94.
47. White, *The Jacksonians*, 13. For a good description of the use of the custom house in the Philadelphia elections of 1856 see the report of the congressional investigation in *House Reports*, vol. 5, doc. no. 648 (Washington, D.C.: Government Printing Office, 1860), 9–22.
48. J.D.B. DeBow, *Compendium of the Seventh Census* (Washington, D.C.: 1854),

153. For other corroborating evidence of the high rates of Southern illiteracy, see Clement Eaton, *The Freedom of Thought Struggle in the Old South*, 64–67. See also the excellent discussion of Southern illiteracy in Wyatt-Brown, *Southern Honor*, 192–95.

49. Eaton, *The Freedom of Thought Struggle in the Old South*, 67–88. Wyatt-Brown suggests that another case of Southern illiteracy was the patriarchs' fear of being superseded by their sons if they educated them. Wyatt-Brown, *Southern Honor*, 195.

50. DeBow, *Compendium of the Seventh Census*, 154–58. See also Wyatt-Brown, *Southern Honor*, 177.

51. On the connection between newspapers and political parties see Roy Franklin Nichols, *The Disruption of American Democracy*, 71–72; and Robert Gray Gunderson, *The Log-Cabin Campaign.*

CHAPTER 4: REPRESENTATION

1. "Resolutions of the General Committee, July 6, 1774," in Elmer Johnson and Kathleen Lewis Sloan, eds., *South Carolina*, 165. See also [William Henry Drayton] *Letter from Freeman of South Carolina to the Deputies of North America Assembled in the High Court of Congress at Philadelphia*, 26–31.
2. Gordon S. Wood, *The Creation of the American Republic, 1776–1787*, 173.
3. Bernard Bailyn, *The Ideological Origins of the American Revolution*, 164–65, for the quotation, see 169.
4. Quoted in ibid., 166.
5. Ibid.
6. Wood, *Creation of the American Republic*, 176–79.
7. Quoted in David Duncan Wallace, *The History of South Carolina*, 2: 69.
8. Wood, *Creation of the American Republic*, 179–80.
9. For a full discussion of the confusions inherent in the usual formulation of the actual representation–virtual representation controversy, see Hannah Fenichel Pitkin, *The Concept of Representation*, 144–67.
10. Wood, *Creation of the American Republic*, 183–88.
11. William A. Schaper, "Sectionalism and Representation in South Carolina," 373.
12. Ibid., 367; Benjamin P. Poore, *The Federal and State Constitutions, Colonial Charters, and Other Organic Laws of the United States*, 2: 1617.
13. Ibid., 2: 1623.
14. Ibid., 2: 1634–35.
15. Wood, *Creation of the American Republic*, 239; Richard Walsh, ed., *The Writings of Christopher Gadsden 1746–1805* (Columbia: University of South Carolina Press, 1966), 225 n.; [Thomas Tudor Tucker], *Conciliatory Hints, Attempting by a Fair State of Matters, to Remove Party Prejudice*; Clement Eaton, "Southern Senators and the Right of Instruction, 1789–1860," 303. The right of instruction of federal senators and the right of instruction of state legislators do not necessarily involve the same principle. It is possible, in other words, to believe in virtual representation on a state level and actual represen-

tation on a national level without being at all inconsistent. Thomas Tudor Tucker, however, distrusted all authority and recognized no distinction between the two levels.

16. Walsh, *Writings of Christopher Gadsden*, 225, 226.
17. Ibid., 226.
18. Jonathan Elliott, ed., *The Debates in the Several State Conventions, on the Adoption of the Federal Constitution*, 4: 332.
19. J. C. Coit, *An Address Delivered to the Freemen of Chesterfield District*, 10.
20. Thomas Cooper, *Two Essays*, 34.
21. Ross J. S. Hoffman and Paul Levack, eds., *Burke's Politics: Selected Writings and Speeches of Edmund Burke on Reform, Revolution, and War* (New York: Alfred A. Knopf, 1949) 116; Richard K. Crallé, ed., *The Works of John C. Calhoun*, vol. 2 (6 vols.; New York: D. Appleton and Co., 1860–83), 177–79.
22. John Townsend, *Reply of Mr. Townsend, in Defense of His Public Conduct, against Certain Charges Made against Him*, 11.
23. For an excellent discussion of Edmund Burke's ideas on the relation between actual and virtual representation, see Pitkin, *Concept of Representation*, 168–89. For the Burke quotation, ibid., 177. For the apparent movement of prerevolutionary Carolinians toward an interest system of representation, see Robert Weir, "Liberty and Property, and No Stamps."
24. For a concise listing of voter and representative property and residence requirements in South Carolina during the colonial period, see Schaper, "Sectionalism and Representation in South Carolina," 350–51. For the requirements after 1776, see Poore, *Federal and State Constitutions*, 2: 1622, 1623, 1628, 1629.
25. David Duncan Wallace, *Constitutional History of South Carolina from 1725 to 1775*, 11.
26. Poore, *Federal and State Constitutions*, 2: 1623, 1628, 1629, 1635.
27. Wallace, *History of South Carolina*, 2: 375; Josiah J. Evans, *South Carolina and Massachusetts*, 11.
28. Joseph W. Cox, *Champion of Southern Federalism*, 27, 28, 35.
29. John Harold Wolfe, *Jeffersonian Democracy in South Carolina*, 129. In other ways, however, Robert Goodloe Harper did indicate a preference for actual representation. He fought for more equitable apportionment within South Carolina. David Hackett Fischer notes: "While Congressional gentlemen of the old school piously declaimed against the dishonesty of representatives who pandered to the prejudices of the people and to the interests of their constituents, Harper sat at his desk writing friendly, folksy letters to the good citizens of Ninety-Six district." But it should be noted that neither Harper nor the good citizens of "Ninety-Six district" ever challenged the idea that a wealthy nonresident could represent the yeoman farmers of the Carolina upcountry. David Hackett Fischer, *The Revolution of American Conservatism*, 37.
30. Schaper, "Sectionalism and Representation in South Carolina," 445. Walter B. Edgar notes: "It was not unusual for an individual to represent more than one election district over a period of time." Walter B. Edgar, ed., *Biographical Directory of the South Carolina House of Representatives*, vol. 1: *Session Lists, 1692–1973*, 626.

31. William W. Freehling, *Prelude to Civil War*, 21.
32. Robert M. Weir, " 'The Harmony We Were Famous For,' " 474–84. See also James M. Banner, Jr., "The Problem of South Carolina," in *The Hofstadter Aegis*, ed. Stanley Elkins and Eric McKitrick, 65–66; Richard Maxwell Brown, *The South Carolina Regulators*, 141.
33. Margaret Kinard Latimer, "South Carolina, a Protagonist of the War of 1812," 914–29.
34. J. Franklin Jameson, ed., "Calhoun Correspondence," *Annual Report of the American Historical Association for the Year 1899*, vol. 2 (2 vols.; Washington, D.C.: Government Printing Office, 1900), 281, 371, 420, 452.
35. F. W. Pickens, *Speech of the Hon. F. W. Pickens*, 3; W. F. Colcock, *Speech of the Hon. W. F. Colcock*, 15; Steven A. Channing, *Crisis of Fear*, 282.
36. Channing, *Crisis of Fear*, 17–57. See also Freehling, *Prelude to Civil War*, 49–86; Banner, "Problem of South Carolina," 67.
37. On the general phenomenon of planter intermarriage, especially cousin marriage, see Catherine Clinton, *The Plantation Mistress*, 57–58.
38. Freehling, *Prelude to Civil War*, 21–23.
39. David Duncan Wallace, *South Carolina*, 107; Jack P. Greene, *The Quest for Power*; Freehling, *Prelude to Civil War*, 95; Schaper, "Sectionalism and Representation in South Carolina," 380; Harold S. Schultz, *Nationalism and Sectionalism in South Carolina, 1852–1860*, 7.
40. Crallé, *Works of Calhoun*, 1: 69.
41. For a slightly different approach to this theme in Calhoun's thought see Pauline Maier, "The Road Not Taken," 1–19.
42. For a description of the inability of some Southerners wholeheartedly to endorse many aspects of the proslavery argument, see Charles Grier Sellers, Jr., "The Travail of Slavery," in Charles Grier Sellers, Jr., ed., *The Southerner as American*, 40–71.
43. [William J. Grayson], *Letters of Curtius*, 6. For the John C. Calhoun quotation, see Richard Hofstadter, *The American Political Tradition and the Men Who Made It*, 83.
44. William Gilmore Simms, *The Letters of William Gilmore Simms*, ed. Oliphant, Odell, Eaves 4: 343.
45. Fletcher M. Green, *Constitutional Development in the South Atlantic States, 1776–1860*, 168–70.
46. Ibid., 201–96. Michael F. Holt, *The Political Crisis of the 1850s*, 108–110, discusses the constitutional conventions of the 1850s, both inside and outside the South. He notes how they resolved longstanding issues of internal state conflict. J. Mills Thornton III, *Politics and Power in a Slave Society*, 3–58, elegantly describes the process by which internal state conflict generated actual representation in Alabama. See also Thomas E. Jeffrey, " 'Thunder from the Mountain,' " 383–84. On the general "democratization of Southern politics" see Fletcher M. Green, *Democracy in the Old South*, 177–92.
47. Chilton Williamson, *American Suffrage from Property to Democracy, 1760–1860*, 225, 228; Michael P. Johnson, *Toward a Patriarchal Republic*, 143–78, quotation on 167; Whitman H. Ridgway, *Community Leadership in Maryland, 1790–1840*.

48. Henry Hughes, "Treatise on Sociology," in Drew Gilpin Faust, ed., *The Ideology of Slavery*, 243, 246, 250, 258–59, 262–64, 267; George Fitzhugh, "Cannibals All! or, Slaves without Masters," in Harvey Wish, ed., *Antebellum* (New York: Capricorn Books, 1960), 151, 152, 154.
49. Holt, *Political Crisis of the 1850s*, nicely describes the gradual end of political conflict in the 1850s in the South, especially in the states of the lower South.
50. Gavin Wright, *The Political Economy of the Cotton South*, 120–25. Of course, ethnic conflict occurred in some parts of the South—Americans versus French in New Orleans, or Americans versus Germans in Texas—but, overall, it was less important than in the North.
51. Stanley Elkins and Eric McKitrick, "A Meaning for Turner's Frontier," 341, 342.
52. Eugene D. Genovese, *The Political Economy of Slavery*, 155–240; Robert E. Gallman and Ralph V. Anderson, "Slaves as Fixed Capital," 24–46. Other historians have argued that cotton cultivation rather than slavery was the decisive factor in stunting urban growth. It was more profitable to use slave labor to grow cotton than to engage in any urban occupation. Whether or not this was true, and whether it is possible to separate (during the antebellum period) cotton from slavery as distinct factors, the argument does not exclude other slavery-related factors inhibiting urban growth. See Robert W. Fogel and Stanley L. Engerman, *Time on the Cross*, for a discussion of these issues.
53. Elkins and McKitrick, "A Meaning for Turner's Frontier," 345, 348.
54. Orlando Patterson, *Slavery and Social Death*, 34, 99, notes the existence of a community of "honor" among free people in a slave society. But he also recognizes it as a community of tension.
55. Calculated from data in W. Dean Burnham, *Presidential Ballots, 1836-1892.*
56. Ralph A. Wooster, *The People in Power*, 10–19.
57. Eugene D. Genovese, "Yeoman Farmers in a Slaveholders' Democracy," 331–42, discusses the various techniques of planter control. See also William L. Barney, *The Secessionist Impulse*, 43–50, 91.
58. Ulrich B. Phillips, ed., "The Correspondence of Robert Toombs, Alexander H. Stephens, and Howell Cobb," 2: 391.
59. Bertram Wyatt-Brown, *Southern Honor*, 345.
60. Phillips, "The Correspondence of Robert Toombs, Alexander H. Stephens, and Howell Cobb," 115.
61. Thornton, *Politics and Power in a Slave Society*, develops a very different analysis of politics in the South. Thornton emphasizes the active role played by the common people in Alabama. But despite the extent of his research and the brilliance of his writing, he is not entirely convincing. What, after all, are we to make of his summary metaphor describing the relationship between rulers and followers? Conceding a great deal of passivity on the part of the masses, he notes: "But as the eunuch shapes the desires of the emperor, as the motion picture mogul gives direction to the tastes of the masses, to that extent, at least, politicians led the people of Alabama" (p. 162). Eunuchs and motion picture moguls seem the wrong kinds of leaders for a democratic political culture based on actual representation.

CHAPTER 5: THE PROSLAVERY ARGUMENT AS AN ANTISLAVERY ARGUMENT

1. Prominent proslavery thinkers included John C. Calhoun, Thomas R. Dew, George Fitzhugh, Henry Hughes, William J. Grayson, Edmund Ruffin, Thornton Stringfellow, George Frederick Holmes, James Henry Hammond, Samuel Cartwright, E. N. Elliott, Josiah C. Nott, William Harper, Albert T. Bledsoe, William Gilmore Simms, James H. Thornwell, Nathaniel Beverly Tucker, Thomas Cooper, James D. B. DeBow and William Porcher Miles.
2. Bernard Bailyn, *The Ideological Origins of the American Revolution*; John Richard Alden, *The South in the American Revolution, 1763–1789.*
3. Richard Walsh, ed., *The Writings of Christopher Gadsden, 1746–1805* (Columbia: University of South Carolina Press, 1966), 95; see also 30, 74, 77; William Tennent, *An Address, Occasioned by the Late Invasion of the Liberties of the American Colonies*, 6; John C. Fitzpatrick, ed., *The Writings of George Washington*, vol. 3 (Washington, D.C., 1931) 242. For similar uses of the word "slavery" see "Papers of the First Council of Safety of the Revolutionary Party in South Carolina, June–November 1775," *South Carolina Historical and Genealogical Magazine* 3 (July 1902): 126; [William H. Drayton], *A Letter from Freeman of South Carolina, to the Deputies of North America*, 29; *Association of 1774*, pamphlet reprinted in 1859, Charleston, S.C., 5.
4. William W. Freehling, *Prelude to Civil War*; Waldo W. Braden, *Oratory in the Old South, 1828–1860*, 19–72; J. Mills Thornton III, *Politics and Power in a Slave Society*; Michael F. Holt, *Political Crisis of the 1850s*, 242, 56, 134–35; Michael P. Johnson, *Toward A Patriarchal Republic*, 36.
5. John C. Calhoun, *The Works of John C. Calhoun*, ed. Richard K. Crallé, 1: 7, 12.
6. Quotations cited in Jack P. Greene, " 'Slavery or Independence,' " 194; Walsh, *Writings of Christopher Gadsden*, 77; see also Robert M. Weir, " 'The Harmony We Were Famous For,' " 474–75; Donald L. Robinson, Slavery in the Structure of American Politics, 1765–1820, 60–61, 463, n.23; Paul K. Conkin, *Self-Evident Truths*, 109–10; Bailyn, *Ideological Origins of the American Revolution*, 233.
7. For good discussions of the connection between slavery and liberty see Edmund S. Morgan, *American Slavery, American Freedom*, especially 363–87; and Greene, " 'Slavery or Independence,' " 193–213.
8. Samuel Johnson, "Taxation No Tyranny" (1775) in Donald J. Greene, ed., *Political Writings: The Works of Samuel Johnson* (New Haven: Yale University Press, 1977), 454.
9. The chain of events that led to the development of the proslavery argument is nicely described in Freehling, *Prelude to Civil War.*
10. For excellent discussions of scientific racism see Stephen Jay Gould, *The Mismeasure of Man*, 30–72; and William Stanton, *The Leopard's Spots.*
11. James H. Hammond, *Speech of Hon. James H. Hammond, of South Carolina, on the Admission of Kansas*, 14; William Henry Trescot, *The Annual Address before the Calliopean and Polytechnic Societies of the Citadel Academy, Charleston, S.C.*, 10.

12. The argument for the importance of scientific racism in Southern proslavery thought can be found in George M. Frederikson, *The Black Image in the White Mind*, 71–96.
13. A Carolinian [Edward J. Pringle], *Slavery in the Southern States*, 7; C. Vann Woodward, ed., *Mary Chesnut's Civil War* (New Haven: Yale University Press, 1981), 381.
14. Anne Middleton to Nathaniel Russell Middleton, August 9, 1852, Nathaniel Russell Middleton Papers, Southern Historical Collection, University of North Carolina.
15. George Frederick Holmes, "Review of Uncle Tom's Cabin," reprinted in Eric L. McKitrick, ed., *Slavery Defended*, 103.
16. William Sumner Jenkins, *Pro-Slavery Thought in the Old South*, 108.
17. James Henley Thornwell, *The Rights and the Duties of Masters*, 24; Edward B. Bryan, quoted in Jenkins, *Pro-Slavery Thought*, 109.
18. Ferdinand Jacobs, *The Committing of Our Cause to God*, 6n.; "Annexation of Texas," *Southern Quarterly Review* 6 (1844) 514; Pringle, *Slavery in the Southern States*, 16.
19. Henry Hughes, "Treatise on Sociology," reprinted in Drew Gilpin Faust, ed., *The Ideology of Slavery*, 247–50.
20. [Daniel Whitaker], *SQR* 2 (July 1842): 163–64.
21. Quoted in Jenkins, *Pro-Slavery Thought*, 112; see other examples of explicitly contractual language in the proslavery argument, 112–13.
22. Hughes, "Treatise on Sociology," in Faust, *Ideology of Slavery*, 244–47.
23. George Fitzhugh, "Sociology for the South, or the Failure of Free Society," reprinted in Harvey Wish, ed., *Antebellum*, 82.
24. A South Carolinian [Edwin C. Holland], *A Refutation of the Calumnies Circulated against the Southern and Western States*, 48; William Gilmore Simms, "The Morals of Slavery," in *Pro-Slavery Argument*, quotation on 216, 228; Hughes, "Treatise on Sociology," in Faust, *Ideology of Slavery*, 250. Southern law, of course, could never quite accomplish all that proslavery theorists expected. See Mark Tushnet, *Considerations of Humanity and Interest.*
25. See for example William Harper, "Harper on Slavery," in *Pro-Slavery Argument*, 31.
26. [Samuel A. Cartwright], "Canaan Identified with the Ethiopian," *Southern Quarterly Review* 2 (1842): 337; a South Carolinian [Henry Middleton], *Economical Causes of Slavery in the United States and Obstacles to Abolition*, 7; [Holland], *Refutation of the Calumnies*, 43–44; Mrs. Henry R. Schoolcraft, *The Black Gauntlet*, 61; Holmes, "Review of Uncle Tom's Cabin." in McKitrick, *Slavery Defended*, 107.
27. Holmes, "Review of Uncle Tom's Cabin," in McKitrick, *Slavery Defended*, 108; [William J. Grayson], *Letters of Curtius*, 6; Calhoun quoted in Richard Hofstadter, *The American Political Tradition and the Men Who Made It*, 83.
28. Hughes, "Treatise on Sociology," in Faust, *Ideology of Slavery*, 251.
29. James O. Breeden, ed., *Advice among Masters*, 28, 40, 43.
30. For some other examples see Harper, "Harper on Slavery," in *Pro-Slavery Argument*, 29–34; Simms, "The Morals of Slavery," in *Pro-Slavery Argument*,

215, 228; *A Glance at the Resources of the South in the Event of Separation and Hostile Collision with the North*, 19; William H. Trescot, *The Position and Course of the South*, [Samuel A. Cartwright], "Canaan Identified with the Ethiopian," 9; 2 (1842): 345; Fitzhugh, "Sociology for the South," in Wish, *Antebellum*, 70, 119. Fitzhugh's ideas are thoroughly discussed in Eugene Genovese, *The World the Slaveholders Made*, 118–244.

31. Richard Furman, *Rev. Dr. Richard Furman's Exposition of the Views of the Baptists*, 10, 11; Hughes, "Treatise on Sociology," in Faust, *Ideology of Slavery*, 266. See also George Fitzhugh, "Sociology for the South," in Wish, *Antebellum*, 92.
32. Edwin G. Burrows and Michael Wallace,"The American Revolution," 177. Locke himself never accepted the analogy between parental authority and other kinds of government. Yet, as Burrows and Wallace show, the American revolutionaries frequently used the analogy as a way of establishing the limits of power and the obligations of Great Britain vis-à-vis the colonies.
33. Simms, "The Morals of Slavery," in *Pro-Slavery Argument* quotation on 217, 244; Edward Thomas Heriot to "My Dear Sir," April 20, 1853, Edward Thomas Heriot Papers, William R. Perkins Library, Duke University.
34. Jacobs, *Committing of Our Cause to God*, 6 n.; Thornwell, *Rights and Duties of Masters*, 26–27.
35. "Channing's Duty of the Free States," *Southern Quarterly Review* 2 (1842): 144; [Louisa S. McCord], "Uncle Tom's Cabin," *Southern Quarterly Review*, n.s., 7 (1853): 119.
36. Proslavery writers even had a tendency to blame instances of cruelty in slavery on threats from outside. See Thomas R. Dew, "The Abolition of Negro Slavery," in Faust, *Ideology of Slavery*, 65; Holmes, "Review of Uncle Tom's Cabin," in McKitrick, *Slavery Defended*, 109.
37. [James Henry Hammond], "The North and the South" *Southern Quarterly Review* 15 (1849): 308; John Lofton, *Insurrection in South Carolina*, 185; Holland, "Refutation of the Calumnies," 12; Simms, "The Morals of Slavery," in *Pro-Slavery Argument*, 223–24; [Edward B. Bryan], *Letters to the Southern People Concerning the Acts of Congress and the Treaties with Great Britain, in Relation to the African Slave Trade*, 45.
38. Bryan, *Letters to the Southern People*, 13. For other examples of this kind of contrast see Josiah J. Evans, *South Carolina and Massachusetts*, 6; Harper, "Harper on Slavery," in *Pro-Slavery Argument*, 6; Simms, "The Morals of Slavery," in *Pro-Slavery Argument*, 222, 272; Samuel G. Stoney, ed., "The Autobiography of William John Grayson," *South Carolina Historical and Genealogical Magazine* 51 (January 1950): 29.
39. [Pringle], *Slavery in the Southern States*, 27; [Middleton], *Economical Causes of Slavery*, 45; [Grayson], *Letters of Curtius*, 7; James H. Hammond, "Hammond's Letters on Slavery," in *Pro-Slavery Argument*, 148.
40. "British Reviewers and the United States," *Southern Quarterly Review* 13 (1848): 203; [Pringle], *Slavery in the Southern States*, 25, 26, 27; Hughes, "Treatise on Sociology," in Faust *Ideology of Slavery*, 269; Hammond, "Hammond's Letters on Slavery," in *Pro-Slavery Argument*, 135. George Fitzhugh

probably most fully developed the Southern critique of "wage slavery." See his "Cannibals All! or Slaves without Masters," in Wish, *Antebellum*, 98–156. See also Genovese, *The World the Slaveholders Made*, 115–244.

41. George A. Gordon to Krilla [?], July 31, 1858, George A. Gordon Papers, William R. Perkins Library, Duke University; Jno. C. Hope, "Faulty History Correcting Itself," *Lexington* (S.C.) *Flag*, September 10, 1857; *Charleston Daily Standard*, October 4, 1853; [Samuel A. Cartwright,] "Canaan Identified with the Ethiopian," *Southern Quarterly Review* 2 (1842): 364–65; "The Danger and Safety of the Republic," 14 (1848): 164; Hughes, "Treatise on Sociology," in Faust, *Ideology of Slavery*, 252, 270; see also 242, 272. William L. Barney, in his study of secession in Alabama and Mississippi, notes the tendency of Southerners to refer to their property as "negroes" rather than "slaves." William L. Barney, *The Secessionist Impulse*, 182.
42. [Pringle], *Slavery in the Southern States*, 20, 21.
43. Louisa S. McCord, "Carey on the Slave Trade," *Southern Quarterly Review*, n.s. 9 (January 1854): 165. William S. Jenkins, *Pro-Slavery Thought*, 116, describes this idea as "the slavery principle of government."
44. George Fitzhugh, "Southern Thought," in Faust, ed. *Ideology of Slavery*, 295. See also Fitzhugh, "Cannibals All!" in Wish, *Antebellum*, 111–15.

CHAPTER 6: FROM ANGLOPHOBIA TO NEW ANGLOPHOBIA

1. Cushing Strout, *The American Image of the Old World*, nicely describes the American ambivalence toward England in his general study of American attitudes toward Europe.
2. William R. Taylor, *Cavalier and Yankee*, xv.
3. J. G. de Roulhac Hamilton, "Southern Members of the Inns of Court," 274. Clement Eaton, *The Freedom of Thought Struggle in the Old South*, 3–31, offers a good description of the English aristocratic pretensions of Southern planters. For the close connection between Southerners and England during the colonial period see Carl Bridenbaugh, *Myths and Realities.*
4. John Richard Alden, *The South in the Revolution, 1763–1789*, 177; John W. Blasingame, "American Nationalism and Other Loyalties in the Southern Colonies, 1763–1775," 54–55.
5. Blasingame, "American Nationalism," 56–57. For the general American condemnation of England see Gordon S. Wood, *The Creation of the American Republic, 1776–1787*; Strout, *The American Image of the Old World*, 14–25; Drew R. McCoy, *The Elusive Republic.*
6. Alden, *The South in the American Revolution*, 186–289; Richard Maxwell Brown, *Strain of Violence*, 67–90; [John C. Calhoun], *Life of John C. Calhoun*, 4; Daniel P. Jordan, "John Randolph of Roanoke and the Art of Winning Elections in Jeffersonian Virginia," 401n.
7. Lisle A. Rose, *Prologue to Democracy*, 105–21; George C. Rogers, Jr., *Evolution of a Federalist*, 99–105; James H. Broussard, *The Southern Federalists, 1800–1816*, 72–77. The leaders of the movement against the Jay Treaty in South Carolina included such figures as Edward and John Rutledge, Charles

Cotesworth Pinckney, John Rutledge, Jr., Christopher Gadsden, Aedanus Burke, and Thomas Tudor Tucker. In Virginia the Lower House of the Assembly condemned the treaty by a vote of 100 to 50.

Southern states led the list of debtors to British merchants before 1795, with Virginia and South Carolina at the top. Samuel Flagg Bemis, *Jay's Treaty*, 140.

On Southern reaction to the *Chesapeake-Leopard* affair see Thomas P. Abernethy, *The South in the New Nation, 1789-1819*, 315–17; and Frank A. Cassell, "The Structure of Baltimore's Politics in the Age of Jefferson, 1795–1812," in Aubrey C. Land, Lois Green Carr, and Edward C. Papenfuse, eds., *Law, Society and Politics in Early Maryland*, 290–91.

8. Abernethy, *The South in the New Nation*, 316–17; Robert L. Meriwether, ed., *The Papers of John C. Calhoun, 1801-1817*, vol. 1 (Columbia: University of South Carolina Press, 1959), 36, 92–93.
9. Margaret Kinard Latimer, "South Carolina, a Protagonist of the War of 1812," 914–29.
10. The connection between American and English antislavery is well described in Betty Fladeland, *Men and Brothers*.
11. Ibid., 124.
12. William W. Freehling, *Prelude to Civil War*, 111-16; Philip M. Hamer, "Great Britain, the United States and Negro Seamen Acts, 1822–1848," 3–28; John M. Lofton, *Insurrection in South Carolina*, 204–30.
13. Lofton, *Insurrection in South Carolina*, 11; Freehling, *Prelude to Civil War*, 115.
14. Alan F. January, "The South Carolina Associations," 191–201.
15. Hamer, "Great Britain, the United States and Negro Seamen Acts, 1822–1848," 7–8, 21.
16. "Samuel Hoar's Expulsion from Charleston," 1–20, quotation p. 8; William H. Trescot, *The Position and Course of the South*, 18.
17. [Robert J. Turnbull], *The Crisis*, 128; Freehling, *Prelude to Civil War* 123–24.
18. Historian William W. Freehling believed that "the English Emancipation Bill was . . . one of the more important reasons for the intensity of the Great Reaction"—the movement of South Carolina toward the extreme proslavery position. Freehling, *Prelude to Civil War*, 307 n.
19. [William Drayton], *The South Vindicated*, 55–56, 166–68; [Alfred] Cuthbert, *Speech of Mr. Cuthbert of Georgia, on the Petition of the Society of Friends of Lancaster County, Pennsylvania, Praying for the Abolition of Slavery in the District of Columbia*; Langdon Cheves, *Letter of the Honorable Langdon Cheves to the Editors of the Charleston Mercury*.
20. [Daniel Wallace], *Letter of Daniel Wallace of South Carolina to His Constituents*, 2–7; "Annexation of Texas," *Southern Quarterly Review* 6 (1844): 502–3.
21. Fladeland, *Men and Brothers*, 257–73.
22. Ibid., 335; *Congressional Globe*, 27th Cong., 2d Sess., 169–76, see especially p. 173.
23. Wilbur Devereux Jones, "The Influence of Slavery on the Webster-Ashburton Negotiations," 49. A good discussion of the *Creole* incident can be found in Howard Jones, "The Peculiar Institution and National Honor, 28–50. A revised

version of this essay can be found in Howard Jones, *To the Webster-Ashburton Treaty*, 69–168. See also Fladeland, *Men and Brothers*, 302–21.

24. Jones, "The Influence of Slavery in the Webster-Ashburton Negotiations," 54.
25. [Edward B. Bryan], *Letters to the Southern People Concerning the Acts of Congress and the Treaties with Great Britain*, 49–61.
26. John McCardell, *The Idea of a Southern Nation*, 232; William J. Cooper, Jr., *The South and the Politics of Slavery, 1828-1856*, 184–86; Frederick Merck, *Fruits of Propaganda in the Tyler Administration*, 3–35; *Niles' Weekly Register* May 4, 1844, 151; May 11, 1844, 164–72.
27. Evidences of the Southern campaign can be found in McCardell, *The Idea of a Southern Nation*, 233; Chauncey Samuel Boucher, "The Annexation of Texas and the Bluffton Movement in South Carolina," 13–15; *Niles' Weekly Register* May 25, 1844, 200; June 8, 1844, 229; July 20, 1844, 327–28.
28. Robert E. May, *The Southern Dream of a Caribbean Empire, 1854-1861*, 31–34, 39, 46–76; McCardell, *The Idea of a Southern Nation*, 254, 340.
29. McCoy, *The Elusive Republic*, 47, 54, 141–42.
30. *The Pro-Slavery Argument*, 23, 135; see also 30–31, 53–54, 135–38. George Fitzhugh, "Cannibals All!" in Harvey Wish, ed., *Antebellum*, 143; see also 142–44.
31. [William Drayton], *The South Vindicated*, 55–56, 166–68; James Franklin Jameson, "Calhoun Correspondence," *Annual Report of the American Historical Association for the Year 1899*, vol. 2 (Washington, D.C.: Government Printing Office, 1900), 137–39, 506, 546; "State of Education and Learning in Cuba," *Southern Quarterly Review* 1 (1842): 396.
32. Jon L. Wakelyn, *The Politics of a Literary Man*, 4; for examples of Anglophobia in the *Southern Quarterly Review*, see "Dickens' American Notes," 3 (1843): 179; "Annexation of Texas," 6 (1844): 501–2; [William J. Grayson] "Slavery in the Southern States," 8 (1845): 326; [John A. Campbell], "Slavery in the United States, " 12 (1847): 97–98; "The Invasion of Cuba," n.s., 5 (1852): 18. On Southern literary nationalism, see McCardell, *The Idea of a Southern Nation*, 141–76.
33. "The Address of the People of South Carolina," in John Amasa May and Joan Reynolds Faunt, *South Carolina Secedes*, 83. The analogy between 1776 and the later struggle for Southern rights was common throughout the South. See J. Mills Thornton III, *Politics and Power in a Slave Society*, 213–17; Michael P. Johnson, *Toward a Patriarchal Republic*, 29–30; McCardell, *The Idea of a Southern Nation*, 261.
34. Michael Hechter, *Internal Colonialism*.
35. Forrest McDonald and Ellen Shapiro McDonald, "The Ethnic Origins of the American People," 179–99. See especially the chart on p. 198. On Southern ethnicity see also Forrest McDonald and Grady McWhiney, "The Celtic South," 11–15; Forrest McDonald, "The Ethnic Factor in Alabama History," 256–65; Forrest McDonald and Grady McWhiney, "The South from Self-Sufficiency to Peonage," 1095–1118; Robert Kelley, *The Cultural Pattern in American Politics*, 99–100.
36. On the Southern hysterical reaction to the Nat Turner rebellion see Henry

Irving Tragle, ed., *The Southampton Slave Revolt of 1831*, 86–87, 89, 94, 98. On the Southern fear of slave revolts see especially Freehling, *Prelude to Civil War*, 49–86, and Steven A. Channing, *Crisis of Fear.*

CHAPTER 7: SECTIONAL CONFLICT

1. Michael F. Holt, *The Political Crisis of the 1850s*, also defines the problem of secession in this way although he offers a different analysis of its cause.
2. Pauline Maier, "The Road Not Taken," 1–19, offers a good discussion of Calhoun's republican values.
3. For a discussion of Calhoun's fear of spoilsmen see William W. Freehling, "Spoilsmen and Interests in the Thought and Career of John C. Calhoun," 25–42; Langdon Cheves, *Speech of the Hon. Langdon Cheves, in the Southern Convention, at Nashville, Tennessee, November 14, 1850*, 15, 19; Lewis M. Ayer, *Southern Rights and the Cuban Question, An Address Delivered at Whippy Swamp, on the Fourth of July, 1855*, 4; Isaac Hayne to Charles Cotesworth Pinckney, Jr., April 23, 1860, Charles Cotesworth Pinckney, Jr., Papers, South Caroliniana Library, University of South Carolina.
4. "Characteristics of the Statesman," *Southern Quarterly Review* 6 (1844): 122; James Franklin Jameson, ed., "Calhoun Correspondence," *Annual Report of the American Historical Association for the Year 1899*, vol. 2 (Washington, D.C.: Government Printing Office, 1900), 1056. See also "The Danger and Safety of the Republic," *Southern Quarterly Review* 14 (1848): 151–53.
5. "The Dignity Departing" [Abbeville, S.C.], *Erskine Miscellany*, June 22, 1850, p. 2; W. Alston Pringle, *An Oration Delivered before the Fourth of July Association, at the Hibernian Hall, July Fourth, 1850*, 14, 15; Henry L. Pinckney, Jr., *An Oration Delivered on the Fourth of July, 1851, before the '76 and Cincinnati Societies*, 4, 6.
6. J. C. Coit, *An Address Delivered to the Freemen of Chesterfield District*," iv.
7. *Unionville* (S.C.) *Journal*, June 22, 1855; *Carolina Spartan*, November 8, 1860. See also *Unionville Journal*, January 15, 1858.
8. Francis W. Pickens to [Armistead Burt?] August 8, 1856, Armistead Burt Papers, William R. Perkins Library, Duke University. For other examples of Pickens's fear of corruption see Pickens to "My Dear Sir," Francis W. Pickens Papers, South Caroliniana Library, University of South Carolina, August 20, 1840; also Pickens to "My Dear Child," April 10, 1842; and Pickens to Milledge Luke Bonham, April 2, 1859, Milledge Luke Bonham Papers, South Caroliniana Library, University of South Carolina.
9. C. B. Northrop, *An Oration Delivered in St. Mary's Church before the Washington Society, on the 4th of July, 1843*, 22; James Hamilton, letter 1844, Jameson, "Calhoun Correspondence," 963, 1089.
10. James Henry Hammond to W. B. Hodgson, January 24, 1847, James Henry Hammond Papers, William R. Perkins Library, Duke University; James Henry Hammond to George Wimberly Jones DeRenne, November 20, 1858, George W. J. DeRenne Papers, William R. Perkins Library, Duke University.
11. Paul Johnston, *The Electoral Question Discussed*, 88; Samuel Gaillard Stoney,

ed., "The Autobiography of William John Grayson," *South Carolina Historical and Genealogical Magazine* 50 (1949): 143.

12. John L. Manning, *An Oration Delivered on the Fourth of July, 1848, before the Cincinnati Society, and the '76 Association*, 13; "Calhoun on Government," *Southern Quarterly Review*, n.s., 7 (1853): 365; John Belton O'Neal to Burt, February 25, 1856, Armistead Burt Papers, William R. Perkins Library, Duke University. For an earlier opinion on the same issue see Ernest M. Lander, "Dr. Thomas Cooper's Views on Retirement," *South Carolina Historical Magazine* 54 (1953): 178.
13. "Editors Table," *Russell's Magazine* 1 (1857): 89.
14. "Characteristics of the Statesman," *Southern Quarterly Review* 6 (1844): 118.
15. Lawrence M. Keitt to "Carrie," February 22, 1860, Lawrence M. Keitt Papers, William R. Perkins Library, Duke University; James Henry Hammond to [South Carolina Legislature?], 1860, James Henry Hammond Papers, South Caroliniana Library, University of South Carolina; Rev. William O. Prentiss, *A Sermon Preached at St. Peter's Church," 17; R. N. Hemphill to W. R. Hemphill, December 14, 1860, Hemphill Family Papers, William R. Perkins Library, Duke University.*
16. Lawrence M. Keitt to Mrs. Frederick Brown, March 4, 1861, Lawrence M. Keitt Papers, William R. Perkins Library, Duke University [from a typed copy]. See also Michael Davis, *The Image of Lincoln in the South*; Martin Abbott and Elmer L. Puryear, eds., "Beleaguered Charleston," 66.
17. [David McCord], "Slavery and the Abolitionists," *Southern Quarterly Review* 15 (1849): 199–200; *Pendleton Messenger*, May 8, 1851; W. F. Colcock, *Speech of the Hon. W. F. Colcock, Delivered before the Meeting of Delegates from the Southern Rights Associations of South Carolina, at Charleston, May 20, 1851*, 15–16.
18. [J. H. Conner?] to Armistead Burt, February 11, 1848, Armistead Burt Papers, William R. Perkins Library, Duke University; Pinckney, *An Oration, Delivered on the Fourth of July, 1851*, 16; William H. Barnwell, *Views upon the Present Crisis*, 10; John Townsend, *The Southern States, Their Present Peril and Their Certain Remedy*, 28; Christopher G. Memminger, *Address of the Hon. C. G. Memminger, Special Commissioner from the State of South Carolina, before the Assembled Authorities of the State of Virginia, January 19, 1860*, 37. See also One of the People [pseud.], *A Letter on Southern Wrongs and Southern Remedies*, 4; Samuel Gaillard Stoney, ed., "The Autobiography of William John Grayson," *South Carolina Historical and Genealogical Magazine* 5 (1949): 19; Robert W. Barnwell, *Southern Rights and Cooperation Documents. No. 2.* 3; William Gilmore Simms, *The Letters of William Gilmore Simms*, ed., Oliphant, Odell, Eaves, 3: 150.
19. Robert Barnwell Rhett, quoted in Harold S. Schultz, *Nationalism and Sectionalism in South Carolina, 1852–1860*, 23. See also Daniel Wallace, *The Political Life and Services of the Hon. R. Barnwell Rhett, of South Carolina*, 10.
20. Armistead Burt, *Southern Rights and Cooperation Documents. No. 3. Letter from the Hon. Armistead Burt*, 2.
21. W. Alston Pringle, *An Oration Delivered before the Fourth of July Association,*

at the Hibernian Hall, July Fourth, 1850, 22; Colcock, *Speech of the Hon. W. F. Colcock*, 15.

22. Prentiss, *A Sermon Preached at St. Peter's Church*, 17; Lawrence M. Keitt to Mr. Frederick Brown, March 4, 1861, Lawrence M. Keitt Papers, William R. Perkins Library, Duke University.
23. Elmer D. Johnson and Kathleen Lewis Sloan, eds., *South Carolina*, 351; Francis W. Pickens to Jefferson Davis, January 23, 1861, Francis W. Pickens Papers, South Caroliniana Library, University of South Carolina.
24. Grayson, "The Confederate Diary of William J. Grayson," ed., Puryear, 63: 143; C. Vann Woodward, ed., *Mary Chesnut's Civil War* (New Haven: Yale University Press, 1981), 7.
25. Quotations can be found in J. Mills Thornton III, *Politics and Power in a Slave Society*, 235–36, 367.
26. Quotations can be found in Michael P. Johnson, *Toward a Patriarchal Republic*, 12, 22, 31, 44, 56, 6.
27. Ulrich Bonnel Phillips, ed., "The Correspondence of Robert Toombs, Alexander H. Stephens and Howell Cobb," 2: 181–82; Haskell M. Monroe, Jr., and James T. McKintosh, eds., *The Papers of Jefferson Davis*, vol. 1 (Baton Rouge: Louisiana State University Press, 1971), 455.
28. William Kauffman Scarborough, ed., *The Diary of Edmund Ruffin*, vol. 1 (Baton Rouge: Louisiana State University Press, 1972), 66, 37–38; *Sumter Watchman*, cited in Harold S. Schultz, *Nationalism and Sectionalism in South Carolina, 1852-60*, 134. Leonard D. White, *The Jacksonians*, 16, concludes that "the South tended to maintain higher standards [in political conduct] than the North or the West." The skill with which Republicans wielded the new techniques of party organization and patronage is nicely described in Harry J. Carman and Reinhard H. Luthin, *Lincoln and the Patronage.*
29. The inevitable tension between the independence and dependence of the master seems at the heart of Hegel's analysis of lordship and bondage. G.W.F. Hegel, *The Phenomenology of Mind*, trans. J. B. Baillie, 228–40.
30. Freehling, "Spoilsmen and Interests in the Thought and Career of John C. Calhoun," offers an insightful analysis of a parallel contradiction in Calhoun's thought. The contradiction is that Calhoun never decided whether the real danger to republican government lay in corrupt spoilsmen motivated by their own material greed or in selfish interest groups. The tension between these two unresolved possibilities is a mirror image of the tension in Calhoun's ideal vision of the relationship between statesmen and their constituents. The statesman had to be independent of but also somehow connected to his constituents. The spoilsman engaged in serving his individual greed, yet he was also the tool of selfish interest groups.
31. Thornton, *Politics and Power in a Slave Society*, offers a detailed description of the way some Alabama statesmen were charged with attempting enslavement.
32. For some examples of this complaint see John Hope Franklin, *A Southern Odyssey*, 243; Robert J. Brugger, "The Mind of the Old South," 285; John McCardell, *The Idea of a Southern Nation*, 68.
33. John Barnwell, ed., "Hamlet to Hotspur: Letters of Robert Woodward Barn-

well to Robert Barnwell Rhett," *South Carolina Historical Magazine* 77, no. 4 (1976): 240, 250, 251.

34. [Robert J. Turnbull], *The Crisis*, 137, 151. Quoted in William W. Freehling, *Prelude to Civil War*, 127–28.
35. Justice Peter Vivian Daniel quoted in Don E. Fehrenbacher, "Roger B. Taney and the Sectional Crisis," 566; Phillips, "Correspondence of Robert Toombs, Alexander H. Stephens and Howell Cobb," 117–24; Holt, *Political Crisis of the 1850s*, 69, see also 54–55; Thornton, *Politics and Power in a Slave Society*, 58.
36. [Turnbull], *The Crisis*, 163; *Niles' Weekly Register*, vol. 33 (September 1827–March 1828): 28–32; J.F.H. Claiborne, ed., *Life and Correspondence of John A. Quitman, Major General, U.S.A. and Governor of the State of Mississippi*, vol. 2 (New York, 1860), 24; Phillips, "Correspondence of Robert Toombs, Alexander H. Stephens and Howell Cobb," 532.
37. *State Papers on Nullification*, 71; *Charleston Mercury*, December 20, 1832; Richard K. Crallé, ed., *The Works of John C. Calhoun*, vol. 2 (New York: D. Appleton and Co., 1853), 235.
38. "The Conspiracy of Fanaticism," *Camden Journal*, May 21, 1850; [William D. Porter], *Separate State Secession*, 22. Some of the quotations are cited in Holt, *Political Crisis of the 1850s*, 56, 242; Johnson, *Toward a Patriarchal Republic*, 36.
39. Thornton, *Politics and Power in a Slave Society*, 78.
40. Freehling, *Prelude to Civil War*, 314–21; James Petigru Carson, ed., *Life, Letters and Speeches of James Louis Petigru, the Union Man of South Carolina*, 167–70.
41. Don E. Fehrenbacher, "The Missouri Controversy and the Sources of Southern Separatism," 665.
42. David M. Potter, *The Impending Crisis, 1848-1861*, comp. and ed. Don E. Fehrenbacher, 113. A full account of the Compromise of 1850 can be found in Holman Hamilton, *Prologue to Conflict*.
43. John V. Mering, "The Slave-State Constitutional Unionists and the Politics of Consensus," 396–405; William S. Hitchcock, "The Limits of Southern Unionism," 60; Daniel P. Jordan, "Mississippi's Antebellum Congressmen," 175.
44. Ollinger Crenshaw, "The Speakership Contest of 1859–1860," 330.
45. Charles Sumner, *Kansas Affairs*, 3, 5, 29. The best account of the Sumner caning episode can be found in David Herbert Donald, *Charles Sumner and the Coming of the Civil War*, 278–311.
46. Donald, *Charles Sumner*, 289.
47. Ibid., 304.
48. Quoted in William E. Gienapp, "The Crime against Sumner," 222. Other samples of Southern opinion can be found in Donald, *Charles Sumner*, 304–7.

Bibliography

PRIMARY SOURCES

MANUSCRIPT COLLECTIONS

Numerous manuscript collections have been consulted. Included here are those cited in the notes.

William R. Perkins Library, Duke University, Durham, North Carolina

- Iveson Lewis Brookes
- Armistead Burt
- George Wymberly Jones DeRenne
- George A. Gordon
- Robert Newman Gourdin
- James Henry Hammond
- Hemphill Family
- Edward Thomas Heriot
- David Flavel Jamison
- Lawrence Masillon Keitt
- Francis Wilkinson Pickens

South Caroliniana Library, University of South Carolina, Columbia

- Milledge Luke Bonham
- James Henry Hammond
- Francis Wilkinson Pickens

Southern Historical Collection, University of North Carolina, Chapel Hill

- Nathaniel Russell Middleton
- Pettigrew Family Papers

PUBLISHED SOURCES

Abbott, Martin, and Puryear, Elmer L., eds. "Beleaguered Charleston: Letters from the City, 1860–64." *South Carolina Historical Magazine* 61 (1960): 65–68.

Ames, Fisher. *Works of Fisher Ames.* Edited by Seth Ames. New York: DaCapo Press, 1969.

Association of 1774, The. Pamphlet reprinted, Charleston, S.C., 1859.

Ayer, Lewis Malone, Jr. *An Address on the Question of Separate State Secession, to the People of Barnwell District.* Charleston, S.C., 1851.

———. *Southern Rights and the Cuban Question: An Address, Delivered at Whippy Swamp, on the Fourth of July, 1855.* Charleston, S.C., 1855.

Baldwin, Simeon E. *Life and Letters of Simeon Baldwin.* New Haven: Tuttle, Morehouse and Taylor Co., 1919.

Barnwell, Robert W. "Hamlet to Hotspur: Letters of Robert Woodward Barnwell to Robert Barnwell Rhett." Edited by John Barnwell. *South Carolina Historical Magazine* 77, no. 4 (1976): 236–56.

———. *Southern Rights and Cooperation Documents. No. 2. Remarks of the Hon. R. W. Barnwell, before the Convention of Southern Rights Associations in Charleston, May 1851.* N.p., 1851.

Barnwell, William H. *Views upon the Present Crisis: A Discourse Delivered in St. Peter's Church, Charleston, on the 6th of December, 1850, the Day of Fasting, Humiliation and Prayer, Appointed by the Legislature of South-Carolina.* Charleston, S.C., 1850.

Brookes, Iveson L. *A Defense of the South against the Reproaches and Incroachments of the North.* Hamburg, S.C., 1850.

Brooks, Preston. "Preston S. Brooks on the Caning of Charles Sumner." Edited by Robert L. Meriwether. *South Carolina Historical and Genealogical Magazine* 52 (1951): 1–4.

[Bryan, Edward B.]. *Letters to the Southern People Concerning the Acts of Congress and the Treaties with Great Britain, in Relation to the African Slave Trade.* Charleston: Walker, Evans and Co., 1858.

Burke, Edmund. *Burke's Politics: Selected Writings and Speeches of Edmund Burke on Reform, Revolution, and War.* Edited by Ross J. S. Hoffman and Paul Levack. New York. Alfred A. Knopf, 1949.

Burt, Armistead. *Southern Rights and Cooperation Documents. No. 3. Letter from the Hon. Armistead Burt.* N.p., 1851?

Calhoun, John C. "Calhoun Correspondence." Edited by James Franklin Jameson. In *Annual Report of the American Historical Association for the Year 1899.* 2 vols. Washington, D.C.: Government Printing Office, 1900.

[Calhoun, John C.] *Life of John C. Calhoun, Representing a Condensed History of Political Events from 1811 to 1843.* New York: Harper and Brothers, 1843.

Calhoun, John C. *The Papers of John C. Calhoun.* 15 vols. Edited by Robert L. Meriwether, Clyde N. Wilson, and W. Edwin Hemphill. Columbia: University of South Carolina Press, 1959–.

Calhoun, John C. *The Works of John C. Calhoun.* 6 vols. Edited by Richard K. Crallé. New York: D. Appleton and Co., 1854–57.

Carson, James Petigru, ed. *Life, Letters and Speeches of James Louis Petigru, the Union Man of South Carolina.* Washington, D.C.: W. H. Lowdermilk and Co., 1920.

Chesnut, Mary Boykin. *Mary Chesnut's Civil War.* Edited by C. Vann Woodward. New Haven: Yale University Press, 1981.

Cheves, Langdon. *Letter of the Honorable Langdon Cheves to the Editors of the Charleston Mercury.* N.p., September 11, 1844.

———. *Speech of the Hon. Langdon Cheves in the Southern Convention at Nashville, Tennessee, November 14, 1850.* N.p. 1850.

———. *Speech of the Hon. Langdon Cheves, Delivered before the Delegates of the Nashville Convention on Friday, November 15, 1850.* Columbia, S.C., 1850.

Coit, J. C. *An Address Delivered to the Freemen of Chesterfield District, on Tuesday, Second Day of Court Week, March 1851.* Columbia, S.C., 1851.

Colcock, W. F. *Speech of the Hon. W. F. Colcock, Delivered before the Meeting of Delegates from the Southern Rights Associations of South Carolina at Charleston, May 20, 1851.* Columbia, S.C., 1851.

Cooper, Thomas. "Dr. Thomas Cooper's Views in Retirement." Edited by Ernest M. Lander. *South Carolina Historical Magazine* 54 (1953): 173–84.

———. *Two Essays: 1. On the Foundation of the Civil Government: 2. On the Constitution of the United States.* Columbia, S.C., 1826.

Cuthbert, [Alfred]. *Speech of Mr. Cuthbert of Georgia, on the Petition of the Society of Friends of Lancaster County, Pennsylvania, Praying for the Abolition of Slavery in the District of Columbia.* Washington, D.C.: Blair and Rives, 1836.

Davis, Jefferson. *Constitutionalist. His Letters, Papers, and Speeches.* 10 vols. Edited by Dunbar Rowland Jackson: Mississippi Department of Archives and History, 1923.

———. *The Papers of Jefferson Davis.* Edited by Haskell L. Monroe and James T. McIntosh. Baton Rouge: Louisiana State University Press, 1971–.

DeBow, James D. B. *Compendium of the Seventh Census.* Washington, D.C., 1854.

[Drayton, William Henry]. *A Letter from Freeman of South Carolina to the Deputies of North America Assembled in the High Court of Congress at Philadelphia.* Charleston, S.C., 1774.

[Drayton, William]. *The South Vindicated from the Treason and Fanaticism of the Northern Abolitionists.* Philadelphia: H. Manly, 1836.

Elliott, Jonathan, ed. *The Debates in the Several State Conventions, on the Adoption of the Federal Constitution as Recommended by the General Convention at Philadelphia, in 1787.* 5 vols. Washington, D.C., 1856.

Evans, Josiah J. *South Carolina and Massachusetts. Speech of Hon. J. J. Evans, of South Carolina, in Reply to Mr. Sumner, of Massachusetts, Delivered in the United States Senate, June 23, 1856.* Washington, D.C., 1856.

Faust, Drew Gilpin, ed. *The Ideology of Slavery: Proslavery Thought in the Antebellum South, 1830–1860.* Baton Rouge: Louisiana State University Press, 1981.

Flagg, Charles E. B. *Oration Delivered before the '76 Association and Society of the Cincinnati, at Hibernian Hall, Charleston, S.C., on the 5th of July, 1858.* Charleston, S.C., 1858.

Funeral Oration Delivered at the Capitol in Washington over the Body of Jonathan Cilley. New York: Wiley and Putnam, 1838.

Furman, Richard. *Rev. Dr. Richard Furman's Exposition of the Views of the Baptists, Relative to the Coloured Population of the United States in a Communication to the Governor of South Carolina.* Charleston, S.C., 1823.

Gadsden, Christopher. *The Writings of Christopher Gadsden, 1746–1805.* Edited by Richard Walsh. Columbia: University of South Carolina Press, 1966.

Gervais, John Lewis. "Letters from John Lewis Gervais to Henry Laurens, 1771–1778." *South Carolina Historical Magazine* 66 (1965): 25–37.

A Glance at the Resources of the South in the Event of Separate and Hostile Collision with the North: Together with a Brief Examination into the Value of the Union to the South. Winnsboro, S.C., 1850.

Grayson, William J. "The Autobiography of William J. Grayson." Edited by Samuel Gaillard Stoney. *South Carolina Historical and Genealogical Magazine* 48 (1947): 125–33, 189–97; 49 (1948): 23–40, 88–103, 163–69, 216–24; 50 (1949): 19–28, 77–90, 131–43, 209–15; 51 (1950): 29–43, 103–17.

———. "The Confederate Diary of William J. Grayson." Edited by Elmer L. Puryear. *South Carolina Historical Magazine* 63 (1962): 137–49, 214–26.

———. *James Louis Petrigru: A Biograghical Sketch.* New York, 1866.

———. *Letters of Curtius.* Charleston, S.C., 1851.

Hamilton, Alexander. *The Papers of Alexander Hamilton.* 26 vols. Edited by Harold C. Syrett and Jacob E. Cooke. New York: Columbia University Press, 1961–79.

Hammond, James H. *Speech of the Hon. James H. Hammond, of South Carolina, on the Admission of Kansas, under the Lecompton Constitution.* Washington, D.C., 1858.

Hanckel, Thomas W. *Government and the Right of Revolution: An Oration Delivered before the '76 Association and the Cincinnati Society.* Charleston, S.C., 1859.

[Holland, Edwin C.] *A Refutation of the Calumnies Circulated against the Southern and Western States Respecting the Institution and Existence of Slavery among Them.* Charleston, S.C., 1822.

Jackson, Andrew. *Correspondence of Andrew Jackson.* 7 vols. Edited by John Spencer Bassett and James F. Jameson. Washington, D.C.: Carnegie Institution, 1926–35.

Jacobs, Ferdinand. *The Committing of Our Cause to God: A Sermon Preached in the Second Presbyterian Church, Charleston, S.C. on Friday, the 6th of December.* Charleston, S.C., 1850.

Johnson, Elmer D., and Sloan, Kathleen Lewis, eds. *South Carolina: A Documentary Profile of the Palmetto State.* Columbia: University of South Carolina Press, 1971.

Johnson, Samuel. *Political Writings: The Works of Samuel Johnson.* Edited by Donald J. Greene. New Haven: Yale University Press, 1977.

Johnston, Paul. *The Electoral Question Discussed, and the Expediency, the Republicanism, and the Constitutionality of Appointing the Presidential Electors by the Members of the General Assembly (as Directed by the Statute of South Carolina of 1792) Vindicated.* Columbia, S.C., 1856.

"Letters on the Nullification Movement in South Carolina, 1830–1834." *American Historical Review* 7 (1901): 736–65.

Lincoln, Abraham. *The Collected Works of Abraham Lincoln.* 9 vols. Edited by Roy P. Basler. New Brunswick, N.J.: Rutgers University Press, 1953–55.

Littell, John Stockton. *Memoirs of His Own Times with Reminiscences of the Man and Events of the Revolution by Alexander Grayden.* Philadelphia: Lindsay and Blakiston, 1846.

McKitrick, Eric L., ed. *Slavery Defended: The Views of the Old South.* Englewood Cliffs, N.J.: Prentice-Hall, 1963.

Mangum, Willie Person. *The Papers of Willie Person Mangum.* 5 vols. Edited by Henry Thomas Shanks. Raleigh: North Carolina State Department of Archives and History, 1955.

Manning, John L. *An Oration Delivered on the Fourth of July, 1848, before the Cincinnati Society, and the '76 Association.* Charleston, S.C., 1848.

Maury, General Dabney Herndon. *Recollections of a Virginian in the Mexican, Indian, and Civil Wars.* London: Sampson Low, Marston and Co., 1894.

Memminger, C. G. *Address of the Hon. C. G. Memminger, Special Commissioner from the State of South Carolina, before the Assembled Authorities of the State of Virginia, January 19, 1860.* N.p., 1860?

Middleton, Henry. *Economical Causes of Slavery in the United States and Obstacles to Abolition.* London, 1857.

Northrop, Claudian B. *An Oration Delivered in St. Mary's Church before the Washington Society, on the 4th of July, 1843.* Charleston, S.C., 1843.

Olmsted, Fredrick Law. *A Journey in the Back Country.* New York: Mason Brothers, 1860.

One of the People [pseud.]. *A Letter on Southern Wrongs and Southern Remedies. Addressed to the Hon. W. J. Grayson, in Reply to His Letter to the Governor of South Carolina on the Dissolution of the Union.* Charleston, S.C., 1850.

Petigru, James Louis. *Oration Delivered on the Third Anniversary of the South Carolina Historical Society, at Hibernian Hall, in Charleston, on Thursday Evening, May 27, 1858.* Charleston, S.C., 1858.

Phillips, Ulrich B., ed. "The Correspondence of Robert Toombs, Alexander H. Stephens, and Howell Cobb." *Annual Report of the American Historical Association for the Year 1911.* Vol. 2. Washington, D.C., 1913.

Pickens, Francis W. *Speech of the Hon. F. W. Pickens, Delivered before a Public Meeting of the People of the District, Held at Edgefield, C.H., S.C., July 7, 1851.* N.p., 1851.

Pinckney, Henry L., Jr. *An Oration Delivered on the Fourth of July, 1851, before the '76 and Cincinnati Societies.* Charleston, S.C., 1851.

Poore, Benjamin P. *The Federal and State Constitutions, Colonial Charters, and Other Organic Laws of the United States.* Part 2. Washington, D.C., 1877.

Porcher, Frederick A. "The Memoirs of Frederick Adolphus Porcher." Edited by Samuel Gaillard Stoney. *South Carolina Historical and Genealogical Magazine* 46 (1945): 25–39, 78–92, 140–58, 198–208; 47 (1946): 32–52, 83–108, 150–62, 214–27; 48 (1947): 20–25.

Porter, William D. *Semi-Centennial Address. An Oration Delivered before the Washington Light Infantry, in the South Carolina Institute Hall, on Monday, February 23, 1857. In Commemoration of the One Hundred and Twenty-fifth Anniversary of the Birth of Washington.* Charleston, 1857.

———. *Separate State Secession, Practically Discussed, in a Series of Articles Published Originally in the Edgefield Advertiser.* Edgefield, S.C., 1851.

[Prentiss, S. S.]. *A Memoir of S. S. Prentiss.* New York: Charles Scribner, 1856.

Prentiss, William O. *A Sermon Preached at St. Peter's Church, Charleston . . . on*

Wednesday, Nov. 21, 1860, . . . on Contemplation of the Secession of the State from the Union. Charleston, S.C., 1860.

[Pringle, Edward J.]. *Slavery in the Southern States.* Cambridge, Mass., 1852.

Pringle, W. Alston. *An Oration Delivered before the Fourth of July Association, at the Hibernian Hall, July Fourth, 1850.* Charleston, S.C., 1850.

The Pro-Slavery Argument; as Maintained by the Most Distinguished Writers of the Southern States Containing the Several Essays on the Subject, of Chancellor Harper, Governor Hammond, Dr. Simms, and Professor Dew. Charleston: Walker, Richards and Co., 1852. New York: Negro Universities Press, 1968.

Quincy, Josiah. *The Journals of Major Samuel Shaw, the First American Consul at Canton.* Taipei: Ch'eng-Wen Publishing Co., 1968.

Quitman, John Anthony. *Life and Correspondence of John A. Quitman, Major General, U.S.A. and Governor of the State of Mississippi.* 2 vols. Edited by J.F.H. Claiborne. New York: 1860.

Ruffin, Edmund. *The Diary of Edmund Ruffin.* 2 vols. Edited by William Kauffman Scarborough. Baton Rouge: Louisiana State University Press, 1972.

Schoolcraft, Mrs. Henry R. *The Black Gauntlet: A Tale of Plantation Life in South Carolina.* Philadelphia, 1861.

Schurz, Carl. *The Reminiscences of Carl Schurz, 1852–1863.* 3 vols. New York: McLure and Co., 1907.

Scudder, H. E., ed. *Men and Manners in America One Hundred Years Ago.* New York: Charles Scribner, 1887.

Simms, William Gilmore. *The History of South Carolina.* Charleston, S.C., 1842.

———. *The Letters of William Gilmore Simms.* 5 vols. Edited by Mary C. Simms Oliphant, Alfred Taylor Odell, and T. C. Duncan Eaves. Columbia: University of South Carolina Press, 1952–56.

———, ed. *The Army Correspondence of Colonel John Laurens in the Years 1777–78.* New York, 1867.

Smith, William Loughton. "The Letters of William Loughton Smith to Edward Rutledge, June 8, 1789 to April 1, 1794." Edited by George C. Rogers, Jr. *South Carolina Historical Magazine* 70 (1969): 1–25, 101–38, 225–42; 71 (1970): 38–58.

State Papers on Nullification Including the Public Acts of the Convention of the People of South Carolina, Assembled at Columbia, November 19, 1832, and March, 1833. Boston: Dutton and Wentworth, 1834.

Sumner, Charles. *Kansas Affairs: Speech . . . in the Senate of the United States, May 19, 1856.* New York: Greeley and McElrath, 1856.

Tennent, William. *An Address, Occassioned by the Late Invasion of the Liberties of the American Colonies.* Philadelphia, 1774.

Thornwell, James H. *The Rights and Duties of Masters. A Sermon Preached at the Dedication of a Church, Erected in Charleston, S.C., for the Benefit and Instruction of the Coloured Population.* Charleston, S.C., 1850.

[Townsend, John]. *The Doom of Slavery in the Union: Its Safety out of It.* Charleston, S.C., 1860.

———. *Reply of Mr. Townsend, in Defense of His Public Conduct, against Certain Charges Made against Him.* Charleston, S.C., 1858.

———. *The Southern States, Their Present Peril and Their Certain Remedy. Why Do They Not Right Themselves? and So Fulfill Their Glorious Destiny.* Charleston, S.C., 1850.

Tragle, Henry Irving, ed. *The Southampton Slave Revolt of 1831.* Amherst: University of Massachusetts Press, 1971.

Trescot, William Henry. *Annual Address before the Calliopean and Polytechnic Societies of the Citadel Academy, Charleston, S.C.* Charleston, S.C., 1856.

———. *Oration: Delivered before the Washington Light Infantry, on the 22d February, 1847.* Charleston, S.C., 1847.

———. *The Position and Course of the South.* Charleston, S.C.: Walker and James, 1850.

Tucker, Thomas Tudor. *Conciliatory Hints, Attempting by a Fair State of Matters, to Remove Party Prejudice.* Charleston, S.C., 1784.

[Turnbull, Robert J.]. *The Crisis.* Charleston, S.C., 1827.

Van Buren, Martin. "The Autobiography of Martin Van Buren." Edited by John C. Fitzpatrick. *Annual Report of the American Historical Association for the Year 1918.* Vol. 2. Washington, D.C., 1918.

[Wallace, Daniel.]. *Letter of Daniel Wallace of South Carolina to His Constituents.* N.p., 1850?

———. *The Political Life and Services of the Hon. R. Barnwell Rhett, of South Carolina. By "a Contemporary." And Also, His Speech at Grahamville, S.C., July 4th 1859.* Cahawba, Ala., 1859.

Washington, George. *The Writings of George Washington.* 39 vols. Edited by John C. Fitzpatrick. Washington, D.C.: Government Printing Office, 1931–44.

Webster, Daniel. *The Papers of Daniel Webster.* 6 vols. Edited by Charles M. Wiltse. Hanover, N.H.: University of New England, for Dartmouth College, 1974.

Wilson, John Lyde. *The Code of Honor or Rules for the Government of Principles and Seconds in Duelling.* Charleston: Thomas J. Eccles, 1838.

Wish, Harvey, ed. *Antebellum: Writings of George Fitzhugh and Hinton Rowan Helper on Slavery.* New York: G. P. Putnam's Sons, Capricorn Books, 1960.

SECONDARY SOURCES

Abernethy, Thomas P. *The South in the New Nation, 1789–1819.* Baton Rouge: Louisiana State University Press, 1961.

Alden, John Richard. *The South in the Revolution, 1763–1789.* Baton Rouge: Louisiana State University Press, 1957.

Alexander, Thomas B. "The Civil War as Institutional Fulfillment." *Journal of Southern History* 47 (February 1981): 3–32.

———, and Beringer, Richard E. *The Anatomy of the Confederate Congress.* Nashville: Vanderbilt University Press, 1972.

Alexander, Thomas B.; Elmore, Peggy Duckworth; Lowry, Frank M.; Skinner, Mary Jane Pickens. "The Basis of Alabama's Ante-Bellum Two-Party System." *Alabama Review* 19 (October 1966): 243–76.

Bailyn, Bernard. *The Ideological Origins of the American Revolution.* Cambridge: Harvard University Press, 1967.

Baldick, Robert. *The Duel: A History of Dueling.* London: Chapman and Hall, 1965.

Banner, James M., Jr. "The Problem of South Carolina." *The Hofstadter Aegis: A Memorial.* Edited by Stanley Elkins and Eric McKitrick. New York: Alfred A. Knopf, 1974.

Banning, Lance. *The Jeffersonian Persuasion: Evolution of a Party Ideology.* Ithaca: Cornell University Press, 1978.

Barney, William L. *The Secessionist Impulse: Alabama and Mississippi in 1860.* Princeton: Princeton University Press, 1974.

Bemis, Samuel Flagg. *Jay's Treaty: A Study in Commerce and Diplomacy.* New Haven: Yale University Press, 1923.

Blasingame, John W. "American Nationalism and Other Loyalties in the Southern Colonies, 1763–1775." *Journal of Southern History* 34 (February 1968): 50–75.

Boorstin, Daniel J. *The Americans: The National Experience.* New York: Vintage Books, 1965.

Boucher, Chauncey Samuel. "The Annexation of Texas and the Bluffton Movement in South Carolina." *Mississippi Valley Historical Review* 6, no. 1 (1919): 3–33.

———. "Sectionalism, Representation and the Electoral Question in Ante-Bellum South Carolina." *Washington University Studies* 4, pt. 2, no. 1 (1916): 3–62.

Braden, Waldo W. *Oratory in the Old South, 1828-1860.* Baton Rouge: Louisiana State University Press, 1970.

Breeden, James O., ed. *Advice among Masters: The Ideal in Slave Management in the Old South.* Westport, Conn.: Greenwood Press, 1980.

Breen, T. H. "Horses and Gentlemen: The Cultural Significance of Gambling among the Gentry of Virginia." *William and Mary Quarterly* 3d ser. 34, no. 2 (1977): 239–57.

Bridenbaugh, Carl. *Myths and Realities: Societies of the Colonial South.* Baton Rouge: Louisiana State University Press, 1952.

Broussard, James H. *The Southern Federalists, 1800-1816.* Baton Rouge: Louisiana State University Press, 1978.

Brown, Richard Maxwell. *The South Carolina Regulators: The Story of the First American Vigilante Movement.* Cambridge: Belknap Press of Harvard University Press, 1963.

———. *Strain of Violence: Historical Studies of American Violence and Vigilantism.* New York: Oxford University Press, 1975.

Brown, Thomas. "Southern Whigs and the Politics of Statesmanship, 1833–1841." *Journal of Southern History* 46, no. 3 (1980): 361–80.

Bruce, Dickson D. *Violence and Culture in the Antebellum South.* Austin: University of Texas Press, 1979.

Bruce, William Cabell. *John Randolph of Roanoke,* 1773–1833. 2 vols. New York: G. P. Putnam's Sons, 1922.

Brugger, Robert J. "The Mind of the Old South: New Views." *Virginia Quarterly Review* 56, no. 2 (1980): 277–295.

Burnham, W. Dean. *Presidential Ballots, 1836-1892.* Baltimore: Johns Hopkins University Press, 1959.

BIBLIOGRAPHY

Burrows, Edwin G., and Wallace, Michael. "The American Revolution: The Ideology and Psychology of National Liberation." *Perspectives in American History* 6 (1972): 167–306.

Campbell, Randolph B. "Planters and Plain Folk: Harrison County, Texas as a Test Case, 1850–1860." *Journal of Southern History* 40 (August 1974): 369–98.

———. "Political Conflict within the Southern Consensus: Harrison County, Texas 1850–1880." *Civil War History* 26 (September 1980): 218–39.

Carman, Harry J., and Luthin, Reinhard H. *Lincoln and the Patronage.* New York: Columbia University Press, 1943.

Chambers, William Nisbet. *Political Parties in a New Nation: The American Experience, 1776-1809.* New York: Oxford University Press, 1963.

———, and Burnham, Walter Dean, eds. *The American Party Systems: Stages of Political Development.* New York: Oxford University Press, 1967.

Channing, Steven A. *Crisis of Fear: Secession in South Carolina.* New York: W. W. Norton and Co., 1970.

Clinton, Catherine. *The Plantation Mistress: Woman's World in the Old South.* New York: Pantheon Books, 1982.

Clubb, Jerome M.; Flanigan, William H.; and Zingale, Nancy H. *Partisan Realignment: Voters, Parties, and Government in American History.* Beverly Hills, Calif.: Sage Publications, 1980.

Coleman, J. Winston. *The Trotter-Wickliffe Duel.* Frankfort, Ky.: Roberts Printing Co., 1950.

Conkin, Paul K. *Self-Evident Truths.* Bloomington: Indiana University Press, 1974.

Cooper, William J., Jr. *The South and the Politics of Slavery, 1828-1856* Baton Rouge: Louisiana State University Press, 1978.

Cox, Joseph W. *Champion of Southern Federalism: Robert Goodloe Harper of South Carolina.* Port Washington, N.Y.: Kennikat Press, 1972.

Crenshaw, Ollinger. "The Speakership Contest of 1859–1860." *Mississippi Valley Historical Review* 29 (1942): 323–38.

Current, Richard N. *Daniel Webster and the Rise of National Conservatism.* Boston: Little, Brown, and Co., 1955.

Dalzell, Robert F., Jr. *Daniel Webster and the Trial of American Nationalism 1843-1852.* New York: W. W. Norton and Co., 1972.

Davidson, Chalmers Gaston. *The Last Foray: The South Carolina Planters of 1860: A Sociological Study.* Columbia: University of South Carolina Press, 1971.

Davis, Michael. *The Image of Lincoln in the South.* Knoxville: University of Tennessee Press, 1971.

Donald, David Herbert. *Charles Sumner and the Coming of the Civil War.* Chicago: University of Chicago Press, 1960.

———, ed. *Why the North Won the Civil War.* New York: Collier Books, 1967.

Duverger, Maurice. *Political Parties: Their Organization and Activity in the Modern State.* New York: John Wiley and Sons, 1955.

Eaton, Clement. *The Freedom of Thought Struggle in the Old South.* New York: Harper and Row, 1964.

———. *Henry Clay and the Art of American Politics.* Boston: Little, Brown and Co., 1957.

———. "Southern Senators and the Right of Instruction, 1789–1860." *Journal of Southern History* 18 (August 1952): 303–19.

Edgar, Walter B., ed. *Biographical Directory of the South Carolina House of Representatives*. Vol. 1. *Session Lists 1692–1973*. Columbia: University of South Carolina Press, 1974.

Elkins, Stanley, and McKitrick, Eric. "A Meaning for Turner's Frontier." *Political Science Quarterly* 69, no. 3 (1954): 321–53, 565–602.

Fehrenbacher, Don E. "The Missouri Controversy and the Sources of Southern Separatism." *Southern Review* (Autumn 1978): 653–67.

———. "Roger B. Taney and the Sectional Crisis." *Journal of Southern History* 43, no. 4 (1977): 555–66.

Fischer, David Hackett. *The Revolution of American Conservatism: The Federalist Party in the Era of Jeffersonian Democracy*. New York: Harper and Row, 1965.

Fladeland, Betty. *Men and Brothers: Anglo-American Antislavery Cooperation*. Urbana: University of Illinois Press, 1972.

Fogel, Robert W., and Engerman, Stanley L. *Time on the Cross: The Economics of American Negro Slavery*. 2 vols. Boston: Little, Brown, and Co., 1974.

Foner, Eric. *Free Soil, Free Labor, Free Men*. New York: Oxford University Press, 1970.

Formisano, Ronald P. "Deferential-Participant Politics: The Early Republic's Political Culture, 1789–1840." *American Political Science Review* 68 (June 1974): 473–87.

———. "Toward a Reorientation of Jacksonian Politics: A Review of the Literature, 1959–1975." *Journal of American History* 63 (June 1976): 42–65.

Foster, William Omer. *James Jackson: Duelist and Militant Statesman, 1757–1806*. Athens: University of Georgia Press, 1960.

Franklin, John Hope. *The Militant South*. New York: Beacon Press, 1956.

———. *A Southern Odyssey: Travelers in the Antebellum North*. Baton Rouge: Louisiana State University Press, 1976.

Frederickson, George M. *The Black Image in the White Mind: The Debate on Afro-American Character and Destiny, 1817–1914*. New York: Harper and Row, 1971.

Freehling, William W. "The Founding Fathers and Slavery." *American Historical Review* 77 (1972): 81–93.

———. *Prelude to Civil War: The Nullification Controversy in South Carolina, 1816–1836*. New York: Harper Torchbooks, 1968.

———. "Spoilsmen and Interests in the Thought and Career of John C. Calhoun." *Journal of American History* 52 (1965): 25–42.

Friedman, Jean E. *The Revolt of the Conservative Democrats: An Essay on American Political Culture and Political Development, 1837–1844*. [Ann Arbor, Mich.]: UMI Research Press, 1979.

Gallman, Robert E., and Anderson, Ralph V. "Slaves as Fixed Capital: Slave Labor and Southern Economic Development." *Journal of American History* 64 (June 1977): 24–46.

Geertz, Clifford. *The Interpretation of Cultures*. New York: Basic Books, 1973.

Genovese, Eugene D. *Roll, Jordan, Roll: The World the Slaves Made*. New York: Pantheon Books, 1974.

———. *The Political Economy of Slavery: Studies in the Economy and Society of the Slave South*. New York: Vintage Books, 1961.

———. *The World the Slaveholders Made: Two Essays in Interpretation*. New York: Vintage Books, 1971.

———. "Yeoman Farmers in a Slaveholders' Democracy." *Agricultural History* 49 (April 1975): 331–42.

Gienapp, William E. "The Crime against Sumner: The Caning of Charles Sumner and the Rise of the Republican Party." *Civil War History* 25, no. 3 (1979): 218–45.

Goldman, Perry M. "Political Virtue in the Age of Jackson." *Political Science Quarterly* 87 (March 1972): 46–62.

Gould, Stephan Jay. *The Mismeasure of Man*. New York: W. W. Norton and Co., 1981.

Green, Fletcher M. *Constitutional Development in the South Atlantic States, 1776-1860: A Study in the Evolution of Democracy*. Chapel Hill: University of North Carolina Press, 1930.

———. *Democracy in the Old South and Other Essays*. Edited by J. Isaac Copeland. Nashville: University of Tennessee Press, 1969.

Greenberg, Kenneth S. "Civil War Revisionism." *Reviews in American History* 7 (1979): 202–8.

———. "Representation and the Isolation of South Carolina, 1776–1860." *Journal of American History* 64 (1977): 723–43.

———. "Revolutionary Ideology and the Proslavery Argument: The Abolition of Slavery in Antebellum South Carolina." *Journal of Southern History* 42 (1976): 365–84.

Greene, Evarts B. "The Code of Honor in Colonial and Revolutionary Times, with Special Reference to New England." *Publications of the Colonial Society of Massachusetts* 26. Boston: Colonial Society of Massachusetts, 1927, 367–88.

Greene, Jack P. *The Quest for Power: The Lower Houses of Assembly in the Southern Royal Colonies, 1689-1776*. Chapel Hill: University of North Carolina Press, 1963.

———. " 'Slavery or Independence.' Some Reflections on the Relationship among Liberty, Black Bondage, and Equality in Revolutionary South Carolina." *South Carolina Historical Magazine* 80, no. 3 (1979): 193–213.

Gunderson, Robert Gray. *The Log-Cabin Campaign*. Lexington: University of Kentucky Press, 1957.

Hamer, Philip M. "Great Britain, the United States and Negro Seamen Acts, 1822–1848." *Journal of Southern History* 1, no. 1 (1935): 3–28.

Hamilton, Holman. *Prologue to Conflict: The Crisis and Compromise of 1850*. New York: W. W. Norton and Co., 1964.

Hamilton, J. G. de Roulhac. "Southern Members of the Inns of Court." *North Carolina Historical Review* 10 (October 1933): 273–86.

Hechter, Michael. *International Colonialism: The Celtic Fringe in British National Development, 1536–1966.* Berkeley and Los Angeles: University of California Press, 1975.

Hegel, G.W.F. *The Phenomenology of Mind.* Translated by J. B. Baillie. New York: Harper and Row, 1967.

Hitchcock, William S. "The Limits of Southern Unionism: Virginia Conservatives and the Gubernatorial Election of 1859." *Journal of Southern History* 47, no. 1 (1981): 57–72.

Hofstadter, Richard. *The American Political Tradition and the Men Who Made It.* New York: Alfred A. Knopf, 1948.

———. *The Idea of a Party System: The Rise of Legitimate Opposition in the United States, 1780–1840.* Berkeley: University of California Press, 1969.

Holman, C. Hugh. "William Gilmore Simms' Picture of the Revolution as a Civil Conflict." *Journal of Southern History* 15 (1949): 441–62.

Holt, Michael F. *The Political Crisis of the 1850s.* New York: John Wiley and Sons, 1978.

Howe, Daniel Walker. *The Political Culture of the American Whigs.* Chicago: University of Chicago Press, 1979.

James, Marquis. *Andrew Jackson, The Border Captain.* Indianapolis: Bobbs-Merrill Co., 1933.

January, Alan F. "The South Carolina Association: An Agency for Race Control in Antebellum Charleston." *South Carolina Historical Magazine* 78, no. 3 (1977): 191–201.

Jeffrey, Thomas E. " 'Thunder from the Mountains': Thomas Lanier Clingman and the End of Whig Supremacy in North Carolina." *North Carolina Historical Review* 56 (October 1979) 366–95.

Jenkins, William Sumner. *Pro-Slavery Thought in the Old South.* Chapel Hill: University of North Carolina Press, 1935.

Jervey, Theodore D. *Robert Y. Hayne and His Times.* New York: Macmillan Co., 1909.

Johnson, Michael P. *Toward a Patriarchal Republic: The Secession of Georgia.* Baton Rouge: Louisiana State University Press, 1977.

Jones, Howard. "The Peculiar Institution and National Honor: The Case of the *Creole* Slave Revolt." *Civil War History* 21, no. 1 (1975): 28–50.

———. *To the Webster-Ashburton Treaty: A Study in Anglo-American Relations, 1783–1843.* Chapel Hill: University of North Carolina Press, 1977.

Jones, Wilbur Deveraux, "The Influence of Slavery on the Webster-Ashburton Negotiations." *Journal of Southern History* 22 (1956): 48–58.

Jordan, Daniel P. "John Randolph of Roanoke and the Art of Winning Elections in Jeffersonian Virginia." *Virginia Magazine of History and Biography* 86, no. 4 (1978): 389–407.

———. "Mississippi's Antebellum Congressmen: A Collective Biography." *Journal of Mississippi History* 38, no. 2 (1976): 157–82.

Kelley, Robert. *The Cultural Pattern in American Politics: The First Century.* New York: Alfred A. Knopf, 1979.

Kendall, John S. "According to the Code." *Louisiana Historical Quarterly* 23 (January–October 1940): 141–61.

Kernell, Samuel. "Toward Understanding 19th Century Congressional Careers: Ambition, Competition and Rotation." *American Journal of Political Sciences* 21, no. 4 (1977): 669–93.

Kibler, Lillian Adele. *Benjamin F. Perry, South Carolina Unionist.* Durham: Duke University Press, 1946.

Kirwan, Albert D. *John J. Crittendon: The Struggle for the Union.* Lexington: University of Kentucky Press, 1962.

Kleppner, Paul. *The Third Electoral System, 1853-1892: Parties, Voters and Political Cultures.* Chapel Hill: University of North Carolina Press, 1979.

Land, Aubrey C.; Carr, Lois Green; and Papenfuse, Edward C., eds. *Law, Society and Politics in Early Maryland.* Baltimore: Johns Hopkins University Press, 1977.

LaPalombra, Joseph, and Weiner, Myron, eds. *Political Parties and Political Development.* Princeton: Princeton University Press, 1966.

Latimer, Margaret Kinard. "South Carolina, a Protagonist of the War of 1812." *American Historical Review* 61 (July 1956): 914–29.

Lofton, John. *Insurrection in South Carolina: The Turbulent World of Denmark Vesey.* Yellow Springs, Ohio: Antioch Press, 1964.

Long, David F. *Nothing Too Daring: A Biography of Commodore David Porter, 1780-1843.* Annapolis: U.S. Naval Institute, 1970.

Lynch, Denis Tilden. *An Epoch and a Man: Martin Van Buren and His Times.* New York: Horace Liveright, 1929.

McCardell, John. *The Idea of a Southern Nation: Southern Nationalists and Southern Nationalism, 1830-1860.* New York: W. W. Norton and Co., 1979.

McCormick, Richard P. *The Second American Party System: Party Formation in the Jacksonian Era.* New York: W. W. Norton and Co., 1973. Originally published Chapel Hill: University of North Carolina Press, 1966.

McCoy, Drew R. *The Elusive Republic: Political Economy in Jeffersonian America.* Chapel Hill: University of North Carolina Press, 1980.

McDonald, Forrest. "The Ethnic Factor in Alabama History: A Neglected Dimension." *Alabama Review* 31, no. 4 (1978): 256–65.

McDonald, Forrest and McDonald, Ellen Shapiro. "The Ethnic Origins of the American People." *William and Mary Quarterly* 37, 3d ser., no. 2 (1980): 179–99.

McDonald, Forrest and McWhiney, Grady. "The Celtic South." *History Today* 30 (July 1980): 11–15.

———. "The South from Self-Sufficiency to Peonage: An Interpretation." *American Historical Review* 85, no. 5 (1980): 1095–1118.

Maier, Pauline. "The Road Not Taken: Nullification, John C. Calhoun, and the Revolutionary Tradition in South Carolina." *South Carolina Historical Magazine* 82 (1981): 1–19.

May, John Amasa, and Faunt, Joan Reynolds. *South Carolina Secedes.* Columbia: University of South Carolina Press, 1960.

May, Robert E. *The Southern Dream of a Caribbean Empire, 1854-1861.* Baton Rouge: Louisiana State University Press, 1973.

Mayo, Bernard. *Henry Clay: Spokesman of the New West.* Boston: Houghton Mifflin, 1937.

Merck, Frederick. *Fruits of Propaganda in the Tyler Administration.* Cambridge: Harvard University Press, 1971.

Mering, John V. "The Slave-State Constitutional Unionists and the Politics of Consensus." *Journal of Southern History* 43, no. 3 (1977): 395–410.

Morgan, Edmund S. *American Slavery, American Freedom: The Ordeal of Colonial Virginia.* New York: W. W. Norton and Co., 1975.

Moss, James E. *Duelling in Missouri History.* Kansas City: Kansas City Posse of the Westerners, 1966.

Nichols, Roy Franklin. *The Disruption of American Democracy.* New York: Macmillan Co., 1948.

Parish, John Carl. *George Wallace Jones.* Iowa City: State Historical Society of Iowa, 1912.

Patterson, Orlando. *Slavery and Social Death: A Comparative Study.* Cambridge: Harvard University Press, 1982.

Paulin, Charles Oscar. *Commodore John Rodgers.* Cleveland: Arthur H. Clark Co., 1910.

———. *Duelling in the Old Navy.* Reprinted from the United States Naval Institute Proceedings. Vol. 35, no. 4, whole no. 132. [Annapolis: U.S. Naval Institute], 1909.

Pessen, Edward. *Jacksonian America: Society, Personality and Politics.* Homewood, Ill.: The Dorsey Press, 1969; rev. ed., 1979.

Phillips, Ulrich B. "The Southern Whigs, 1834–1854." *Turner Essays in American History.* New York: Henry Holt and Co., 1910.

Pitkin, Hannah Fenichel. *The Concept of Representation.* Berkeley: University of California Press, 1967.

Pitt-Rivers, Julian. "Honor." *Encyclopedia of the Social Sciences,* 2d edition. Vol. 6. New York: Macmillan Co., 1968, 503–511.

Pocock, J.G.A. "Machiavelli, Harrington, and English Political Ideologies in the Eighteenth Century." *William and Mary Quarterly,* 3d ser., 22 (1965): 549–83.

———. *The Machiavellian Moment: Florentine Political Thought and the Atlantic Republican Tradition.* Princeton: Princeton University Press, 1975.

Potter, David M. *The Impending Crisis, 1848-1861.* Compiled and edited by Don E. Fehrenbacher. New York: Harper and Row, 1976.

Pye, Lucian W., and Verba, Sidney, eds. *Political Culture and Political Development.* Princeton: Princeton University Press, 1965.

Randall, James G. "The Blundering Generation." *Mississippi Valley Historical Review* 27 (1940): 3–28.

Remini, Robert V. *The Election of Andrew Jackson.* Philadelphia: J. B. Lippincott Co., 1963.

Rhea, Linda. *Hugh Swinton Legaré: A Charleston Intellectual.* Chapel Hill: University of North Carolina Press, 1934.

Ridgway, Whitman H. *Community Leadership in Maryland, 1790-1840: A Comparative Analysis of Power in Society.* Chapel Hill: University of North Carolina Press, 1979.

Robinson, Donald L. *Slavery in the Structure of American Politics, 1765-1820.* New York: Harcourt, Brace, Jovanovich, 1971.

Rogers, George C., Jr. *Evolution of a Federalist: William Loughton Smith of Charleston (1758–1812).* Columbia: University of South Carolina Press, 1962.

Rose, Lisle A. *Prologue to Democracy: The Federalists in the South, 1789–1800.* Lexington: University of Kentucky Press, 1968.

Rutledge, William S. "Dueling in Antebellum Mississippi." *Journal of Mississippi History* 26, no. 3 (1964): 181–91.

Sabine, Lorenzo. *Notes on Duels and Duelling, Alphabetically Arranged, with a Preliminary Historical Essay.* Boston: Crosby, Nichols and Co., 1856.

"Samuel Hoar's Expulsion from Charleston." *Old South Leaflets No. 140.* Boston: Directors of the Old South Work, n.d.

Scarborough, William Kauffman. *The Overseer: Plantation Management in the Old South.* Baton Rouge: Louisiana State University Press, 1966.

Schaper, William A. "Sectionalism and Representation in South Carolina." *Annual Report of the American Historical Association for the Year 1900.* 2 vols. Washington, D.C., 1901.

Schultz, Harold S. *Nationalism and Sectionalism in South Carolina, 1852–1860: A Study of the Movement for Southern Independence.* Durham: Duke University Press, 1950.

Sellers, Charles G., Jr. "Who Were the Southern Whigs?" *American Historical Review* 59, no. 2 (1954): 335–46.

———, ed. *The Southerner as American.* Chapel Hill: University of North Carolina Press, 1960.

Silbey, Joel H. *A Respectable Minority: The Democratic Party in the Civil War Era, 1860–1868.* New York: W. W. Norton and Co., 1977.

———; Bogue, Allan G.; Flanigan, William H., eds. *The History of American Electoral Behavior.* Princeton: Princeton University Press, 1978.

Stanton, William. *The Leopard's Spots: Scientific Attitudes toward Race in America, 1815–1859.* Chicago: University of Chicago Press, 1960.

Strout, Cushing. *The American Image of the Old World.* New York: Harper and Row, 1963.

Swieranga, Robert P., ed. *Beyond the Civil War Synthesis.* Westport, Conn.: Greenwood Press, 1975.

Taylor, Rosser H. *Ante-Bellum South Carolina: A Social and Cultural History. James Sprunt Studies in History and Political Science.* Vol. 25, no. 2. Chapel Hill: University of North Carolina Press, 1942.

Taylor, William R. *Cavalier and Yankee: The Old South and American National Character.* Garden City, N.Y.: Doubleday, Anchor Books, 1963.

Thornton, J. Mills, III. *Politics and Power in a Slave Society: Alabama, 1800–1860.* Baton Rouge: Louisiana State University Press, 1978.

Turner, Victor. *The Drums of Affliction: A Study of Religious Processes among the Ndembu of Zambia.* Ithaca: Cornell University Press, 1981.

Tushnet, Mark. *Considerations of Humanity and Interest: The American Law of Slavery, 1810–1860.* Princeton: Princeton University Press, 1981.

Wakelyn, Jon L. *The Politics of a Literary Man: William Gilmore Simms.* Westport, Conn.: Greenwood Press, 1973.

Wallace, David Duncan. *Constitutional History of South Carolina from 1725 to 1775.* Abbeville, S.C., 1899.

———. *The History of South Carolina.* 4 vols. New York: American Historical Society, 1934.

———. *The Life of Henry Laurens.* New York: G. P. Putnam's Sons, 1915.

———. *South Carolina: A Short History, 1520–1948.* Chapel Hill: University of North Carolina Press, 1951.

Walton, Brian G. "Elections to the United States Senate in North Carolina, 1835–1861." *North Carolina Historical Review* 53 (April 1976): 168–92.

Weir, Robert M. " 'The Harmony We Were Famous For': An Interpretation of Pre-Revolutionary South Carolina Politics." *William and Mary Quarterly,* 3d ser., 26 (1969): 473–501.

———. "Liberty and Property, and No Stamps: South Carolina and the Stamp Act Crisis." Ph.D. dissertation, Western Reserve University, 1966.

"When Knighthood Was in Flower." *Louisiana Historical Quarterly* 1, no. 4 (1918): 367–71.

White, Leonard D. *The Jacksonians: A Study in Administrative History, 1829–1861.* New York: Free Press, 1954.

Williamson, Chilton. *American Suffrage from Property to Democracy, 1760–1860.* Princeton: Princeton University Press, 1960.

Wolfe, John Harold. *Jeffersonian Democracy in South Carolina.* Chapel Hill: University of North Carolina Press, 1940.

Wood, Gordon S. *The Creation of the American Republic, 1776–1787.* Chapel Hill: University of North Carolina Press, 1969.

Wooster, Ralph A. *The People in Power: Courthouse and Statehouse in the Lower South, 1850–1860.* Knoxville: University of Tennessee Press, 1969.

———. *The Secession Conventions of the South.* Princeton: Princeton University Press, 1962.

Wright, Gavin. *The Political Economy of the Cotton South: Households, Markets, and Wealth in the Nineteenth Century.* New York: W. W. Norton and Co., 1978.

Wyatt-Brown, Bertram. *Southern Honor: Ethics and Behavior in the Old South.* Oxford: Oxford University Press, 1982.

Yearns, Wilfred Buck. *The Confederate Congress.* Athens: University of Georgia Press, 1960.

Index